T0350775

Liability-Driven Investment

Founded in 1807, John Wiley & Sons is the oldest independent publishing company in the United States. With offices in North America, Europe, Australia and Asia, Wiley is globally committed to developing and marketing print and electronic products and services for our customers' professional and personal knowledge and understanding.

The Wiley Finance series contains books written specifically for finance and investment professionals as well as sophisticated individual investors and their financial advisors. Book topics range from portfolio management to e-commerce, risk management, financial engineering, valuation and financial instrument analysis, as well as much more.

For a list of available titles, visit our Web site at www.WileyFinance.com.

Liability-Driven Investment

From Analogue to Digital, Pensions to Robo-Advice

DANIEL TAMMAS-HASTINGS

WILEY

This edition first published 2021
Copyright © 2021 by Daniel Tammas-Hastings. All rights reserved.

Registered office
John Wiley & Sons Ltd, The Atrium, Southern Gate, Chichester, West Sussex, PO19 8SQ,
United Kingdom

For details of our global editorial offices, for customer services and for information about how
to apply for permission to reuse the copyright material in this book please see our website at
www.wiley.com.

All rights reserved. No part of this publication may be reproduced, stored in a retrieval system,
or transmitted, in any form or by any means, electronic, mechanical, photocopying, recording or
otherwise, except as permitted by the UK Copyright, Designs and Patents Act 1988, without the
prior permission of the publisher.

Wiley publishes in a variety of print and electronic formats and by print-on-demand. Some material
included with standard print versions of this book may not be included in e-books or in print-on-
demand. If this book refers to media such as a CD or DVD that is not included in the version you
purchased, you may download this material at http://booksupport.wiley.com. For more information
about Wiley products, visit www.wiley.com.

Designations used by companies to distinguish their products are often claimed as trademarks.
All brand names and product names used in this book are trade names, service marks, trademarks
or registered trademarks of their respective owners. The publisher is not associated with any product
or vendor mentioned in this book.

Limit of Liability/Disclaimer of Warranty: While the publisher and author have used their best efforts
in preparing this book, they make no representations or warranties with respect to the accuracy
or completeness of the contents of this book and specifically disclaim any implied warranties of
merchantability or fitness for a particular purpose. It is sold on the understanding that the publisher is
not engaged in rendering professional services and neither the publisher nor the author shall be liable
for damages arising herefrom. If professional advice or other expert assistance is required, the services
of a competent professional should be sought.

Library of Congress Cataloging-in-Publication Data

Names: Tammas-Hastings, Daniel, author.
Title: Liability-driven investment : from analogue to digital, pensions to
   robo-advice / Daniel Tammas-Hastings.
Description: Hoboken, New Jersey : Wiley, [2021] | Series: Wiley finance |
   Includes index. | Summary: "The project aims to outline the usefulness
   and explain the growing popularity of Liability-Driven Investing (LDI).
   The ultimate aim of Liability Driven Investing is to ensure that
   investors have sufficient funds to pay liabilities.
This is a targeted approach that moves beyond the simple asset value maximization framework
   which is prevalent in the academic literature."—Provided by publisher.
Identifiers: LCCN 2020055881 (print) | LCCN 2020055882 (ebook) | ISBN
   9781119441953 (cloth) | ISBN 9781119441984 (adobe pdf) | ISBN
   9781119441960 (epub) | ISBN 9781119441977 (obook)
Subjects: LCSH: Investments. | Liabilities (Accounting)
Classification: LCC HG4521 .T295 2021 (print) | LCC HG4521 (ebook) | DDC
   332.6—dc23
LC record available at https://lccn.loc.gov/2020055881
LC ebook record available at https://lccn.loc.gov/2020055882

Cover Design: Wiley
Cover Image: © Tetra Images/Getty Images

Set in 10/12 pt Sabon LT Std by SPi Global, Chennai, India
Printed and bound by CPI Group (UK) Ltd, Croydon, CR0 4YY

10 9 8 7 6 5 4 3 2 1

Dedicated to my wife Dominica for her support throughout this process and to Angela Tammas for forty years of support and education.

Contents

Preface xi

CHAPTER 1
Liability-Driven Investment and Multi-Asset Class Investing 1
Moving Beyond Modern Portfolio Theory: Introducing the World of
    Liability-Driven Investment 1
The Cult of Equity 6
The Pension Protection Fund 7
Summary 13

CHAPTER 2
Introduction to Investment Risk 15
Risk Management 18
The Importance of Risk vs Return 18
Quantifying Risk 19
Systematic and Nonsystematic Risk 19
Creating A Risk Profile 20
Summary 21
    Some Basic Rules of Investment Risk 21

CHAPTER 3
Introductory Steps into the World of Multi-Asset Class Investment 23
Some Handy Definitions 25
The Starting Point 26
Introducing Modern Portfolio Theory 27
More Handy Definitions 29
But How Does the Asset Allocation Decision work? 30
Home Country Bias: 32
Developing a Strategy for Multiple Asset Classes 33
    Handy Definitions 34
Quick Aside: 36
Summary 36

CHAPTER 4
Building Investment Portfolios   **39**
   (Fundamental, Technical and Quantitative Techniques)   39
   An Introduction to Single Stock Selection   40
   The Types of Analysis   40
   Fundamental Analysis of Securities   41
       Introducing Ratio Analysis   42
       Liquidity and Solvency Ratios   43
       Current Ratio   43
       The Quick Ratio or Acid Test   43
       Cash Ratio   44
       Financial Leverage or Debt Ratios   44
   Technical Analysis of Securities   45
       The Main Assumptions of Technical Analysis   46
   Quantitative Analysis   47
       Passive Investors   48
   The Passive vs Active Debate   48
       Introducing the Efficient Market Hypothesis   48
       So Why Use Active Managers?   51
   So Passive or Active?   56
   Summary   57

CHAPTER 5
Building Investment Portfolios   **59**
   Choosing the Manager   61
   Moving on to Operational Due Diligence   63
   A Sample (Non-Exhaustive) List of Operational Checks   63
       Quick Aside: Replicating Private Equity and a Passive Venture
           Capital Fund   65
   Part 3 Portfolio Selection   69

CHAPTER 6
Moving Towards Liability Driven Investing   **73**
   The Time Value of Money   73
       More Extreme than the Extreme   76
   The Basics Continued: Real Versus Nominal Discounting   77
   A Simple and Brief Look at Bonds   78
       Some Other Types of Bonds   79
       How to Price a Bond   80
       Key Terms   80
   Immunisation Theory and Frank Redington   81
   An Introduction to Interest Rate Swaps   82
       What Is an Interest Rate Swap?   83
       The Mechanics   83

Some Terms Used in the Market   83
A Quick Aside: Forward Rate Agreements (FRAs)   84
An Introduction to Inflation-Linked Securities   85
Why Do Governments Issue Inflation-Linked Bonds?   87
The Basic Mechanics   88
Inflation-Linked Swaps   89
The Global Market   90
Payers vs Receivers   91
The Zero-Coupon Swap   91

CHAPTER 7
The Defined Benefit Pension Plan and Explicit Liabilities   **93**
The Boots Example   95
The Stakeholders in a Typical Plan   97
A Checklist for Trustees   97
What Are the Liabilities?   98

CHAPTER 8
ESG, Governance and the Pensions Industry   **101**
The UN PRI   103
The Increasing Importance of ESG   105
What Does ESG Represent?   106
The Main Approaches to Ethical Investing   107
Screening and Beyond   107
ESG: A Screening Approach   108
Implementing a Screen   110
ESG: An Integration-Based Approach   111
Best in Class Positive Screening   112
Impact-Based ESG Investing   114
Engagement-Based ESG Investing   117
ESG in History   119
The Case of Cowan vs Scargill   119
Incorporating ESG into the SIP   121
The Revised Statement Should   122

CHAPTER 9
Moving Beyond Liability-Driven Investment   **123**
The World of CDI   123
What is the Difference Between LDI and CDI?   125
Credit Where It's Due   126
Moving into Illiquid Credit   126
Cash Flow-Driven Investment in Action   128
The ABC Scheme   128
What Are the Objectives of Our Typical CDI Scheme?   129

CHAPTER 10
The Statement of Investment Principles   **131**
  Drawing up a Statement of Investment Principles   131
    What the SIP must include   131
    Preparing the SIP   132
  A Sample Statement of Investment Principles   132
  Statement of Investment Principles for the ABC Plan   132
    Investment Objective and Strategy   133
    Investment Strategy   133
    Investment Restrictions   134
    Investment Risk   134
    Realising Investments   135
    Responsible Investment   135
    Additional Voluntary Contributions (AVCs)   136

CHAPTER 11
Liability-Driven RoboAdvice and the Development and Digitisation of the Industry   **139**
  WealthTech: How Wealth Managers and their Clients are Embracing
    New Technologies   139
  From WealthTech to Robo-Advice   143
    Robo-Advice in Ten Points   143
  A Brief Introduction to Robo-Advice   145
    Pricing Structures for Digital Advice   147
  Advice or Guidance: Robo-advice or Partially Automated
    Digital Guidance   148
    From the FCA   150
  Further Developments in LDI   151
    The Evolution of LDI and the Creation of Cash Flow-Driven
      Investment   151
  What is Cash Flow-Driven Investment?   151
  The Evolution of LDI   152

INDEX   **155**

Preface

Welcome to the first edition of 'Liability Driven Investment'. This is my first experience of writing a book, and I'm grateful to John Wiley and the team for the commission. Plus of course the support and expertise received from the editors there; thank you Purvi for input, advice and changes. All mistakes are of course my own.

This book is an introduction to creating investment portfolios using a broad range of asset classes and shows how finance professionals increasingly use Liability Driven Investment frameworks to do this. Liability Driven investment for convenience is commonly known as LDI. LDI is sometimes also described as Asset-Liability Management (ALM) or in the States Dedicated Portfolios. We live in a world where the bulk of our pension money, in the UK at least, is invested with an LDI strategy at its core. In the rest of the developed world the techniques and frameworks are gaining increasing acceptance and market share. It is likely that this trend will continue. However despite its importance the strategy is unknown to even most financial professionals. With most of the advanced portfolio management textbooks focusing on the peculiarities of Fixed Income Wiley felt a broader guide was overdue. To describe how LDI works we look at the major asset classes, the basics of fund selection and management, and how to use these building blocks to create a diversified portfolio. We also look at the regulatory and ethical issues involved in creating multi-asset class portfolios and how these will impact the industry in the future.

The book can be used as a guide for pension fund trustees as they negotiate an increasingly complex regulatory landscape, but the text is very much aimed at the lay person with the aim of building up an investment strategy from first principles. It is first and foremost a book about investment theory, addressing the risk management frameworks currently used in capital markets across the globe to create modern investment portfolios. Later, we move on from purely investment matters to explain the some of regulatory systems in which financial professionals work in, and the regulatory obligations that are placed on professionals and amateurs alike when advising on investments. We also go on to look at the impact technology has had on how and when we invest, and how technology is likely to create further changes in the near future.

I will attempt to explain the numerous theories that underpin modern finance: in particular, Modern Portfolio Theory and the theoretical work of Harry Markowitz that underpins how the bulk of our pensions are invested. We then expand from MPT to look at risk frameworks that take into account both sides of an investor's balance sheet. Incredibly elegant and taught on every undergraduate finance course, MPT is the most influential financial theory in use today, and it will remain so tomorrow. It starts with the assumption that risk-averse investors will construct portfolios to maximise expected returns based on a certain level of market risk. However, Modern Portfolio Theory stems from original work in 1952 and some of the assumptions are not ideal for the needs of a pensioner in the twenty-first century. By neglecting one side of an individual or pension plan's balance sheet, MPT could be said to be looking at half the problem. (Although this is perhaps mean, as the assumptions are clearly laid out and there are frameworks explicitly developed from MPT that do include Liabilities.)

The field of Liability Driven Investment is particularly relevant to anyone with a pension, which in the UK at least is effectively all of us. We have seen talk in the press of 'Peak LDI' in the last few years as more and more pension schemes utilise cash flow driven frameworks. But growth has continued, indeed at the time of writing hedging of institutional portfolios against changes in UK interest rates and against inflation has increased to another record high. Growth will also continue in markets with limited take up, it is also likely that Digital or FinTech solutions will create a trickle down affect to the High Street.

The core idea behind LDI frameworks is that rational investors would not look to maximise real assets, subject to risk constraints as in traditional frameworks – usually defined as volatility with total portfolio value. Rather an investor would seek to maximise the profit – subject to constraints on the variability of the surplus, and subject to meeting cashflows that are defined as needs rather than wants. This approach can make a huge difference to portfolio construction and user outcomes. It also shifts the focus of investors from equity prices to long-term treasury or government yields because the volatility of the present value of the liabilities is related to the volatility of the funding status.

Across the world falling bond yields have created pension fund deficits since the global financial crisis. This is despite rising stock prices and limited portfolio impact from credit loss. Rising asset prices have not been enough to counteract the increase in liabilities for a large number of pension schemes, as funding deficits have increased despite an equity bull market. This is due to under-hedging of the liabilities. The implication is that a focus on asset-price optimization may not be enough in a world of long-dated liabilities and that LDI might be the solution.

This book has three parts to it, broadly matching the subtitles Pensions, Regulations and Robo-advice, although we may also have described the focus as: i) Investment and Risk; ii) Regulation and ethical considerations; iii) The Impact of Technology.

The first part, which stretches through the first half of the text, consists of an introduction to the asset classes available to the modern investor. Alongside an introduction to investment funds, why they are important and how to choose them. There is also a brief explanation of both discounted cash flows and investment management frameworks which should be familiar territory for anyone who has taken a finance or economics class in the past.

The second part looks at regulation, the changing regulatory landscape, and the obligations upon stakeholders in the investment world. Regulation is more important to finance professionals than it has ever been, and we expect to see continued growth in the number of, and complexity of, regulations as markets become more and more complex. We also look at ESG (Environmental, Social and Governance) criteria and investigate how finance is more than a simple question of risk and return. With ESG criteria incorporated into regulations and the investment process, we expect social considerations to become an increasingly important part of the investment process.

The third part looks at the digital landscape and the impact of technology. The rise of WealthTech and the likelihood of digital disruption (so far it is early days), including the distribution of advice and financial products such as LDI, is likely to change dramatically over the next few years as processes become less human-led and more commoditised. This will bring mass distribution of investment solutions and lower costs to us as consumers of financial products – but it also creates risks.

We hope you find this book useful.

Daniel Tammas-Hastings

CHAPTER 1

Liability-Driven Investment and Multi-Asset Class Investing

MOVING BEYOND MODERN PORTFOLIO THEORY: INTRODUCING THE WORLD OF LIABILITY-DRIVEN INVESTMENT

In the last few decades, and the last few years particularly, volatile asset markets, shifting demographics, increased living standards and changing consumer expectations have created a demand for better savings products and resultantly more advanced financial risk management. These changes, coupled with a world which has an ageing population across many industrialised nations, but in which we anticipate secularly declining asset returns, has meant that there has been an increased focus on understanding investors' exact needs and the risks that they face.

Events such as the Global Financial Crisis or GFC, have meant that investors young and old have had first-hand experience of capital loss and the effect of market uncertainty on Savings Outcomes. The events of the crisis and its aftermath has changed permanently our estimates of society's ability and willingness to tolerate financial risk, as well as skewering central bankers and regulators belief in the efficiency of the capital markets. The Efficient Market Hypothesis (EMH), which had dominated the thoughts of academics, regulators, central bankers and investors alike, has now lost its primacy and the need for regulation to tilt markets towards better outcomes has become much more accepted. As a result of the large capital losses caused by the crisis, there has naturally been a need for a better understanding of what 'risk' means: where it resides and how best to manage it.

Particularly as it has been shown that the definition and acceptability of risk may not be constant between differing stakeholders in the capital markets. Due to these changes in circumstances and understanding modern investment management has come to encompass a more 'holistic' approach to saving. These new 'holistic' frameworks rely on more than simply maximising returns or 'profits', on a risk-adjusted basis, and instead look at long-term investor outcomes and specific goals.

In the United Kingdom and continental Europe this new broader approach to investment has been typified by the rise of Liability-Driven Investment Strategies. These frameworks are more commonly shortened to LDI and now dominate long-term institutional investing in Europe. These methodologies put loss mitigation ahead of simpler risk, return optimisation techniques, and are thought to lead to less dramatic swings in user outcome. The more traditional approach towards saving and investment, which still dominates many types of financial advice and capital allocation, relies on asset value optimisation (given a risk constraint) or risk minimisation (given a return constraint) for the construction of investment portfolios. Even today professional Financial Advice often solely relies on a set of frameworks that have become known as Modern Portfolio Theory. This is despite advances in the understanding of investment risks and the capital markets in the six decades since MPT was initially proposed by Dr. Harry Markowitz.

It seems strange that, nearly two decades after what is considered to have been the first successful implementation of a Liability-Driven Investment structure (the immunisation of the Boots Pension Scheme in 2001, the implementation of which is briefly discussed in a later chapter), that Liability Driven Investing is not more popularly understood and accepted amongst the wider finance community, particularly those giving financial advice. Indeed, for some practitioners it is still a controversial subject. This is partly due to what some argue are the high long-term costs of reduced equity exposure, and for other investors / trustees there is a reluctance to embrace fixed income investment at a time of historically low yields.

However, given the tremendous risk-adjusted and absolute outperformance of LDI style strategies in their (still limited) trading history many holdouts are slowly choosing to move (or being forced to move) to more risk focused strategies. Although many financial market practitioners have long been vocal advocates of the Liability Driven approach, there is often resistance to the unfamiliar in the world of investment. Unfamiliarity will reduce take-up and engagement of any innovation, not just financial, unless coupled with a simple and easily understood message of superior outcomes. Currently, the communication of the abstract concepts within LDI is a focus of the industry as they try to increase take-up. Explaining the abstract concepts simply and effectively is something the industry as a whole has failed to do. The move to LDI has been led by the Investment Consultants, Actuaries and Fixed Income Specialists with the benefit of growing regulatory support. For investment consultants in particular, advising on LDI has become an important driver of revenue as the more traditional consulting revenue streams of manager and fund selection on behalf of institutional clients have been disrupted by the increasing acceptance of passive investment strategies and the rise of low-cost Exchange Traded Funds (ETFs). This matches an end user change in focus from selection 'within' asset classes to selection 'of' asset classes. We live in a world where before the GFC approximately 80 per cent of advisor research was for the narrow selection of funds within asset classes and only 20 per cent was devoted to asset allocation. But perversely 80 per cent of returns are generated from the selection of asset classes, and returns within asset classes should be a secondary consideration when the asset allocation decision is the main driver of return and ultimately investor utility.

Liability driven investment has been increasing in market share globally and in some areas of the institutional pension market (in the UK DB market at least) take-up is nearing 100%. Indeed, in the UK at least, some are talking of Peak LDI. However, in many other areas of long term investment, (for example retail saving and digital asset management) take-up of these holistic techniques and frameworks is as yet negligible if not non-existent. A partial explanation of this is the opacity of the products and techniques. Complex investment strategies are often held back by a lack of understanding at both user and even advisor level. Complexity and unfamiliarity have meant that many pension fund trustees and IFAs have stayed invested in more traditional investment styles. This is despite the gathering evidence of superior outcomes from more novel strategies. Even the idea of cash flow hedging and the utilisation of Interest Swaps and other Financial Derivatives to match future liabilities can be intimidating to some advisors. Quantitative analysis and advanced risk management are skill sets that are often far away from advisors' comfort zones. The implementation of these strategies is unlikely to gain as much traction as possible whilst the concept alone can be so off-putting to potential advocates. One of the aims of this work is to reduce the appearance of complexity and explain how and why liability driven investing strategies can work for a variety of goal driven investment styles. Ultimately, it seems that user and advisor education are one of the catalysts needed to stimulate the growth of superior risk management, boosting the knowledge base of potential beneficiaries, should take-up increase and lead to improved outcomes. With better understanding of Liability Driven Investing what is currently an investing solution only for the largest institutions will start trickling down to become a solution for the smallest saver.

The smallest retail accounts receiving the same strength of risk management as the world's largest institutions would represent the democratisation of Risk Management, although realistically this is unlikely to happen in the near future. However, we do believe that, in the long term, the style of Financial Advice that is currently the domain of Investment Consultants and Pension Actuaries should be available to the retail user: either through a High Street Independent Financial Advisor (IFA) or the increasingly popular Digital Advice platforms, which are also colloquially known as Robo-Advisors. These platforms and increasing use of similar technology by individual advisors may permanently change the way financial advice is distributed – hopefully for the better – by both lowering the cost of provision and by increasing the quality of advice proffered.

(Examples of these digital advice platforms are numerous but include Nutmeg in the UK and Betterment in the States, alongside Scalable Capital, Moneyfarm and many others throughout Europe, more and more High Street Banks are also adding a 'robo-advisor' to their product mix. As of 2019 none were providing explicitly LDI driven strategies, but the use of ETFs such as Vanguard's Life Strategy and Target Retirement product suite, implies that similar concepts are gaining ground.)

There has been concern in the academic literature and from financial regulators around the world that the more traditional Portfolio construction techniques popularised by Modern Portfolio Theory (MPT) may be too simplistic. MPT, whilst mathematically elegant, may not be the most practical for investors who are more worried about the unavoidable costs of living rather than asset or wealth optimisation. By only investigating the risk–return profiles of assets rather than the explicit needs of investors MPT can potentially create portfolios that are unsuitable for those savers with large unavoidable living costs. Intuitively many investors are more concerned with the avoidance of poverty and financial ruin rather than maximising their wealth.

These risk-averse individuals represent an investor base that would logically include the majority of the world's savers.

Although the model is incredibly elegant and widely accepted by economists and finance academics alike, Modern Portfolio Theory is far from perfect. As with all theoretical models, it must rely on a set of assumptions. MPT is an investment theory based on the core assumption that risk-averse investors will construct portfolios to optimise or maximise expected return based on a given level of market risk. It is arguably the most important financial theory in use today and has applications across many fields of risk modelling, Corporate Finance as well as in Wealth Management. However, the model's simplistic assumptions may not hold in all cases. Modern Portfolio Theory – sometimes shortened to simply 'Portfolio Theory' – was first derived in a significantly different economic and social landscape from today. The theories originated and were advanced in 1950s America (1952 Chicago to be precise) and resultantly the model developed reflected a vastly different world to that of today, and relied on multiple assumptions which may not hold in the present day. In the United States of the 1950s retirement needs and retirement expectations alongside estimates of long term healthcare costs were both different from and not as significant as they are now. The investment universe was also immeasurably smaller, which may have naturally suggested a simpler solution to the asset allocation problem.

Just how different society and its corresponding savings and investment needs were can be seen in demographic data from the Office of National Statistics (ONS). The ONS being the recognised national statistical institute of the United Kingdom. A British citizen now reaching pensionable age at sixty-five can happily expect to live for another decade if not more compared to someone retiring sixty years ago. Indeed, there exist similar trends in longevity in all other economies with developed financial markets. This is because increases in wealth and advances in medical technology have led to increased life expectancy globally. These demographic changes have created a much more complex set of investor wants and needs.

Developments in financial markets have also meant that these more complex investor preferences must also be managed from a much more complex set of financial instruments and securities than were available in the middle of the last century. An individual now seeking retirement is likely to live three times longer and have considerably greater costs whilst in retirement than a similar individual 65 or 70 years ago. Similar to other developed financial markets, advances in medicine and society have contributed to pensioners in the United Kingdom and similar nations living far longer than would have been expected last century. This is a trend set to continue, amplifying the need to understand the greater upcoming liabilities (pensions, healthcare etc) and how best to hedge and manage these cash flows.

Sometimes also known as 'The Markowitz Theory of Portfolio Management', Modern Portfolio Theory is famous for creating an 'efficient frontier' of securities. This efficient frontier offers the maximum possible expected return for a given level of risk. So, under MPT an efficient portfolio is defined as – a portfolio that has either:

i. more return than any other portfolio with a similar risk profile (equivalent to other assets with the same standard deviation of returns), or equivalently

ii. less risk than any other portfolio with the same return.

Investments that match these criteria are often referred to as Markowitz Efficient. This is after the aforementioned Professor Harry Markowitz, the Nobel prize winner who created two-parameter portfolio theory.

However, in both finance and economics; elegant solutions aren't always practical solutions, and it might be said that by neglecting one side of an individual (or pension plan's) balance sheet MPT is only looking at half (or less of) the problem. Indeed, for many savers a sensible investment plan would start by looking, not at what assets they have, but at what they will need in the future. These are the liabilities.

So more modern Liability-driven investment frameworks have arisen that by explicitly including current and future liabilities attached to the investor as well as assets, could be looked at as a more complete approach. Indeed, the word 'holistic' is often used in the literature. There is a growing consensus in the wholesale capital markets that the LDI toolkit is the appropriate way to create portfolios for many investors' requirements, and whilst there has been particular interest for retirement needs, we feel that LDI should not be limited to this. It is our belief that this two-sided methodology should and will filter down to the retail market and from Defined Benefit pension plans to Defined Contribution plans.

This expansion of scope could be both from the emergence of LDI style passive (and active) multi-asset class funds, and through advisor and user education creating further demand for a larger LDI style product base.

Currently further development of an LDI product suite is a focus for most large asset managers in the United Kingdom as they attempt to take market share from the three largest players. More competition would certainly be welcome as currently the top three asset managers in the space BlackRock, Legal & General Investment Management (LGIM) and Insight Investment (owned by BNY Mellon) currently take roughly 90% by AUM of the mandates available. As such more and more asset managers are likely to become familiar with the underlying methodologies and the space will become more competitive. In recent years multi-asset class investing has become much better understood, and users will often ask for a holistic solution at outset.

In short, the liability-driven investment template can be thought of as an investment framework for any company or individual where cash flows needed to fund future liabilities are explicitly included. Techniques like this are sometimes referred to asset-liability management (ALM) and indeed LDI is in fact a direct descendant of ALM. Asset Liability Management just like LDI, has the drawback that it requires far more expertise in Fixed Income than the traditional approach to investing, which has typically focused on the Equity Markets and the selection of Investment Funds or Single Securities within the equity markets. The need for fixed income knowledge is created, because the liabilities could be considered analogous to fixed income instruments, specifically a short position in a bond maturing when the liability is due. Modelling a set of liabilities hence becomes similar to modelling a short position in a bond portfolio, which may require a different skillset for advisors to learn.

Unfortunately, bond mathematics can be intimidating both for pension fund trustees and advisors, as fixed income investment and analysis can often be counterintuitive. For example, in the current markets for financial instruments there are many government securities yielding negative returns (both real and nominal), and most investment grade bonds would be expected to lag inflation implying an expected loss of value. Securities such as these with a guaranteed loss of purchasing power in the long term are not an obviously attractive addition to a savings portfolio, particularly if the return objective is significantly in advance of inflation (hint: they usually are). The want or need for rising equity markets is far easier to understand and follow for the average investor than the relevance of fluctuating bond yields, the importance of long term interest rates or the need for advanced risk management. Indeed, some pension fund trustees will still show surprise at the fact that rising bond yields will usually do more to fight pension fund deficits than strongly rising stock markets.

THE CULT OF EQUITY

Investment Advisors specialising in or advocating Fixed Income based solutions must also fight the 'Cult of Equity'. Many investors and advisors believe that in the long-term equity is the most appropriate means to achieve high returns. As well as perhaps the only way to consistently outperform inflation.

The trend towards increased equity investment by pension funds became dominant in the 1950s alongside the rise of Markowitz. Many proponents of the 'Cult of Equity' were also early supporters of Modern Portfolio Theory. One significant figure from the period was George Ross Goobey, manager and Chief Investment Officer (CIO) of the Imperial Tobacco Pension Fund between 1947 and 1970. He invested his mandate entirely in the stock market in 1955 and supported the cult of equity by advocating stock investment as the natural home for long term capital. Today whilst belief in the power of equities is still strong, years of underperformance in developed markets, and the Japanese experience of negative multi-year stock returns have demonstrated both the need for diversification amongst asset classes and the possibility of weak equity performance.

In the past due to its original development in the pension market it was often assumed that the Liability Driven Investing framework requires cash flows that are known with a reasonable amount of accuracy, the classic example of a suitable port-folio for the approach being a defined-benefit (DB) pension scheme. However, due to the validity of the approach we are increasingly seeing similar frameworks being used for Defined Contribution schemes. This is because the needs of individuals within DC schemes often mirror the needs of those in DB schemes, even if the investing approaches differ. For those in DC pensions (where the contribution is known but not the benefit) the cash flow needs are implicit rather than explicit. The idea being that an individual who is rational would not look to maximise real assets, subject to risk constraints (usually but not always defined as volatility with total portfolio value). But instead to maximise the economic surplus, or the surplus of their basic funding needs, subject to constraints on the variability of the surplus. This makes a difference because the volatility of the present value of the liabilities is related to the volatility of the funding status. It also turns the focus of investors' attention from the level of the stock markets and a constant desire for asset appreciation to the more esoteric long-term treasury market or the level of government bond yields.

As an example of how Stock appreciation on its own is not enough to meet investors' expectations. We can see how falling bond yields have caused deficits for

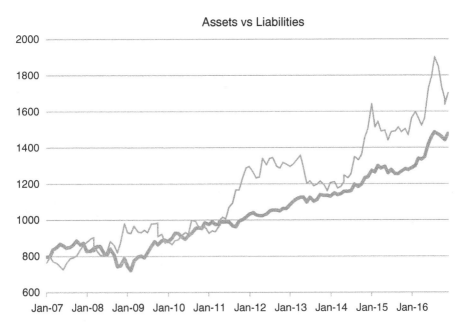

FIGURE 1.1 Assets vs. Liabilities

many pension funds to increase in the last five years despite benign market positions with continuously rising stock prices and limited portfolio impact from credit loss. Figure 1.1 shows how rising asset prices have not been enough to counteract the increase in liabilities for the UK Pension Protection Fund, as funding deficits have increased despite an equity bull market. This effect is due to under-hedging of the liabilities. The implication being that a focus on asset-price optimisation may not be enough in a world of long dated liabilities.

THE PENSION PROTECTION FUND

> 'the Pension Protection Fund's main function is to provide compensation to members of eligible defined benefit pension schemes, when there is a qualifying insolvency event in relation to the employer, and where there are insufficient assets in the pension scheme to cover the Pension Protection Fund level of compensation. The Pension Protection Fund is a statutory fund run by the Board of the Pension Protection Fund, a statutory corporation established under the provisions of the Pensions Act 2004.'

For eligible firms who have a final salary pension scheme in the United Kingdom, membership of the PPF is compulsory and the payment of a compulsory levy, its funding status and movements and assets and liabilities often reflect the health of its constituents.

	Assets	Liabilities									
Jan-07	797.2	765.2	31.9	261	312.2	−51.2	5,619	536.1	453.1	83.1	2,132
Feb-07	798.6	795.5	3.2	329.6	395.1	−65.5	5,924	469	400.4	68.6	1,827
Mar-07	837.7	770	67.8	214.4	252.9	−38.5	4,690	623.3	517.1	106.2	2,853
Apr-07	851.3	763.1	88.3	195.5	228.2	−32.7	4,402	655.9	534.9	121	3,141
May-07	868	742	126	133.6	157.3	−23.7	3,845	734.5	584.7	149.7	3,698
Jun-07	858.1	727.7	130.3	122.8	145.1	−22.3	3,745	735.2	582.6	152.6	3,798
Jul-07	844.8	761.5	83.2	197.4	231.3	−34	4,453	647.4	530.2	117.2	3,090
Aug-07	848.8	789.7	59.1	248.2	291.1	−42.9	4,803	600.6	498.6	102	2,740
Sep-07	865.7	790.6	75.1	214.3	252.6	−38.3	4,613	651.4	538	113.4	2,930
Oct-07	884.5	800.5	84	211.5	248.4	−36.9	4,507	673	552.1	120.9	3,036
Nov-07	861.5	835.5	26.1	312.1	370.3	−58.2	5,208	549.4	465.1	84.3	2,335
Dec-07	872.6	860.9	11.7	347	413.6	−66.6	5,361	525.6	447.2	78.4	2,182
Jan-08	827.3	876	−48.7	443.4	541.3	−98	5,960	383.9	334.6	49.2	1,583
Feb-08	829.8	896.8	−67	464.5	574	−109.5	6,112	365.3	322.7	42.5	1,431
Mar-08	844.8	903.3	−58.5	499.4	612.6	−113.2	5,790	345.5	290.7	54.8	1,621
Mar-08	834.7	857.5	−22.9	410.7	492.2	−81.5	5,378	424	365.3	58.7	2,033
Apr-08	856.4	829.3	27.1	309.9	365.8	−55.9	4,815	546.5	463.5	83	2,596
May-08	856	805	51	286.6	331.6	−45	4,514	569.4	473.4	96	2,897
Jun-08	816.4	803.4	13	313	373.3	−60.3	4,946	503.4	430.1	73.3	2,465
Jul-08	811.3	830.1	−18.8	392.3	470	−77.7	5,297	419	360.1	58.9	2,114
Aug-08	840.2	879.5	−39.3	429.7	522.4	−92.7	5,507	410.5	357.1	53.4	1,904
Sep-08	805.7	857.9	−52.2	464.3	562.7	−98.4	5,618	341.4	295.2	46.2	1,793
Oct-08	743.6	821.2	−77.6	450.6	563.1	−112.5	5,832	293	258	34.9	1,579
Nov-08	749.5	873.4	−123.9	529.2	678.2	−149	6,135	220.3	195.3	25	1,276
Dec-08	789.2	979.8	−190.6	645.9	854.7	−208.7	6,443	143.2	125.2	18.1	968
Jan-09	744.6	928.2	−183.6	607.6	807.7	−200.1	6,438	137	120.5	16.4	973
Feb-09	723.1	927.8	−204.7	597.4	815.3	−218	6,507	125.7	112.4	13.3	904
Mar-09	772.7	964.9	−192.2	620.9	829.5	−208.6	5,603	151.8	135.4	16.5	1,050
Apr-09	795.3	934.8	−139.5	607.6	770.4	−162.9	5,357	187.8	164.4	23.4	1,296
May-09	800.8	931.1	−130.2	606.9	761.8	−155	5,307	193.9	169.2	24.7	1,346
Jun-09	794.1	943.4	−149.2	611.8	783.4	−171.6	5,400	182.3	160	22.4	1,253

Date											
Jul-09	819.8	928.5	−108.7	587.8	725.8	−138	5,167	232	202.7	29.3	1,486
Aug-09	856.4	981.2	−124.8	629	782.8	−153.8	5,236	227.4	198.4	29	1,417
Sep-09	880.2	978.9	−98.8	619.7	753.1	−133.4	5,066	260.5	225.9	34.6	1,587
Oct-09	865.1	983.2	−118.1	629.9	778.6	−148.7	5,198	235.3	204.7	30.6	1,455
Oct-09	865.1	909.1	−44	503.5	596.7	−93.2	4,632	361.6	312.4	49.2	2,021
Nov-09	884.7	922.4	−37.7	497.7	587.6	−89.9	4,575	387	334.7	52.2	2,078
Dec-09	892.2	872.2	19.9	370.6	425.7	−55.1	3,991	521.6	446.5	75	2,662
Jan-10	880.3	879.4	0.9	397.8	462.4	−64.6	4,208	482.5	417	65.5	2,445
Feb-10	901.1	864	37.2	306.2	353.3	−47.1	3,801	594.9	510.7	84.2	2,852
Mar-10	926.2	887.9	38.3	293.3	342.4	−49.1	3,770	632.9	545.5	87.4	2,826
Apr-10	925	889.4	35.6	303.4	353.6	−50.2	3,808	621.6	535.8	85.8	2,788
May-10	908.9	913.3	−4.4	429.8	499.7	−69.9	4,258	479.1	413.6	65.5	2,338
Jun-10	892.7	931.2	−38.5	498.9	590.2	−91.4	4,534	393.9	341	52.9	2,062
Jul-10	911.7	922.2	−10.5	444.3	518	−73.7	4,292	467.4	404.2	63.2	2,268
Aug-10	924.4	998.2	−73.8	559.5	678.1	−118.6	4,757	364.9	320.1	44.8	1,803
Sep-10	951.7	991.9	−40.2	528.9	624.6	−95.7	4,498	422.8	367.3	55.5	2,062
Oct-10	957.1	962.2	−5.1	457.1	530.6	−73.4	4,244	500	431.6	68.3	2,316
Nov-10	951.1	952.1	−1	446.2	516.9	−70.7	4,202	504.8	435.2	69.7	2,358
Dec-10	983.4	961.7	21.7	374.7	435.7	−61	3,953	608.7	526	82.7	2,607
Jan-11	973.3	927.2	46.1	301.9	350.7	−48.8	3,696	671.5	576.5	95	2,864
Feb-11	986	937.5	48.4	307.9	356.7	−48.8	3,675	678	580.8	97.2	2,885
Mar-11	973.5	936.6	36.9	343.9	404.9	−61	3,607	629.6	531.8	97.9	2,825
Apr-11	973.5	969.7	3.8	389	465.5	−76.5	3,945	584.5	504.2	80.3	2,487
Apr-11	987.4	995.6	−8.2	417.1	501.3	−84.3	4,052	570.3	494.3	76	2,380
May-11	989.3	1,013.80	−24.5	461	554.6	−93.7	4,164	528.4	459.2	69.2	2,268
Jun-11	988.8	1,006.60	−17.7	455.3	545	−89.7	4,122	533.5	461.5	72	2,310
Jul-11	989	1,067.00	−78	587.1	716.7	−129.6	4,571	401.8	350.2	51.6	1,861
Aug-11	966.6	1,092.70	−126.1	646.7	811.2	−164.5	4,891	319.9	281.5	38.4	1,541
Sep-11	960.4	1,165.90	−205.5	746.5	978.2	−231.7	5,258	213.9	187.7	26.2	1,174
Oct-11	993.4	1,165.20	−171.8	748.5	953.1	−204.6	5,084	244.9	212.1	32.9	1,348
Nov-11	1,001.40	1,236.00	−234.6	792.8	1,053.50	−260.8	5,305	208.6	182.4	26.1	1,127
Dec-11	1,013.10	1,283.90	−270.8	820.3	1,114.10	−293.9	5,412	192.9	169.8	23.1	1,020
Jan-12	1,031.20	1,296.80	−265.6	827.4	1,117.30	−289.9	5,388	203.8	179.5	24.3	1,044

(Continued)

	Assets	Liabilities									
Feb-12	1,041.30	1,263.50	−222.2	810.6	1,062.00	−251.4	5,235	230.7	201.4	29.2	1,197
Mar-12	1,026.80	1,231.10	−204.2	806.4	1,037.40	−231	5,022	220.5	193.7	26.8	1,294
Apr-12	1,022.10	1,237.10	−215	817.2	1,057.50	−240.2	5,073	204.8	179.6	25.3	1,243
May-12	1,024.50	1,341.50	−317	870	1,202.80	−332.9	5,404	154.6	138.7	15.9	912
Jun-12	1,032.60	1,304.10	−271.6	846.9	1,138.40	−291.5	5,267	185.7	165.7	20	1,049
Jul-12	1,048.90	1,341.50	−292.6	867.6	1,179.00	−311.4	5,314	181.3	162.6	18.7	1,002
Aug-12	1,053.10	1,343.50	−290.3	869.4	1,179.00	−309.5	5,300	183.7	164.5	19.2	1,016
Sep-12	1,055.50	1,294.90	−239.4	847.5	1,110.60	−263.1	5,128	208	184.3	23.7	1,188
Oct-12	1,052.50	1,288.20	−235.7	850.3	1,110.60	−260.2	5,160	202.2	177.7	24.5	1,156
Nov-12	1,063.80	1,316.00	−252.2	861.6	1,137.30	−275.7	5,205	202.2	178.7	23.5	1,111
Dec-12	1,065.60	1,310.30	−244.7	861	1,130.10	−269.1	5,173	204.6	180.2	24.4	1,143
Jan-13	1,084.30	1,295.50	−211.2	859.9	1,100.40	−240.4	5,031	224.4	195.1	29.3	1,285
Feb-13	1,104.60	1,306.10	−201.5	865.5	1,098.60	−233.1	4,973	239.1	207.5	31.6	1,343
Mar-13	1,118.50	1,329.20	−210.8	852.9	1,098.70	−245.8	4,806	265.6	230.6	35	1,344
Apr-13	1,127.40	1,358.80	−231.3	878.4	1,142.70	−264.3	4,882	249.1	216.1	32.9	1,268
May-13	1,126.30	1,284.70	−158.4	806.1	1,008.20	−202.1	4,570	320.1	276.5	43.7	1,580
Jun-13	1,098.00	1,202.90	−104.9	692.3	850.4	−158.1	4,327	405.7	352.5	53.2	1,823
Jul-13	1,126.10	1,214.40	−88.3	689.6	837.6	-147.9	4,178	436.5	376.8	59.7	1,972
Aug-13	1,105.90	1,186.20	−80.3	667	807.8	−140.8	4,145	438.9	378.4	60.5	2,005
Sep-13	1,114.00	1,199.00	−85	677.9	822.7	−144.8	4,173	436.1	376.3	59.8	1,977
Oct-13	1,139.10	1,214.70	−75.6	677.5	817.6	−140.1	4,063	461.6	397.1	64.5	2,087
Nov-13	1,132.90	1,192.50	−59.7	642.3	770.7	−128.4	3,952	490.5	421.8	68.7	2,198
Dec-13	1,133.00	1,160.50	−27.6	590.5	697.4	−106.9	3,701	542.5	463.1	79.4	2,449
Jan-14	1,130.40	1,206.80	−76.5	673.5	813.2	−139.7	4,108	456.9	393.7	63.2	2,042
Feb-14	1,148.60	1,209.80	−61.2	647.6	778	−130.4	3,947	501	431.7	69.3	2,203
Mar-14	1,137.50	1,176.80	−39.3	616.8	735.8	−119	3,834	520.7	441	79.7	2,223
Apr-14	1,143.30	1,184.00	−40.8	623.4	744.1	−120.7	3,827	519.9	439.9	80	2,230
May-14	1,159.10	1,208.30	−49.2	646.3	773.9	−127.7	3,873	512.8	434.4	78.4	2,184
May-14	1,159.10	1,247.50	−88.4	704	855	−151	4,132	455.1	392.5	62.6	1,925
Jun-14	1,155.70	1,232.50	−76.8	692.1	834.4	−142.3	4,078	463.6	398.1	65.5	1,979
Jul-14	1,161.30	1,254.50	−93.2	721.1	875.7	−154.6	4,178	440.2	378.8	61.5	1,879

Aug-14	1,195.50	1,347.00	−151.6	817.1	1,019.20	−202.1	4,493	378.4	327.9	50.5	1,564
Sep-14	1,186.00	1,330.30	−144.3	806	1,001.60	−195.6	4,472	380	328.7	51.3	1,585
Oct-14	1,198.50	1,363.50	−164.9	832	1,045.00	−213	4,570	366.5	318.4	48.1	1,487
Nov-14	1,232.90	1,454.00	−221.1	895.1	1,156.70	−261.6	4,781	337.8	297.3	40.4	1,276
Dec-14	1,236.60	1,502.90	−266.3	957	1,257.70	−300.7	4,936	279.6	245.2	34.3	1,121
Jan-15	1,273.80	1,641.20	−367.5	1,037.40	1,430.00	−392.6	5,175	236.4	211.2	25.2	882
Feb-15	1,263.40	1,512.10	−248.7	958.8	1,245.60	−286.8	4,849	304.5	266.5	38.1	1,208
Mar-15	1,298.30	1,542.50	−244.2	965.3	1,250.60	−285.3	4,677	333	291.9	41.1	1,268
Apr-15	1,286.70	1,489.60	−202.8	935.1	1,184.70	−249.6	4,526	351.6	304.8	46.8	1,419
May-15	1,294.50	1,495.40	−200.9	939.3	1,187.90	−248.6	4,515	355.2	307.5	47.8	1,430
Jun-15	1,259.50	1,441.60	−182.2	876.7	1,107.60	−230.8	4,473	382.7	334.1	48.7	1,472
Jul-15	1,278.40	1,487.10	−208.7	932.1	1,186.30	−254.2	4,556	346.3	300.8	45.5	1,389
Aug-15	1,256.40	1,489.60	−233.3	931.7	1,205.20	−273.4	4,678	324.6	284.5	40.2	1,267
Sep-15	1,253.90	1,513.90	−260	952.8	1,249.10	−296.3	4,780	301.1	264.8	36.3	1,165
Oct-15	1,269.90	1,486.70	−216.8	930	1,190.20	−260.2	4,604	339.9	296.4	43.5	1,341
Nov-15	1,281.70	1,503.20	−221.4	938.7	1,203.90	−265.2	4,606	343.1	299.3	43.8	1,339
Dec-15	1,275.20	1,469.80	−194.6	892.7	1,134.90	−242.1	4,521	382.5	335	47.5	1,424
Jan-16	1,286.80	1,563.60	−276.8	985.4	1,298.70	−313.3	4,811	301.3	264.9	36.4	1,134
Feb-16	1,301.00	1,595.50	−294.5	1,012.90	1,342.60	−329.7	4,848	288.2	253	35.2	1,097
Mar-16	1,341.40	1,563.10	−221.7	933.1	1,206.60	−273.5	4,499	408.4	356.5	51.8	1,295
Apr-16	1,333.10	1,521.80	−188.7	899.7	1,145.70	−246	4,383	433.5	376.2	57.3	1,411
May-16	1,350.10	1,563.70	−213.6	937.6	1,205.30	−267.7	4,468	412.5	358.3	54.2	1,326
Jun-16	1,420.30	1,724.80	−304.5	1,077.10	1,427.20	−350.1	4,685	343.2	297.5	45.6	1,109
Jul-16	1,458.40	1,791.80	−333.5	1,129.00	1,506.60	−377.5	4,734	329.3	285.3	44.1	1,060
Aug-16	1,486.30	1,899.40	−413.1	1,182.70	1,633.80	−451.1	4,834	303.6	265.6	38	960
Sep-16	1,474.60	1,848.10	−373.5	1,159.50	1,573.70	−414.2	4,792	315.1	274.4	40.7	1,002
Oct-16	1,460.00	1,735.90	−275.9	1,046.90	1,374.80	−327.9	4,566	413.1	361.1	52	1,228
Nov-16	1,443.10	1,667.20	−224.2	998.2	1,282.10	−283.9	4,429	444.8	385.1	59.7	1,365
Nov-16	1,443.10	1,637.80	−194.7	968.6	1,232.20	−263.6	4,272	474.5	405.6	68.9	1,522
Dec-16	1,476.40	1,700.30	−223.9	1,012.50	1,302.70	−290.2	4,339	464	397.6	66.4	1,455

For any investors with similar objectives, for those whom protecting the downside is more important than simply maximising wealth, then an LDI framework should be appropriate as a risk management tool. The hope of LDI practitioners is that a better understanding of Asset-Liability Management and similar techniques will lead to better risk-adjusted outcomes for a greater number of long term investors. The popular framework in the academic literature of expected value optimisation given a risk constraint, is in our view ripe for evolutionary change or even disruption. Our belief is that the trickle-down effect can and should bring these more advanced techniques to the mass market in the medium term. Technology and the FinTech revolution may be part of the solution as lower cost automated processes could make institutional strength risk management available to retail savers, and digital solutions can dis-intermediate expansive and operationally intensive parts of the distribution process.

Currently for many forms of financial advice the expense of reaching the mass-market just doesn't justify the reward. In the United Kingdom, there exists a genuine 'financial advice gap'. This has been caused by the large insurers, the high street banks, investment management firms and the IFA community withdrawing services for those who aren't part of the mass-affluent, often defined as those with less than £100,000 to invest. Arguably those are the potential clients that would benefit the most from comprehensive financial advice. The industry argues the cost of servicing these customers has become too high. This is in part due to regulation forcing increased transparency, that revealed chronic over-charging and poor value for money. But also due to the increased cost and difficulty of keeping up to date with ever changing regulation.

In part this 'financial advice gap' was an unintended consequence of well-intentioned regulation. In particular the UK regulators (FCA) Retail Distribution Review (2012). The Retail Distribution Review, known as RDR for short, created a set of new rules and procedures to protect consumers that have been in practice since 2013. Their aim: to ensure there is more transparency and fairness in the investment industry.

Showing the slow pace of regulatory change, the RDR was initially launched by the Financial Services Authority (FSA), the antecedent body of the FCA, as far back as 2006. In their words:

> 'The rules aimed to make the retail investment market work better for consumers. They raised the minimum level of adviser qualifications, improved the transparency of charges and services and removed commission payments to advisers and platforms from product providers.'

The consequence of these changes was two-fold, some wealthier clients benefited from lower fees as more accurate disclosures led to more competitive pricing. Unfortunately some segments of the market were diminished. Many retail savers became uneconomic clients of financial service firms and resultantly many less affluent individuals were excluded from the system.

There is some hope that better use of existing technology could help bridge this financial advice gap. In fact new technologies and firms with new business models such as Digital asset management (also known as robo-advice) could create a solution. As these new businesses are expanding quickly, although from a low base (currently Robo-advisors account for a fraction of 1% of AUM in developed markets) to a more significant stake of the Retail Market. The regulators believe that Robo-Advice and digital platforms could be well placed to distribute Financial Advice to savers that are currently either underserved or unserved by the financial services community. Innovators and regulators believe that Financial Technology or FinTech could bring low cost high quality financial advice to the mass market. Alongside holistic and Liability Driven Investment solutions enabling small savers to allocate capital effectively and efficiently using similar methodologies to the most sophisticated institutions. We expect and hope to see the industry move further in this direction over the next few years and decades.

SUMMARY

- Multi-Asset Class Investment frameworks are used to allocate capital across asset classes and securities.
- The theories behind MACI began with the work of Harry Markowitz in the 1950s and the development of Modern Portfolio Theory (MPT). LDI is a Multi-Asset Class Investment framework.
- Many modern investment strategies have been directly developed from Modern Portfolio Theory and directly from Markowitz et al.
- The simplicity and elegance of MPT make it a great entry point for understanding investment management, but the limitations of a model which only looks at one side of an entity (individual or institutional)'s balance sheet may need a re-think to match the needs of the modern investor.
- Explicitly incorporating the liabilities or needs of an entity, move the investor's interest from asset optimisation to directly hedging those liabilities. These liabilities can be modelled in a similar way to bond portfolio and resultantly investors have found a need for more fixed income expertise.
- The need for liability matching is explicit and clear for defined benefit pension schemes, but we can see intuitively that there is an implicit need for similar outcomes both defined contribution pension schemes and individual investors.
- There has been a funding crisis in the pensions world across Developed Markets, caused by low yields inflating the cost of liabilities and exacerbated by poor equity returns since the start of the millennium.
- The rise in pension deficits, which has been a global phenomenon, has led to more interest in managing these deficits pro-actively and protecting the needs of pensioners.
- Liability Driven Investment has become dominant in the institutional world but has yet to filter down to the retail market. Whilst investment consultants in the square mile are specialists and awareness is high, for the retail market independent financial advisors rarely embrace LDI and awareness is low to non-existent.
- Technology may change the current lack of retail take-up, and LDI may filter down to the retail market as new digital platforms help close the 'Financial Advice Gap.'
- The democratisation of liability driven frameworks should come from the lower costs and more efficient distribution methods caused by the FinTech and low cost revolution.

CHAPTER 2

Introduction to Investment Risk

The key question when analysing financial assets is what are the risks? But what is risk? Well, this depends on who you ask. Skydiving is 'risky' but in a different way, so is walking down the street. Some investors will avoid the stock market, because it's risky, but may occasionally gamble on sports, or they might leave cash in the bank or under the couch where it's value could be whittled away by inflation. One thing we can agree on though, is that:

'Risk is a four letter word!'

(In the English language, at least)

No book on investment, liability driven or otherwise, would be complete without gently circling the idea of investment or financial 'risk' and attempting to define it. Risk is in many ways a strange word, the very concept of risk can and will mean different things to different people at different times in their lives. Users and abusers of financial services will have markedly different perceptions of what 'risk' is, what 'risk' was and the risks ahead. Even across different sectors of the investment industry what a practitioner may consider as 'risk' can also differ markedly.

Unhelpfully, the securities markets and financial market practitioners everywhere, alongside the world of financial risk management, have created many multiple definitions of risk which can add to, but also sometimes confuse our real-world understanding of the concept. It will be shown that risk is a word that is difficult to define exactly and has many different meanings depending on who you are talking to and when.

Some examples of risk definitions are:

'Risk is any uncertainty with respect to your investments that has the potential to negatively affect your financial welfare.'

From FINRA – the US-based Financial Regulatory Authority

'In finance, risk refers to the degree of uncertainty and/or potential financial loss inherent in an investment decision. In general, as investment risks rise, investors seek higher returns to compensate themselves for taking such risks.'

From the SEC – The US Securities and Exchange Commission

For the purposes of this book our main concern is 'market risk', but many other forms of investment risk exist and can impact and confuse the investing process. In common usage, 'risk' is usually pejorative and has somewhat negative connotations – in everyday life unemployment, injury, ill health are all considered risks, and risk is usually not described in a positive manner.

The sentences below use the word 'risk' in an understandable way, but also in a way that seems unusual due to the lack of a negative outcome:

   i. There is a risk my health will improve
  ii. There is an increasing risk that I'll be a millionaire by Tuesday
 iii. There's a risk the holiday will be amazing
  iv. The risk of winning

The Oxford English Dictionary defines risk as '*A situation involving exposure to danger.*'

In finance, we tend to think a little differently. To the economist or investment manager 'risk' is a more neutral term and refers purely to the possibility of more than one outcome. In other words, in financial language 'risk' is similar to 'uncertainty' and danger is implicit not explicit.

When investing we can look at risk as a deviation from expected or known returns. This difference from the expected return can and will be either positive or negative. As risk managers we are concerned with the probability and magnitude of the deviation from expectations and understanding the probability of various outcomes. In particular for Liability Driven Investing the main concern or greatest risk is the likelihood of not achieving our goals.

Many people or investors, when they hear the term investment 'risk', may think of volatile equity markets (or potentially even worse risks, such as the possibility of being defrauded and losing everything) and the frequency or potential for large stock market losses. The investors may also be concerned with the possibility of not getting all of their investment back when saving for the future. Whilst this 'capital' risk is important, it isn't the only type of risk that investors experience. Other types of risk to consider include potential loss of income, uncertainty over cash flows and the changing nature of money over time.

Often a lack of clarity in our definition of risk can lead to unclear communication between investment practitioners and savers or stakeholders. This can be particularly true in the world of Defined Benefit pensions where Liability Driven Investment has become so dominant. Pension trustees are often highly qualified and experienced in their own fields, but rarely have extensive experience of investment risk management. As such it can often be a refreshing and useful exercise for investment consultants and plan trustees to agree what they mean by risk before creating a plan for the future, which is often specified in the '*Statement of Investment Principles*'. This, of course, is also relevant to retail investors who may be unclear as to whether they wish to optimise the value of their assets – or to better mitigate their liabilities and ensure that a minimum income level can be obtained.

Ultimately, when you as an investor put capital to work in the financial markets or 'at risk'. It can be difficult to say with any precision what returns will be like over any investment horizon. Particularly when investing over the long term, or over multiple time horizons.

Whilst the cult of equity means that for many long-term investors, substantial allocations to stocks and shares mean there is little consideration of timing and cash flow issues. For other investors it is unclear even if, and when they may need to withdraw the investment. Over any holding period asset prices are likely to fluctuate, often substantially, interest rates will vary and inflation is likely to erode the purchasing power of any cash or fixed cash flows in the portfolio. Currently we are globally in a low interest rate regime. These low interest rates have created high prices almost universally across asset classes, but interest rates can change and asset price increases are not guaranteed to stay high. Investing is an inherently risky endeavour. But perversely when investing for the long term, it can be seen that under-investment and taking too little risk can also be dangerous. Usually under-investment will lead to worse outcomes than even a partially invested portfolio, as over time inflation (usually) erodes the value of money.

Here are some points on risk for an investor or their advisors to consider:

- Do they know what their primary savings goals are?
- Do they know their primary, secondary, etc. goals and the relative importance of each?
- Do they understand the risks associated with the primary savings goal?
- Has this risk been constant or at least reasonably predictable overtime?
- If circumstances were to change dramatically, is it possible to change the portfolio, quickly and easily and at low cost? The need for change could be due to asset market dynamics or a dramatic change in the lifestyle or needs of the saver.
- For the riskier parts of the portfolio, is there adequate compensation or likely expected extra return for the extra risk undertaken?
- Is the downside limited, understood and where practical mitigated?
- Is there potential for significant outperformance?
- Is there potential for significant underperformance?
- Does the risk of any new investment add to or diversify away from other risks already existing in the portfolio?
- Does risk need to be taken? Short- or medium-term goals available with cash assets may mean the extra reward cannot be justified.

Questions like these help us comprehend our goals and provide a framework against which we can start making investment decisions. This helps develop our understanding of which risks to avoid, which to accept, and which (if any) to embrace.

To understand risk in a financial context an investor must identify their outcome preferences and their ability to withstand loss. When assessing risk on behalf of investors, investment advisors often breakdown their clients' preferences and needs into two distinct categories:

1. <u>Risk Tolerance:</u> This is considered the level of risk that the investor is comfortable taking. It is subjective and can (has to) be measured in an arbitrary way. It refers to an attitude about risk; particularly with regard to short term fluctuations in portfolio value. For the small saver, an individual investor's risk tolerance is usually measured using a template risk survey, many of which don't fully capture the nuances of investor psychology. For a financial institution, more sophisticated, but still subjective frameworks are used.

Questions used to estimate risk tolerance include: What level of risk would an investor be willing to accept? What would be considered a bad result? How aggressive should the portfolio be to achieve these desired return objectives, or simply to avoid a defined 'bad result'? Is the investor – whether an individual, or trustees acting on behalf of beneficiaries – likely to panic and make sub-optimal decisions at critical times?

2. Risk Capacity: This is less subjective and risk capacity can often be more critical as it measures the level of risk an entity or investor is actually able to withstand. Hence, unlike risk tolerance, which is an estimate of the amount of risk that an investor is comfortable with, risk capacity reflects the amount of risk that is required to reach investment goals.

RISK MANAGEMENT

Risk Management is perhaps the most important part of any investment framework. In times of crisis or financial stress, strong risk controls can make the difference between firm survival and bankruptcy or firm extinction. Lehman Brothers are the classic example of an entity with weak Risk Management that should have had much stronger risk frameworks in place given the complexity of the underlying business. In the case of the individual, managing risk wisely can be the difference between prosperity and destitution. Due to this importance the Risk department will (or should) form the backbone of many financial services firms, and the position of Chief Risk Officer or CRO is one of the most important in any institution, typically reporting directly to the board, if not a board member in their own right.

However, in quieter times, with benign market conditions, the Risk department can often be seen as a cost centre and a drain on resources, removing capital from business development and more productive opportunities with a tangible and immediate return on capital.

Let's look at what we consider to be fair risks and see how our understanding of the term 'risk' as investment professionals differs from common usage.

A fair return on investment is defined as one that compensates the investor for the risk incurred in making the investment. In investment management risk-adjusted returns are sometimes more important than absolute returns. Particularly when compensating risk-takers for the returns they have generated.

An excess return is a return on investment that over-compensates the investor for the risk taken. Investors will seek investments likely to pay an excess return and wish to avoid investments that are likely to pay less than a fair return.

THE IMPORTANCE OF RISK VS RETURN

An investor's appetite for risk is perhaps the most critical component of future outcomes. The likely reward of an investment must be considered against the risk profile of the investor and the anticipated probability distribution of outcomes. An investment with a relatively high expected return could still be undesirable if the risk is considered too high. However, for many institutions, risk may not be quantified in a deliberate manner and a quantitative trade-off of risk vs. return is not meaningful if reasonable estimates of risk are not made *a priori*.

QUANTIFYING RISK

When measuring investment risk, the most common methodology is volatility, which is defined as the standard deviation of returns. It is helpful therefore to try and quantify risk by looking at a simple example of volatility in a stochastic (where the future is unknown) context. Let's take a simple example where we look at possible returns from investing in a stock index. We'd like to know the likelihood, or probability, of each of the possible alternative outcomes.

Suppose that we are investing in the shares of an ETF which tracks a broad stock market index, when doing this we would like to know:

What is my expected return?

What is the mean or average expected total return for the next year?

How 'risky' is the investment?

How can we measure this risk?

We might begin by checking the history books. There exists a great deal of data for broad index returns and collecting data about total returns on an index for an extended time period, say 30 years or longer, we could make reasoned estimates of what an investor may expect in return to compensate for the 'riskiness' of a stock market investment.

The standard measure used to 'simply' quantify risk is the standard deviation of asset prices, and is a statistical measure equal to the square root of the variance.

Mathematically,

$$SQRT(E(X)^2 - E(SQRT(X^2))).$$

For simplicity, risk managers will often assume asset prices for a Normal Distribution.

In practice, financial assets exhibit leptokurtosis, more commonly known as 'fat tails'. This means that using a Normal Distribution is likely to underestimate the possibility of extreme events. An example of this in practice is during the global financial crisis (GFC), bank risk models would often suggest that some of the extreme daily moves observed were only likely to occur once in 10,000 years. Unfortunately, reality was suggesting their models were wrong.

Investment Risk is often broken into two.

SYSTEMATIC AND NONSYSTEMATIC RISK

As explained elsewhere, investment risks (particularly) market risk is often de-composed into systematic or nonsystematic components. This is financial jargon but what they describe can be simplified:

Systematic risk refers to risk in the overall securities markets.

Non-Systematic refers to risks that aren't systematic, or more crudely risks specific to individual securities.

Asset Classes vary in risk.

It is crucial when investing or simply analysing investment risk to understand that each asset class has different risks and rewards. An investor who understands what these risks and rewards are, and how they change over time, will generally be able to construct an investment portfolio or savings plan that better matches their needs.

The risk profiles of the main asset classes are:

Equities – These are characterised as High Risk, High Return and suit the long-term investor;

Fixed Income – More commonly known as Bonds. Bonds are generally considered medium- to low-risk investments *(although some bonds are high risk, eg High Yield or distressed debt)*.

Cash – No nominal risk but minimal return. (In practical terms, the value of cash can be eroded over time, hence not even cash can be considered completely without risk.)

Equity is the driver of returns in most long-term portfolios. Equity securities are considered permanent and don't have a nominal value that will likely be returned with a specific timeframe. Instead, equity prices, at least in the short term, reflect changing investor demand in the markets and estimations of future economic returns. This leads to volatility with a likelihood of significant price changes in short time periods. These short-term significant fluctuations are believed to be rewarded with increased return, this belief is backed up by substantial amounts of academic research and historical data.

Fixed Income. Fixed Income Securities or Bonds have a fixed value. Typically, either 100 or 1,000 per instrument. This is known as par or nominal value. An investor who owns a bond until maturity would expect to receive the nominal or par value back, plus the interest rate defined by the coupon. This is, of course, unless the issuer of the bond security defaults on the loan, or fails to pay a coupon or principal payment. In developed nations the probability of default on government debt is considered for practical purposes to be zero.

Just like stocks, bonds will exhibit price volatility, but significantly less than comparable equities.

The price of fixed income securities varies with interest rates, expected changes in interest rates and investor demand.

Cash. On cash investments the return will be known. But importantly only in nominal terms. The primary risk with cash investments is the loss of purchasing power due to the long term and compounding effects of inflation.

Many other asset classes exist, notably real estate, hedge funds, emerging markets, Forex and commodities.

CREATING A RISK PROFILE

Modern Portfolio Theory and most investment frameworks make an assumption that an investor can and will make a rational and knowledgeable trade-off between the risk and return to be expected from a portfolio of securities. But investment knowledge is never perfect, and investors will always make imperfect decisions on imperfect data, the growing field of Behavioural Finance describes how investors behave irrationally and how emotions can affect the investment process. Traditional financial and economic models often rely on perfect and rational knowledge. However, *homo economicus* does not exist in reality, and panic fear and greed will impact all of our decision making. These effects are especially pronounced for less sophisticated investors or those not from a finance background. However, only once the payoffs between risk and return are understood can an optimal portfolio be constructed.

Definition, *Homo Economicus*:

From the Oxford English Dictionary '*using rational assessments, Homo economicus attempts to maximize utility as a consumer and economic profit as a producer*'; essentially a person whose every action is made unemotionally on perfect information. This person is unlikely to exist in the real world, which may imply that many economic models are flawed at the outset.

SUMMARY

Some Basic Rules of Investment Risk

- The word risk means different things to different people, and its use in financial markets and investment is different to that of everyday life.
- The greater return required or desired, the greater the risk that will have to be taken.
- High Investment Risk implies higher expected return, but it does not guarantee it.
- For short-term investment, risking principle may be unwise. The security of cash (no downside) can often be more important than a small loss in expected portfolio return.
- For long-term investment, more risk can be appropriate; indeed, the effects of inflation mean that underinvestment has been more risky than over-investment in a broad array of investment environments.
- Equity investment has historically been the best way for creating long term value, with generous returns in both nominal and inflation adjusted terms. With a long time horizon there is more time to recover from periods of weak stock market performance and for the equity risk premium to take effect.

CHAPTER 3

Introductory Steps into the World of Multi-Asset Class Investment

'Don't put all your eggs in one basket'

– Harry Markowitz and many others

Every investor, be it a young professional starting their savings journey, or the stereotypical rich industrialist (possibly wearing a top hat) allocating billions will have to make similar decisions when they put their money to work.

They will be confronted with a bewildering and near infinite choice of investments. A stream of difficult questions lies ahead of them as they begin putting their capital into the financial markets. Or, more formally, the investor implements the asset allocation process. The numerous decisions that will have to be made include:

Should the investor directly invest in individual securities?

Should he or she buy into actively managed funds for easy diversification and risk management?

Should they purchase a basket of ETFs (Exchange Traded Funds) as this technique becomes increasingly popular?

What asset classes are appropriate?

Is it best to go **passive or active** (to be discussed)?

Is he or she more interested in capital growth or security?

Importantly, how does the investor feel about the risk?

What is their risk capacity and how does it compare to their risk tolerance?

For any investor an important question is: Is the return **of** capital, more important than the return **on** capital?

Clearly there are a multitude of options available to the average investor. Even more importantly we ask: How can the modern investor answer these questions and make the best decisions, and what guidance, if any, will they require?

What should be obvious from the above, is that the asset allocation decision is complex and that to make the most appropriate allocations an investor must be informed of a wide range of possible investments across multiple asset classes. We can see that successfully managing multi-asset portfolios demands an exceptionally broad array of skills. Possibly too many for one person!

When you leave your savings in the hands of professionals you are (hopefully) gaining access to a set of experienced and educated investors with insights in all investable asset classes – including the better-known such equities, fixed income, real estate, infrastructure, private equity, but then also many, many more esoteric investments.

But an in-depth comprehension of all asset classes may only be the start, having chosen the securities and assets and creating an investment universe, yet another skill is necessary. This is the expertise to blend these investments in just the right proportions and then form the right portfolio for the investor's needs, matching both their risk capacity and their risk tolerance.

The starting point for many professional investors, when on-boarding a new investor and approaching portfolio construction, is Modern Portfolio Theory and iterations there-of, but this is now seen by many in the investment community as a too simplistic approach. As discussed, in its simple form it only looks at one side of the investor's balance sheet. Resultantly the holistic approach of Liability Driven Investing (LDI) is gaining favour.

In the last decade interest in Multi-Asset Class investing (MACI) has increased both as a field of academic study and as a practical concern in the capital markets with dedicated teams forming to specialise in investing across the various different asset classes. In Europe the loosely defined multi-strategy sector has seen significant growth this decade, approximately trebling in size from 5% of worldwide assets in 2010 to 15% of global assets in 2017. In the institutional markets, this uptake has partly been due to the rise of LDI. In the last five years there has been more interest in liability-driven investments, as part of multi-asset bespoke solutions both due to the increased underfunding of many pensions and growing awareness of the product from advisors and investors.

This increased interest in investing across multiple asset classes has led to an increased awareness of Liability-Driven Investment Strategies which rely on a holistic view of entire investment portfolios. LDI tools will often act as an overlay to these MACI structures. In this book, I aim to provide an introduction to and reference for liability driven investment (LDI). My hope is that readers can build a base from which they can develop a deeper understanding of modern investing and the importance of risk management, whilst avoiding an overly quantitative approach that has often failed to resonate with end-users.

Over the last fifteen years Liability Driven Investment has come to dominate institutional investment markets in the United Kingdom, with near total market share in the defined benefits pensions market and increasing relevance for all large multi-asset allocation decisions. It is also gaining increasing acceptance globally with the emergence of increasing numbers of European and American practitioners. However, in many ways it is still early days in the switch to LDI frameworks with global uptake still low and the low-yield environment making strategies unattractive to many investors. The concept of Liability Driven Investment is still virtually unknown to Retail Investors and even to the vast majority of Financial Advisors. But like many in the field I believe this will change over time due to both investor education and LDI's developing track record of superior user outcomes. Although the catalyst for a change to LDI style techniques may be greater use of technology and a regulatory regime that increasingly favours a more holistic approach to risk management rather than end-user demand.

It seems intuitive to us as risk managers and investors that future cash flow needs can be as important as current assets when assessing our risk appetite. Further, that only by incorporating liabilities into the asset allocation decision can we fully understand an investor's needs and risks. It is this understanding at the heart of LDI. It could be said that by only looking at the asset side of investor balance sheets:

'traditional frameworks see less than half the problem'.

There is growing hope that technology will lower the cost associated with financial analysis and democratise Institutional Risk Management. It is likely that the Financial Technology or FinTech Revolution will see greater understanding and uptake of these advanced techniques, with sophisticated risk management filtering down to the smaller institutional investors and then finally to retail. Leading to an end result of better consumer and social outcomes. Many in the field also see regulatory pressure favouring more refined investment techniques, such as LDI for firms offering regulated financial 'advice'. For example, in Europe, under MiFiD II (which was amalgamated into EU law on 3 January 2018), traditional analysis which does not incorporate an investor's debts and liabilities into the investment decision may be generating non-'**Suitable**' portfolios.

Liability Driven Investment is ultimately a framework for asset allocation and goes hand in hand with portfolio construction. LDI is more concerned with risk management than excess return. As such it could be considered a form of multi-asset class investing which even for an experienced investor, given the number of ways to construct a portfolio, can be intimidating. As we shall see the number of available investments is practically infinite in both breadth and depth. In the professional and even retail investing universe, there exist hundreds of stock exchanges scattered across the globe, listing thousands of individual stocks denominated in many different currencies. There are many thousand issuers of fixed income securities or bonds in the United Kingdom alone, each offering many different seniorities, durations, maturities and coupons. All these exist alongside a cavalcade of distinct asset classes, from the well-known such as Real Estate and Fixed Income, to the more esoteric possibilities, which include Structured Notes, Volatility Products and Cryptocurrencies.

The purpose of this discussion is to expand on more traditional risk / return optimisation frameworks and introduce the non-asset or liability side of the balance sheet to the investment equation. My aim is to show that Liability Driven Investment which is often considered helpful only for Defined Benefit pension schemes is in fact relevant for all investors. As many investors have the same long term cash flow needs, this theory is not as revolutionary as it might seem, and we are seeing increasing use of LDI techniques in Defined Contribution or general saving schemes which would in the past have likely used a more traditional asset-optimisation risk-adjusted return framework derived from Modern Portfolio Theory.

SOME HANDY DEFINITIONS

Defined Benefit: A pension scheme typically sponsored by an employer in which the employee receives a recurring payment (which is usually linked to inflation, but can be fixed), or benefit, during retirement or upon a fixed date.

The amount of that payment is determined by a formula based on salary history and years of service at the company. This is considered the gold standard for most pensioners as the employer or trust assumes all the investment risk and has an obligation to pay the employee the defined benefit regardless of the investment performance of their assets or the economic condition of the sponsor.

In Defined Benefit schemes, the size of the payment received is known but the cost of the obligation is not.

Defined Contribution: This refers to a pension scheme in which fixed contributions are invested on behalf of the beneficiary, but the amount to be received on retirement is not fixed. Instead investment returns will ultimately decide the payment and if and when the employee is in a position to retire.

In most cases the beneficiary will have some responsibility in deciding how the contributions are invested (although in practice investment choices are often limited to a small range of funds, on a specified platform). These schemes are preferred by corporate sponsors as investment risk is handed to the employee and employer contributions are known and thus easier to manage. The asset allocation decision for a defined contribution (DC) scheme is often considered similar to that of a general long-term savings account.

In direct contrast to Defined Benefit schemes, in Defined Contribution schemes, the size of the sponsor obligation is known but the size of the future payments is not.

Suitability: The requirement that any investing strategy or portfolio is appropriate to the financial capacity and investment objectives of an investor. In the modern markets, for financial advisors, designing, implementing and executing an asset allocation strategy there must be a defined process. There are obligatory assessments which vary by regulatory regime, which are used to test for suitability. To test for client suitability in retail space, advisors need a detailed analysis of the financial situation of the client, including the client's investment knowledge, experience, investment objectives and capacity for loss.

THE STARTING POINT

The Asset Management industry and Financial Services sector are arguably the most important allocators of capital in the modern economy, but it is important to ask what processes ultimately drive asset allocation and what the underlying rationales are.

Many lay people imagining the investment industry at work, would picture 'Wall Street' – both the film and the place – with traders, salesmen and researchers hunting the latest 'great stock' and finding an interesting story, a broad theme or a hot trading tip to buy into. Whilst there is a hint of truth in this image, it is only a tiny part of a gigantic picture. In actual fact the financial markets have a much sounder theoretical basis, and stock selection is only a small part of the modern investment process. For the vast majority of investors, the major driver of returns is in fact asset allocation, not picking the right stock or security or even the right fund manager. Understanding which asset classes are appropriate for investors' needs, and when, is the foundation of modern multi-asset class investing and financial risk management.

It can help to decompose the asset allocation process into three steps, in which we as liability driven investors are mainly concerned with the last. And, of course, to state our assumptions as and when we develop our model.

Step 1: Individual Security Analysis: This focuses on the selection of individual stocks and bonds using traditional financial techniques such as balance sheet analysis, financial and accounting ratios and the detailed analytical research of individual stocks and issuers. The chosen stocks and securities are then pooled to form a fund. Interestingly, the rise of **passive investing** is decreasing the importance of this part of the process.

Step 2: Fund Selection: Instead of investing in individual securities (stock-picking) within an asset class, many professional investors or advisors are restricted to individual funds. These funds are baskets of investment instruments, which can represent a specific asset class. This guarantees exposure to, but diversification within, each asset class. Factors which are of importance when selecting funds include, but are not limited to: managerial competence, operational stability, relative value, liquidity concerns, expected outperformance (known as Alpha), volatility (both absolute and relative to an index), fees, and transparency as well as tax considerations. For the retail investor buying the right fund can give broad market exposure and risk management in one simple step.

Step 3: Portfolio Construction: Here the end task is to decide, what is the optimal selection of funds and securities for the end investor? This was typically done as return optimisation with a risk constraint, or as risk minimisation given an expected return constraint. However, the advent of Asset Liability Management (ALM) and Liability Driven Investment (LDI) have seen a portfolio selection methodology of minimising the cost of matching expected cash flows gaining acceptance.

INTRODUCING MODERN PORTFOLIO THEORY

The investment industry has typically used Modern Portfolio Theory (MPT) as the underpinning of its risk management and portfolio selection process, and indeed many asset managers and even many Financial Technology or FinTech firms refer to MPT-style techniques as the basis of their asset allocation framework.

Before developing an understanding of current investment frameworks, it is important to understand Modern Portfolio Theory, its explanatory power and its limitations. The conceptual beginnings of MPT were introduced to the world in a 1952 essay by a 24-year-old graduate student at the University of Chicago, Harry Markowitz. Who in 1990, for this and further articles in finance and economics was awarded the Nobel Prize for Economics (or more properly the Bank of Sweden Award in Memory of Alfred Nobel). In the intervening decades until he received the award, he had helped establish and refine his portfolio theory and popularised numerous financial concepts such as **Beta** within the industry, as well as being a key player in the development of contemporary risk management frameworks and the development of Finance as an academic subject separate from accounting or economics.

Historically, individual security-selection models focused primarily on the returns generated by investment opportunities. Financial analysis was concerned with identifying those securities that offered the largest return for a unit of risk and then constructing a portfolio from these. There was little discussion of the effect of individual investments on the portfolio. Investment was not 'holistic', inter asset correlations were not discussed let alone modelled rigorously. But there was some understanding of the benefits of diversification.

Markowitz himself said, quoting Shakespeare in the Merchant of Venice:

'My ventures are not in one bottom trusted,
Nor to one place; nor is my whole estate
Upon the fortune of this present year;
Therefore, my merchandise makes me not sad.'

This passage shows an intuitive understanding of the concept of covariance, and diversification through time, investment, and geography. Despite being centuries old, many of the basic concepts of Finance are implicitly included. Markowitz's contribution was not then to introduce the concept of diversification to portfolio analysis, but to look at the effects of risk and return holistically, and then quantify those effects more rigorously than previous financiers or academics.

The original 1952 Markowitz paper showed that as you add assets to an investment portfolio the total risk of that portfolio – as measured by the volatility of the portfolio's value (or standard deviation) – declines continuously, but that the expected return of the portfolio, which is a weighted average of the expected returns of the individual assets, need not be compromised. In other words, by investing in portfolios rather than individual assets, investors could lower the total risk of investing without necessarily sacrificing return; this is considered the one free lunch in Finance.

Harry Markowitz summed up his discoveries rather neatly:

'Don't put all your eggs in one basket.'

Of course, although this is a nice (and concise) summary his work went past this one liner. Markowitz's numerous essays provided a quantitative understanding of the risk – reward framework and became the underpinning of early quantitative risk management systems. By developing Modern Portfolio Theory, Markowitz alongside others provided a rigorous understanding of what diversification is and how it works to improve investment opportunities. MPT also showed how to create a portfolio that is as 'diverse' as possible for a selected amount of risk: This became known as 'the market portfolio'. In doing so, Markowitz et al created a tool that was immediately applicable to investors large and small. Modern Portfolio Theory told us exactly which risk assets to hold and in what proportions given an investor's risk appetite.

Intuitively, there has always been a pay-off between risk and return. We also know that risk and rewards are dealt with differently. Most investors also suffer from loss aversion, with the pain of losses likely to be felt harder than the benefit of gains. Modern Portfolio Theory and investment has therefore become about finding the right balance between either maximising returns given a risk constraint (often described as a risk budget), or minimising risk given a desired return. The objective is to select your investments in such a way as to diversify your risks while not reducing your expected return. Although, as we shall see later, other techniques can complement this approach.

MORE HANDY DEFINITIONS

Beta: Beta measures the responsiveness of a security's price to changes in the overall market. By multiplying the beta value of a security with a movement in the market or index, the expected change in the value of the stock can be determined. For example, if a beta is 0.8 and the market had crashed 20 per cent, then the stock would be expected to move minus 16 per cent (0.8 times minus 20 per cent). Similarly, for a lower risk stock with a Beta of 0.5, the expected loss would be 10 per cent (0.5 times minus 20 per cent).

Market Portfolio: The Market portfolio is a portfolio consisting of a weighted sum of every asset in the financial markets, with weights in the proportions that they exist in the market. The expected return of the market portfolio is identical to the expected return of the market as a whole.

Passive Investing: This form of investing aims to generate the same rate of return as an underlying market index. Investors will use a fund or derivative to replicate the performance of a specific index, avoiding the cost of active management. The focus on fund selection for investors opting for passive portfolios is primarily cost, but also includes issues such as 'tracking error', liquidity and counterparty risks.

Return: Usually expressed as a percentage, this includes either capital appreciation or loss (the price of the asset rising or falling) and payments (dividends, coupons, etc). For Fixed Income investments, the return may include price appreciation, fixed or floating payments of interest, and the payment or partial payment of the principal. Investors also talk of nominal returns and 'real' returns which have been adjusted for inflation.

Risk: The Oxford English Dictionary defines risk as:

'A situation involving exposure to danger' or 'The possibility that something unpleasant or unwelcome will happen'.

For us as investors risk is a difficult and nuanced concept. Traditional portfolio management is based on mean-variance optimisation and uses the statistical concept of standard deviation (also called volatility) to measure investment risk. In this book we use risk as the measure of variability in the expected return as well as the variability in asset prices.

In many cases, discussions of investment portfolios and relevant legislation will discuss the need for 'risk management' and the avoidance of unnecessary risks. But very rarely will they define it. For example, MiFiD II (the second Markets in Financial Instruments Directive), which is changing European markets, currently talks about diminishing risks but does not define risk mathematically or rigorously.

Volatility: This is now the standard risk measure for financiers and is simply the standard deviation of returns. The standard deviation (which can be synonymous with volatility in finance) is a statistical measure of dispersion and is defined as the square root of the variance. The variance is defined as the expected squared deviation of the return on an investment from its expected return.

BUT HOW DOES THE ASSET ALLOCATION DECISION WORK?

How can the asset allocation decision help investors reach their goals?

Simply put, the decision tells you how much of your portfolio you should place into various categories of investments, after adjusting for return expectations/needs and risk appetite/capacity. In most cases the asset allocation decision will be more important to outcomes than which stocks are selected and the which exact blend of asset managers is chosen. A key part of the decision concerns the break between the parts of the portfolio that generate return, and the parts that mitigate risk. Specifically, how much money to place into riskier assets such as equities, and therefore how much to place in safer investments such as short-term deposits, the money market and AAA-rated government bonds.

As an example, if an investor were in an investment universe with only two assets, Stocks and Bonds, her investment strategy might be to allocate 70% to Stocks, the rest would then implicitly have to be allocated to Bonds, giving what is known as a 70/30 Portfolio.

A standard 70/30 portfolio is often used as a benchmark for medium risk portfolios.

In modern markets, there are of course many more than two asset classes, and investors view the asset allocation decision as determining investment levels in many categories of risk assets. The main risk assets being equities, fixed income, private equity, venture capital, real estate (commercial and residential), emerging markets and Forex. More sophisticated or curious investors will also look to what are considered alternative investments such as hedge funds, infrastructure, commodities, and even more esoteric stores of value such as digital currencies.

An example of the main asset classes that could be used by a modern investor is included in the table below. Although this list is certainly non-exhaustive, and for the private investor art, wine and classic cars etc (collectables) can form a large and important part of an investment portfolio or total assets whilst also being consumables.

The dual purpose of some collectables – fun and funding – is sometimes considered to be similar to the convenience yield from owning commodities:

- Equities (Home Market / Domestic)
- Equities (Developed Markets)
- Equities (Emerging Markets)
- Equities (Small Cap – for example, in the United Kingdom stocks on the Alternative Investment Market; AIM)
- Cash
- Cash Equivalents
- Fixed Income – Short dated
- Fixed Income – Long dated
- Fixed Income – Inflation Linked
- Fixed Income – Inflation and Credit Linked
- Fixed Income – Investment Grade Credit
- Fixed Income – High Yield Credit
- Fixed Income – Asset Backed Securities

- Fixed Income – Structured Notes
- Real Estate
- Commercial Real Estate
- Private Equity
- Venture Capital
- Precious metals (including gold, silver, etc)
- Commodities
- Emerging Markets
- Foreign Exchange
- Alternative Investments
- Hedge Funds (although it is sometimes debated, whether Hedge Funds are an asset class in their own right or simply a changing set of strategies utilising other asset classes)

The total investment universe could then be used to create a **Market Portfolio.** The Market portfolio is defined as a portfolio consisting of a weighted sum of every asset in a specified market, with weights in the proportions that they exist in that market. The market portfolio is an abstract concept and much discussion can ensue over what contains an 'investable' asset. In practice, investors will often limit themselves to highly liquid securities such as the shares in multinational firms and High Quality Corporate/ Government bonds.

Although in some applications of the theory to create a market portfolio for investment purposes an investor would need to include every asset class and security in the universe. In practice a portfolio could not necessarily include every single possible available asset, many of which are not practically investable. These potential assets could include – but are not limited to – real estate, precious metals, Foreign Exchange, stamp collections, fine art, antique furniture, jewellery, fine wine and even cryptocurrencies.

'Any item or potential store of value, from the smallest trinket to the Empire State Building would be included in the theoretical complete market portfolio.'

As such, what constitutes the market portfolio is open to debate. Meaning that, rather unfortunately given our needs, there is no index or benchmark that can accurately represent this idealised market portfolio. However index and benchmark providers will create indices for different asset classes which can be used as a proxy for the broader market, well known examples would include the FTSE 100 in the United Kingdom alongside the S & P 500 in the US for equities, the Barclay's Global Aggregate for Fixed Income and the S & P GSCI (formerly the Goldman Sachs Commodity Index) index for Commodities.

Although as for practical purposes the market portfolio must be limited to investable assets, meaning very few investors will or could have holdings in every conceivable asset class. Similarly, few investors, hold a proportion of domestic and foreign assets directly proportional to their aggregate values. With the observed global phenomenon that investors are often happiest and most comfortable with their own market and often over-allocate there. This is known as 'Home Country Bias.'

A Quick Aside.

HOME COUNTRY BIAS:

This refers to investor's consistent and globally observed preference for investing more in their home country than financial theory would predict. This is despite professional risk managers and investment practitioners being aware of the benefits of diversified international portfolios. Some of the factors or possible explanations are listed below:

Liability Driven Investing or Asset Liability Management – The need to hedge certain cash flows in either the short or long term can lead to a home-country bias, and this effect is particularly pronounced for fixed income investors. Domestic investor cash flow requirements or return objectives are often influenced more by factors in the home economy than events abroad. Resultantly, the diversification benefits attained through expanding the investment universe may actually constrain the investor's ability to meet their objective. For a full LDI or ALM mandate, a practitioner may also be restricted by the availability of appropriate instruments. For example, an individual hedging the cash flow needs of an inflation linked GBP denominated pension scheme, would likely be limited to Inflation products issued by the UK government or derivatives thereof.

It should be noted that this cannot be the only reason and that liability concerns are unlikely to be the driving factor behind Home Country Bias as Liability Hedging has become dominant only this millennium, but the home country bias has been documented alongside Modern Portfolio Theory for over half a century.

Familiarity – End users often feel more comfortable with their home market and allocate investments accordingly, even if this is non-optimal in a risk return framework. A case of less stress but less return.

Governance – Investors will often feel comfortable with their own economic system and the governance standards within their domestic market but be wary of the unknown. In particular, investors worry about differing approaches to governance in emerging markets. This is despite improving standards of governance and understanding of investor concerns in many nascent markets. In addition to the fact that emerging market or EM economies are playing an increasingly important role in the global economy. Given their significantly higher economic growth potential and strengthening trade links EM markets are likely to become increasingly important in the decades to come. Emerging economies now account for nearly 40 percent of global gross domestic product, but are still under-represented in investor portfolios, both as a share of Market Capitalisation and GDP. A large part of this shortfall is thought to be due to perceived risk around accounting standards, property rights and shareholder protections in developing nations. Investors can mitigate some of their worries about lower standards of governance by selecting multi-national firms or purchasing stocks with local listings that may abide by higher (or more familiar) standards of corporate governance. But governance concerns are genuine and typically lead to EM stocks trading at a discount to developed market equities.

Exposure to Multi-nationals – Multinational companies sell and consume goods and services around the globe, which means that they provide exposure beyond the domestic economy. For many of the world's largest firms the majority of both revenues and costs are non-domestic, and the domicile of stock listing is almost an historical accident rather than an economic reality. Investors may feel that through exposure to the world's largest corporations, they are able to gain access to international investment opportunities and risk premia, but at low cost and more familiar standards of corporate governance. For many advisors/trustees the existence of Multi-nationals can substitute for the need to gain in-house emerging market or international specialists. Multi-nationals can offer exposure similar risk profiles but at lower cost and with higher liquidity.

Costs – For many investors with pre-existing relationships within their own markets, the cost of forming new relationships and developing new skill sets is perceived to outweigh the benefit. In addition, in the new era of transparency and full disclosure of charges, investing in foreign and esoteric markets that have both higher transaction costs and less liquidity is unattractive as these charges will be observable on Total Expense Ratio's TERs. High TERs could then make a firm's offering look uneconomic. For an investor solely focused on gaining exposure to risk assets at the lowest possible cost, many international markets offer; higher transaction charges; higher costs due to slippage; higher asset management charges; greater monitoring costs in addition to poorer liquidity. It's not surprising that this kind of investor will likely stay at home.

Conversely, those Investors based in costly or generally illiquid markets could benefit significantly from increased global diversification because their investments would be shifted into lower cost regimes. For example, for all non-US investors a large proportion of assets would be directed towards the US stock market, which has the most liquid and lowest costs available globally. A push for better regulation and cost transparency is also detracting from investors investing in less liquid markets. In Europe the PRIIPs regulations have sought to improve transparency and comparability through greater disclosure of costs to clients. Resultantly managers are very keen to lower the costs of trading and costs not related to their own fees.

Currency – Exposure to assets denominated in foreign currencies can add another risk exposure for those straying away from their home markets. Although much of the volatility in foreign investing can be attributed to exchange-rate fluctuations, and can be negatively correlated with domestic assets, the presence of an extra risk factor can be off putting. For retail or non-professional investors the cost of exchanging currencies can also add significantly to transaction costs, far outweighing any marginal benefit from diversification.

DEVELOPING A STRATEGY FOR MULTIPLE ASSET CLASSES

As a simplified example of a multi-asset strategy, let's think of a simplified investment portfolio and consider an idealised but typical retail investor; a still working professional in good health in their mid-40s in the accumulation (ie, still saving) stage of their investing career with a large and growing retirement fund.

He or she may be advised to allocate 60 percent of their money towards risk assets, the most obvious choices being assets such as diversified mutual funds or equity ETFs with the remaining 40 percent in a combination of cash, investment-grade bond funds, and government debt (both nominal and inflation-linked).

This 60/40 split is often considered to be the typical split for a cautious mid-career investor with many years until potential retirement. Many financial advisors would benchmark their returns versus a stylised portfolio similar to this. For this individual; if the stock market were to rise or fall by 10 percent, their total portfolio could reasonably be expected to move in tandem approximately 6 percent. This is as the stock positions comprising 60 percent of the portfolio will rise or fall in line with the market, but the low-risk bond funds will barely move, and might even be expected to rally if there is a switch into less risky assets or a flight to quality. For the modern investor with the wide array of investable asset classes available to them, it is difficult if not impossible to classify a total portfolio solely in terms of the percentage stocks and percentage bonds. But here for explanatory purposes it can aid comprehension to consider a simple mix of stocks and low-risk bonds. (Sometimes described as risk and risk-less assets.) This can be helpful as asset allocations can be viewed as having an exposure to risk assets or the broader market that is similar to the exposure of a particular combination of stocks and bonds.

Handy Definitions

Risk-less assets: are securities in which the returns and/or cash flows are known with certainty. The certainty generally comes from the stability of the issuer of the asset; for example, in the United States, USD Treasury securities are considered risk-free because the American government ultimately controls the currency, and it is thought that they or their agents can always print more dollars to match unfunded obligations. Similarly, in the United Kingdom, the debt of the British Government, commonly called Gilt-edged securities are considered the risk-less asset.

However, some market theorists believe there is no such thing as a risk-free asset because in theory even stable Governments could default. Indeed, governments can default on debt in their own currency. A noted example is the Russian Government in 1998.

Similarly, investors may ask if assets are risk-less in the presence of inflation, with the value of cash being eroded overtime some discussions of risk move from 'nominal' to 'real' cash flows. However, for our purposes and most interpretations of Modern Portfolio Theory securities described as riskless assets have such a low level of default that it can be considered effectively zero.

Now think of a similar investor, with similar needs, but a more complex portfolio with varied exposures and diverse investments in many other different markets. Alongside large concentrated positions in individual securities in multiple asset classes. By watching market moves, both individual and aggregate, if the second investor sees similar changes in market value as the first investor it can aid comprehension to think of their portfolio as having a level of risk equivalent to a 60/40 equity/bond split even if the portfolio contains many other asset classes and has a markedly different composition.

Similar to this simple example, every portfolio could be viewed as having an asset allocation that has the same responsiveness to market fluctuations as a portfolio comprised of R percent Stocks and (100-R) percent Bonds. This risk is known as **Market Risk**. It is also sometimes referred to as **Systematic Risk**.

Sensitivity to market fluctuations is the first risk factor in Modern Portfolio Theory. Next we look at the other type of risk: **Idiosyncratic Risk**.

Idiosyncratic risks are considered all fluctuations in portfolio value due to anything other than overall movements in the broader market. These risks are generally single stock or sector specific. Examples within a portfolio could include a strike at an airline, an impending lawsuit, or the bankruptcy of small company. A well-diversified portfolio of stocks and bonds, such as the first example, could contain little or no idiosyncratic risk – this is as the largest individual position may influence less than one per cent of the portfolio. But the second portfolio could contain substantial idiosyncratic risks. If the overall market or market portfolio were to suddenly drop 20 per cent, the first portfolio would be expected to drop approximately 12 per cent (60 per cent of 20 per cent) because it is well diversified portfolio that and can (risk-adjusted) be expected to follow the market. For the second portfolio, the moves would be expected to be similar in magnitude but the volatility of the moves will likely be higher. Sometimes the portfolio value will move substantially lower, sometimes slightly lower and in extreme cases the value could even increase. This deviation in returns is due to the idiosyncratic risks contained in the individual asset positions. The higher or lower returns are caused by events unrelated to the market's level that are causing profits or losses in some of the individual holdings.

But it can be helpful to view all portfolios as having a level of market risk that is equivalent to being a proportion invested in Stocks, say R percent, and conversely (100-R) per cent in Bonds (i.e., the so-called riskless asset). This variable, R (usually expressed as a decimal such as 0.60 or 0.8), is called the 'beta' of the portfolio and is the measure of market risk.

So, a diversified portfolio that has 60 percent stocks and 40 percent risk-free bonds, and any investment with a similar level of market risk, is said to have a beta equal to 0.60. A portfolio entirely invested in a broad stock market portfolio would be said to have a beta of 1.0, conversely Cash, which has no volatility and a deterministic value, has a Beta of 0.0.

The concept of beta can be applied to individual stocks, mutual funds and overall portfolios, and has uses not just in asset allocation but also in Corporate Finance and Risk Management.

Beta is represented mathematically below:

$$R_e = \beta \times [R_m - R_f] + R_f \ \text{ or } \ R_e - R_f = \beta \times [R_m - R_f]$$

$$R_e = \textbf{Stock Return}$$

$$\beta = \textbf{Beta Coefficient}$$

$$R_m = \textbf{Market Return}$$

$$R_f = \textbf{Risk} - \textbf{Free Rate}$$

Where:

$$\beta = \frac{\text{Covariance } (R_e, R_m)}{\text{Variance } (R_m)}$$

$$\text{Covariance } (R_e, R_m) = \sum \frac{(R_{e,n} - R_{e,avg}) \times (R_{m,n} - R_{m,avg})}{(n-1)}$$

$$\text{Variance } (R_m) = \sum \frac{(R_{m,n} - R_{m,avg})^2}{n}$$

QUICK ASIDE:

A Very Simple Rule, the 100 per cent minus age guide, aka the Rule of 100

Before we enter the world of MPT and LDI, it's worth looking at a very simple (perhaps the simplest) asset allocation framework designed for the independent investor. The rule of 100. Before the work of Markowitz et al provided mathematical rigour to the investment and asset allocation problem, it was still well understood that the young were (in general) capable of taking more investment risk than the not so young, and that the young were less in need of stability of income and cash flows from investments as their assets were smaller and they had time on their side to accumulate capital.

This commonly cited rule can be a handy benchmark on whether risk levels are appropriate, and if you were to look at the portfolio recommended to you by a financial advisor or digital platform you may find that the asset allocation suggested is not too different from this simple method. The rule of 100 suggests that investors should maintain a percentage of risk assets equal to a hundred per cent minus their age. So, for a typical 60-year-old, 40 per cent of the portfolio should be in risk asset (usually) equities, for a forty-year-old 60 per cent (100–40%) would be in risk assets. If you were to rely solely on this system, every year on your birthday (or more practically every few years on a day that was convenient) you would look to decrease your allocation to stocks, lowering the volatility of the value of the assets and the risk level of your investment portfolio.

The rule is obviously over simplistic but has some explanatory power. Criticisms are numerous, one particular example being that in many cases wealthier investors can look to increase (not decrease) their equity allocation as they grow older as their ever-growing investment portfolios allow them to take more and more risk and their liabilities become less important relative to the value of their assets.

An example would be a wealthy couple who have paid their mortgages, have good medical insurance and little outgoings. In these circumstances they would likely be seeking to maximise their assets, rather than minimise risk, to hand the wealth down to future generations or charitable endowments.

The advantage of course is that it is easy to understand. For an enthusiastic amateur or D-I-Y investor the rule is potentially a good test that an asset allocation decision has not gone too far 'off-piste'.

Another simple rule that leads to a similar portfolio is 'The age in Bonds rule'. This is recommended by Jack Bogle, the founder of Vanguard, instigator of the low cost revolution, and probably the individual with the largest positive effect on financial services in our times.

SUMMARY

- Historically Multi-Asset Investment Decisions have been made using Modern Portfolio Theory which was developed from the work of Harry Markowitz at the University of Chicago.
- In its basic form, MPT only looks at asset optimisation, neglecting the other side of the investors' balance sheet, i.e., the liabilities.

- Investors have multiple asset classes available to them, but it can aid our intuitive understanding to split them into risky and risk-less assets.
- Under MPT risks can be split between systematic and idiosyncratic risk. The key understanding of Markowitz was that idiosyncratic risk need not be compensated.
- Beta is a measure of market risk; it aims to capture the risk of an asset in terms of its exposure to the broader market portfolio.
- The implication of idiosyncratic risk not leading to excess return is that it should be minimised with a well-diversified portfolio.

CHAPTER 4

Building Investment Portfolios

Part 1: Security Selection

We move from Individual Security Selection, then approach Fund Selection before building up to Portfolio Construction
In Simple Steps
Aka Stock-picking

(FUNDAMENTAL, TECHNICAL AND QUANTITATIVE TECHNIQUES)

The basic building blocks of our asset allocation decision must be individual securities. They are the simplest units on which we must build our investment positions, express our investment views and look to hedge our future liabilities. In today's world a diverse, professionally managed portfolio could contain exposure to as many as ten thousand individual stocks, all of which will have only marginal effects on the total value of our positions.

Clearly, in practice, it will be difficult for all but the largest investors to gain exposure to so many assets individually, and investors will therefore engage with financial advisors, asset managers and professional investment teams to select individual securities such as stocks and corporate bonds on their behalf.

Although individual stock selection is not the primary focus of this book, in this chapter we will introduce the most widely known approaches including some of the more common techniques and methodologies that practitioners use. As well as introducing the seminal texts in the field for those interested in finding out more about single stock investing, as well as briefly discussing the history of financial thought.

In this section we will outline the basics of individual security or stock selection, also known as stock-picking. The techniques discussed are widely used by fund managers to create the investable funds which form the core of most retail investors and pensioners investment portfolios. Then we move onto fund or manager selection where the focus moves on from the micro economics of individual stocks to macro-economic factors and more subjective qualitative judgements on manager aptitude. Fund selection can be considered an art in its own right and comes with its own unique set of challenges. Although we should note that many investors are sceptical of 'manager selection' as an art form and believe that allocating resources to fund selection is likely to lead to a loss of portfolio value after costs. It is even currently debated whether manager selection is necessary at all in developed financial markets where low cost passive funds can provide exposure to major asset classes, and increasingly minor ones. We discuss this debate in the section 'Passive vs Active'.

Then we move onto portfolio construction or fund aggregation, which is the main focus of liability-driven investing. The portfolio construction techniques we discuss will then explicitly include both sides of the balance sheet and hence be a demonstration of liability-driven investment or asset liability management.

AN INTRODUCTION TO SINGLE STOCK SELECTION

To start our investment process, we should be able to agree that fund managers and advisors will pick individual stocks and bonds if they believe that outperformance of that security is likely on a risk-adjusted basis. Investors like to find a bargain and hate to overpay.

The literature often splits the basic stock selection frameworks into two parts. Although the goal is always the same.

'Buy low, sell high.'

THE TYPES OF ANALYSIS

Fundamental Analysis

i. In Fundamental Analysis; the market may incorrectly price an asset in the short-term but in the long-term fair value will be reached. Excess return can therefore be made by identifying 'cheap' securities using extensive research and then waiting for the asset price to reach fair value.

By contrast,

Technical Analysis

ii. Technical analysis suggests that all information is reflected already in the price of a security. Technical analysts or chartists look for trends and believe that market sentiment is somewhat predictable, being a reflection of human nature. Market participants' emotional responses to volatility will lead to recognisable price chart patterns. For a 'Technician' pattern recognition can be more important than a detailed understanding of economics.

The most traditional and well understood method of searching for likely outperformers is Fundamental Analysis.

FUNDAMENTAL ANALYSIS OF SECURITIES

The Fundamental Analysis of equities is usually regarded as the most respected form of Stock picking. To utilise Fundamental Analysis frameworks can require deep specific knowledge of individual stocks, sectors and issuers alongside broad expertise in the financial, economic and regulatory environment. For those interested in learning more on this topic, a good starting point, to expand your knowledge of Fundamental Analysis techniques and more generally the history of finance, is the writings of Benjamin Graham. His seminal texts include Security Analysis (1934) – which is possibly the most influential financial book ever. It has sold more than a million copies over the course of eight decades, and at the time of writing is still in print. Also, consider The Intelligent Investor, written in 1949. Both were fascinating and insightful at the time and both are still very much relevant today. The Intelligent Investor which Warren Buffett described as 'the best book about investing ever written' sits on my desk as I write this today.

Also of interest, for both practical and historical reasons, are the works of John Burr Williams. His best-selling book, The Theory of Investment Value (Harvard University Press, 1938) is also still in print today and popularised dividend discount models as a method of security valuation. The book, which was a development of his Harvard PhD thesis, introduced the dividend discount model as a framework for equity valuation. He had been motivated by explaining the Wall Street Crash of 1929 and hoped in part to help avoid a repeat of the depression that followed. His desire was that a more rigorous framework for investing and valuation would ensure that stock prices could be set accurately by detailed analysis and that the excess volatility of the stock market would be diminished. Decades later, we may have increased the rigour but the volatility in asset markets continues.

John Burr Williams is perhaps considered by some to be the founder of Fundamental Analysis. Interestingly Harry Markowitz the developer of Modern Portfolio Theory later wrote that he developed his theories as a rejection of some of Burr Williams conclusions. Particularly the implication that an investor who sought 'to maximise the value of a portfolio would invest solely in one security', this he stated was not a reflection of reality and didn't account for the benefits of diversification or the fact that investors have non-linear utility functions.

Let us begin by looking at how Fundamental Analysis works in practice. At the start of the stock selection process, an investment team performing fundamental analysis on an individual stock could begin by thoroughly investigating the balance sheet and key accounting ratios of a firm and make subjective assessments of the quality of management and the competitive landscape. They might visit factories and talk to staff and stakeholders, then interview customers, suppliers, and competitors, before trying to build a detailed model of the company, its culture, its past, present and ultimately its future. From this they can understand its fair value now and aim to predict its value in the future. As you can imagine, although possibly intellectually rewarding, this pursuit of knowledge can be both difficult and time-intensive. In addition, it is operationally difficult and becomes rather expensive due to the high level of expertise required. Because of the high costs involved, rigorous fundamental analysis has been falling out of favour in the industry, as in the present day for many financial institutions the aim of cutting costs is often paramount to supporting a rigorous research process. In any competitive industry short term focus on costs can impact long-term value creation, and in recent years the investment management industry has moved away from a focus on investing skill to improving distribution and cutting costs.

The fees charged for investing have been falling for decades. The clear driver in my view has been the incredible success of Vanguard, and the rise of passive investing. But technology has led to ever increasing transparency, which in turn has turned a spotlight on the hidden costs that investors are now (rightly) rejecting. In addition, 'better' and larger data sets being readily available has led to more concentration on lower-cost quantitative techniques, which can be provided at lower cost and scale more easily. In turn these falling costs have been turning investors away from the high expense ratios associated with operationally intensive fundamental analysis.

Some examples of active asset managers currently performing fundamental analysis include Terry Smith, the eponymous Fundsmith in the United Kingdom and of course Warren Buffett and Charlie Munger at Berkshire Hathaway in the United States.

A typical fundamental analyst might focus on calculating an exact fair price for a stock. They can then compare their 'theoretical value' with the price observed in the market to generate buy, hold and sell signals. A core part of this analysis will focus on examining a corporation's balance sheet and looking at key accounting ratios or financial metrics to assess the value of organisation. Many equity analysts in this field will have a good knowledge of accounting and should be able to manipulate a balance sheet to identify potential companies or sectors of interest.

Many fundamental analysts will have achieved or be studying towards the Chartered Financial Analyst charter, usually abbreviated to CFA, which has a strong fundamental focus, and can include up to 30% Accounting within its exams.

Introducing Ratio Analysis

A good starting point to begin Fundamental Analysis is **Ratio Analysis**. Ratio Analysis involves investigating the accounting statements of target firms and creating metrics with this data that can then be used to identify mis-priced stocks, or credits that may be approaching bankruptcy. These ratios, tools, and techniques can be used to compare the relative strengths and weaknesses of multiple companies quickly and easily and can form the basis of comparative security valuation.

After an analyst has identified relevant and compelling ratios, comparisons could be made with the security to the broad market, the sector or the industry the firm operates in. Further comparisons could be made to the same metric in prior reporting periods to assess the firm's momentum. Or the same metric from a similar firm's Financial Statements to assess relative value. Choosing the most appropriate ratios to test the valuation hypothesis is one of the most important steps for an analyst in their attempts at deriving an estimate of fair value. Choosing which ratio to use, and for which stock, is where the analysis can become an artform.

The ratios can of course be used for more than just simple valuation. Financial ratios are useful to assess factors such as: the financial health of individual divisions, the operating efficiency of each division, the firm's relative profitability and return on investment (ROI), and many more points of interest. The change in accounting ratios over time can often create a narrative or storyboard for a skilled analyst to deduce a firm's health and future. With some ratios being used to accurately predict likely growth, other ratios being used to assess upcoming sources of peril. For example, consistent profit growth with little underlying volatility, could be an example of management smoothing earnings, or a very healthy and well-run enterprise. In this case, a rosy picture in the eyes of one analyst could be a red flag in the eyes of another more cynical investor. By the same token, rapidly decreasing inventory, could be a harbinger of supply issues in the next accounting period, or a dramatic increase in demand. With the differing interpretations having markedly different inferences for future asset prices and whether to buy sell or hold.

Financial ratios are generally divided into five broad categories: Liquidity or Solvency, Financial Leverage or Debt, Asset Efficiency or Turnover, Profitability, and Market Value ratios.

Liquidity and Solvency Ratios

Some examples of Liquidity Ratios

Liquidity and Solvency refer to an organisation's capacity to meet obligations as and when they become due. With liquidity ratios being more focused on short term cash needs. Managers and analyst have to ensure that upcoming obligations can be met with the working capital, inventory and cash reserves available to them to avoid the risk of insolvency.

Current Ratio

The current ratio measures the ability of a firm to pay obligations in the short term where the short term is regarded as under a year. It is perhaps the most common measure of the short-term liquidity of a corporation. The ratio is used not just by investors but also bankers or trade financiers considering lending credit, or a supplier worried about payment. As well as management looking at upcoming liquidity needs.

To calculate the current ratio an analyst divides the value of all current assets by the value of all current liabilities.

The formula is:

$$Current\ ratio = Current\ assets/Current\ liabilities$$

where current asset and liabilities are cash and near cash instruments that are expected to be repaid within a year.

- Current Assets are Cash, Cash Advances, Receivables, Other Current Assets, Inventories, Marketable Securities.
- Current Liabilities are Accounts Payable, Accrued Liabilities, Short-Term Debt, Interest Payable, Current Tax Payable.

The Quick Ratio or Acid Test

The quick ratio measures the ability of a firm to pay obligations in the short term, where the short term is considered near immediate. We remove inventories from the current assets, as unwinding inventory and stock positions may not be instantaneous, and for a firm struggling with financial viability it is likely that the inventory will not realise a value near book value.

To calculate the quick ratio an analyst divides the value of all current assets with the exception of inventories by the value of all current liabilities.

The formula is:

$$Quick\ Ratio = (Current\ assets - Inventories)/Current\ liabilities$$

where current asset and liabilities are cash and near cash instruments that are expected to be repaid within a year.

A quick ratio of higher than one implies solvencies and a strong financial position as all upcoming payments could be made from upcoming received payments and readily realisable assets. Conversely, a quick ratio less than one implies financial weakness and is a potential red flag to an investor or commercial lender.

Creditors will often use the acid test as it shows the percentage of a firm's upcoming debts that could be readily paid off from converting assets into cash. Clearly the more liquid the firm's assets, the easier it is to adapt to changing economic conditions.

In general, the higher the quick ratio the better, as it shows that the firm is solvent and likely to remain so. However, an overly high ratio may in itself be a red flag (isn't everything?!) as it can show that the firm's treasury is not effectively utilising cash reserves and this can act as a drag on return on equity (ROE). It may also indicate that a corporate capital structure utilising more debt may be appropriate to take advantage of the tax efficiencies of borrowing.

Cash Ratio

The Cash Ratio is a measure of the cash and cash equivalents of a firm versus its current liabilities. It is almost a worst-case liquidity ratio or credit measure since only cash and cash equivalents are compared with the current liabilities.

The formula is:

$$Cash\ Ratio = (Cash + Cash\ Equivalents)/Current\ Liabilities.$$

All three of these solvency ratios shown use Current Liabilities as the denominator. The cash ratio is the most cautious or conservative of the three, allowing only the most liquid of assets, cash and readily realisable securities to offset against liabilities. The current ratio is perhaps the widest used. These solvencies ratios are perhaps most appropriate to credit or fixed income analysis than equity selection but can help paint a picture across the capital structure.

Financial Leverage or Debt Ratios

Debt-to-Assets Ratio = Total Debt/Total Assets
Debt-to-Equity Ratio = Total Debt/Total Equity
Debt-to-Capital Ratio = Today Debt/(Total Debt + Total Equity)
Debt-to-EBITDA Ratio = Total Debt/Earnings Before Interest Taxes Depreciation & mortisation (EBITDA)
Interest Coverage Ratio = Earnings Before Interest & Taxes (EBIT)/ Interest Expense

TECHNICAL ANALYSIS OF SECURITIES

There is a large group of professional investors known as Technicians or Chartists. They will select their investments based on 'Technical Factors' using the framework known as technical analysis. Technical analysis (sometimes also known as Charting) refers to the study of securities through price and volume data. Technical analysis assumes that a security's price already reflects all publicly available information. The chartist will then focus on the statistical analysis of price movements. For the chartist, pattern recognition is the key. In many ways looking for and recognising patterns in price movements from data, can be similar to or a replacement for years of market experience, if the assumption that price movements are independent is true.

Economists and academics have historically been sceptical of this approach, (indeed many still are). But many academics now include the key technical feature of 'price momentum' as a risk factor and a potential source of outperformance in many of their explanatory models, and over the last few years the academic literature is becoming increasingly inclusive of price history driven approaches to stock selection.

The field of Behavioural Economics often tries to describe how the anomalies detected by Technical Analysis can exist and even persist after they become known to the broader market.

However, we should note that some investors and economists are still uncomfortable with this framework. One reason for this discomfort: This approach directly contradicts efficient market theory (EMH) which forms the base of many academic models of the economy and the Capital Markets, and which we will investigate later in this chapter.

Formally, technical analysis is a method of selecting the most liquid securities by analysing the statistics generated from trading, of which the most important data points are past prices and traded volume information.

Counter-intuitively for any economists reading, a Technical analyst is not interested in a security or stock's intrinsic value but instead he or she will use pattern recognition, volume data, and oscillators alongside other tools to predict and profit from future price movements.

Despite its perceived lack of intellectual rigour there are many advantages to using these statistical frameworks. Given that technical analysis doesn't require specialist expertise in a stock or sector it can be applied to virtually any trading instrument on any market and in any timeframe. This widens the investor's opportunity set or investment universe significantly. As a technician might be comfortable trading in multiple markets concurrently where as a fundamental analyst or trader would generally only be able to cover one narrow sector. Charting can be used to analyse any deep, liquid markets that generate large data sets on which they can perform the statistical analysis or 'data mining'. The markets that are suitable for the modern Chartist include but aren't limited to, individual stocks, funds, ETFs, commodities, bonds, forex, and many more. Limited only to popular technical indicators and chart patterns and with commercially available and inexpensive software, a trader or speculator could apply technical tools to find potential trading opportunities almost anywhere in the global financial markets and would not need to perform the detailed and time-consuming research necessary with other approaches.

A financial market would be less readily suited to technical analysis if it was infrequently traded or if there was a paucity of data. Residential real estate could be an example of an infrequently traded market. Perhaps unsurprisingly an FX broker or trader would talk convincingly of technical indicators, oscillators and price signals as part of his or her sales talk. But an estate agent in a less liquid market is likely to focus on more fundamental metrics.

Obviously, the market advice from both your estate agent and your FX broker should be taken with a pinch of salt.

Many Chartists also claim that Charts are time invariant: that you can analyse a daily chart or the tick data (individual trade level) and look for and recognise the same patterns. Some market professionals, particularly day traders, use technical analysis frameworks without incorporating any fundamental techniques. However, most professionals will use a mixture of the templates available to them. For example, many 'Fundamentalists' will use technical analysis to create a set of clear rules and guidelines to assist in the decision of when, where and how to enter and exit a position. For example, using technical analysis to find a support or resistance level might complement the work of an equity research analyst who had found an undervalued asset or a potential takeover target.

The most important application of technical analysis is currently the search for 'momentum'. This is also known as trend-following. Also further described as the *'Trend is your friend'* school of investing. Market participants can use technical analysis to inform them of the direction or trend of asset prices. Statistical Analysis has shown that financial markets are not completely random, and that there is a correlation between the direction and size of price movements over consecutive time-periods. For many speculators searching for a trend is the main rationale for investing. Many investors will allocate capital whenever and wherever they see a trend appearing. This can make trend formation almost a self-fulfilling prophecy.

The Main Assumptions of Technical Analysis

1. The price is all you need

The main weakness of technical analysis is that it only considers price movement, ignoring the fundamental factors of any financial instrument or the economic environment in which it functions. This is because a pure Chartist assumes that, at any given time, an asset's price reflects all available information, even the fundamental factors. Corporate fundamentals, along with broader economic factors and the general market conditions, are all reflected in the price. This has the benefit of removing the need to actually consider fundamental factors separately. This makes the analysis of price movement paramount, and technicians view price as a product of the fluctuating supply and demand for an asset and hence a reliable predictor of future demand.

2. Prices Move in Trends

Chartists believe that markets are generally directional, and that finding and identifying trends can be beneficial. The trend is the technician's friend. In the current financial markets vast amounts of capital are allocated to Funds that invest solely or primarily in Technical Analysis frameworks. These fund managers are often known as CTAs or Commodity Trading Advisors (CTAs).

3. History Rhymes!

Perhaps the most important assumption of Technical Analysis is that whilst history will never repeat itself exactly, it can rhyme. The non-stochastic nature of price movements and the nature of pattern formations is caused by the behaviour of human market participants being somewhat predictable whilst the markets change around them. Whilst academics have been wary of giving credence to technical analysis the new field of Behavioural Finance has sprung up and attempts to explain growing evidence of how recognisable price patterns form and create profitable trading opportunities in direct contradiction of the Efficient Market Hypothesis. Behavioural Finance attributes pattern formation to investor psychology and differing incentive sets for market participants. This new field is belated recognition from the academic world that deep understanding of the price action in Capital Markets can lead to excess return.

For those interested in risk management of large institutional portfolios, technical analysis forms an interesting aside but is not the primary focus. In most cases practitioners look to make long term decisions and the potential benefits of marginally superior trade entry points are negated by the expected increased returns caused by of decades of compounding.

Other financial advisors or investment managers see their priority as identifying potential risks or liabilities for end users and then creating the most efficient portfolios given these constraints. For pension fund trustees and those with a responsibility of allocating capital effectively, market-timing can be seen as counterproductive as keeping assets in cash or cash equivalents whilst waiting for better entry levels will weigh on returns.

QUANTITATIVE ANALYSIS

Quantitative analysts and portfolio managers, colloquially known as 'quants' have become an increasingly visible figure on trading floors and throughout investment firms since the turn of the century. This is due to the advent of integrated systems capable of handling large amounts of data quickly and easily. Quants are often seen as geekier than their fellow front-office colleagues in sales or investment banking. They will in many cases have post graduate qualifications in the hard sciences. Typical examples being Doctorates in physics or mathematics or master's degrees in subjects such as statistics or computer science. Their scientific expertise will be employed to develop a variety of statistical techniques and programmes to price securities and derivatives and implement trading and risk management programmes. The quantitative approach combines the technical and fundamental approaches to picking stocks and generating trade signals. This investing methodology has become increasingly popular since the Global Financial Crisis (GFC), both as new technologies make accurate data easier to source and analyse, but also as Quantitative analysis is scalable and easier to automate in an era where, as stated previously, Financial Institutions are actively seeking to cut the cost of their services.

Quantitative Practitioners typically use a top-down approach, where the quantitative investor or 'quant' will synthetically replicate a benchmark and then use quantitative signals to find sources of extra return. The objective of quantitative strategies is usually to outperform a given index by overweighting and underweighting assets that quantitative signals deem likely to outperform.

Like more traditional managers, quantitative investors will perform fundamental analysis aimed at identifying trade signals and indicators of asset mis-pricings. They will also incorporate economic models and consider the economic environment surrounding asset prices. In common with Fundamental managers, but in contrast to chartists, the intrinsic value of assets is important.

In practice, those investors who believe in the value of individual stock selection are likely to be allocated to fund managers that utilise a mixture of all three approaches.

Passive Investors

A further set of investors believe that the value of Stock-Picking in efficient markets is negligible. Analysing the market and then picking individual securities and timing the purchase or sale of these investments in an attempt to 'beat the market' will, in their view, not increase long-term investment returns. But conversely will increase operating and monitoring costs and is hence likely to detract from performance. These investors therefore wish to gain exposure to asset classes or risk factors as easily as possible. This approach is known as passive investment. Passive investors will typically seek to add exposures to different asset classes in the lowest cost most efficient way possible.

THE PASSIVE VS ACTIVE DEBATE

In Multi-Asset Class investing – the investor seeks exposure to an asset class, market factor or risk premium and will often attempt to do this in the most efficient way possible (where efficient in this sense will generally mean low-cost). In recent years, for many cost sensitive investors, the active versus passive debate has become a debate between high and low cost rather than an insight into efficient market theory. So, with the compound effect of the extra costs of research and trading weighing down returns from active managers, passive investment is becoming increasingly popular, particularly in developed markets. Hence many investors are seeing real benefits from switching to passive investment strategies solely on the grounds of expense. Much of the academic literature suggests that by switching to passive replication of active strategies, an investor will lower costs without sacrificing return, indicating that for all but the most informed investor passive could be the way forward.

Here we will outline some of the reasoning behind the Passive versus Active debate and demonstrate that there are valid arguments on either side.

Introducing the Efficient Market Hypothesis

Alongside the work of Dr. Markovitz, the belief in efficient markets has been a core part of Financial Theory and has enabled the academic community to build elegant models that describe the capital markets in most cases reasonably well. The efficient market hypothesis (EMH) is one such theory. It has been the subject of a great deal of research, and in the past many academics would insist on its validity. This has led to a widely held viewpoint that markets in financial assets operate efficiently and that prices instantaneously reflect all available public information.

In efficient markets, asset prices are fair, and stocks will not be undervalued or overvalued. All stocks will be priced accurately for the risks that they represent. In this 'efficient' world there can be no benefit to extensive research or diligent fundamental analysis! As all prices are an accurate reflection of the information available.

Under EMH there is no benefit to research!

These academic models however rely on many assumptions, some of which are only partially true at best. One such assumption is that all market participants are assumed to be rational and have access to the same data sources. If this is true, it follows that price fluctuations should be unpredictable and asset prices should respond only to genuinely new information. Unfortunately, real world experience will tell us that not all market participants are well informed or rational, with many professional investors performing little or no fundamental research nor investing solely in the hunt for superior risk-adjusted returns. In the real world, many professional investors may be more concerned with career risk and salary maximisation rather than their fiduciary duty or the risk profiles of their end users. However, a belief in efficient or mostly efficient markets has been a core part of the rationale behind passive investing. Although recent consistent and superior observed performance from passive strategies could be said to dispense with the need for theoretical justification.

My apologies for the use of so many three letter acronyms (TLAs). EMH is fundamental to MPT (and also LDI / ALM). Belief in reasonably efficient markets (through EMH) that distribute risk to rational and informed investors are the basis that underpins much financial decision making.

The EMH was first developed and then expanded by Professor Eugene Fama of the University of Chicago who argued that assets will always trade at a price that accurately reflects the value, making it impossible for investors to either purchase undervalued securities or sell holdings at greater than fair value. His theory was developed in the 1960s when for the first time the computing power became available to test financial hypotheses such as this, that relied on large data sets. (He later won the 2013 Nobel Prize for Economics for this work and other contributions to Finance theory.)

Fundamental to Fama's model of efficient markets are an investor class who always behave rationally and asset prices that instantaneously reflect all available information. This is sometimes described as a random walk as all subsequent price changes will reflect a random departure from previous prices. This process is also often described as Geometric Brownian Motion. Since in this framework prices reflect all the available information, news and price changes must be unpredictable.

This is good news for retail investors and the deliberately uninformed. As for both a professional and an amateur investor, holding a diversified portfolio will obtain comparable returns regardless of the varying levels of investment expertise. This is due to the fact that it is impossible for the professional to find an undervalued stock or an investing edge.

However, some of Fama's assumptions do not hold in the real world. For example, as we know in practice, not every buyer or seller of assets has access to the same data and analytics, and certainly not at the same time.

In recognition of investors having different information sets Professor Fama further refined his theory, and resultantly defined three different forms of market efficiency; strong form, semi-strong form, and weak form.

The first of which, **strong form market efficiency,** is where all information, both public and private, is reflected in all asset prices. In a market environment where this was true, an investor would be unable to achieve a competitive trading advantage even from using inside knowledge, as this information would already be reflected in any tradable price. This degree of market efficiency implies that above average returns cannot be achieved even if an investor has access to non-public information. In practice, it is unlikely that many believe that markets are an all-knowing omniscient creature. The existence of profitable opportunities existing for 'insider trading' would demonstrate that EMH is not valid in the strong form. In its strongest form market efficiency suggests that no form of analysis can lead to extra return. It would also suggest that insider trading legislation is pointless and irrelevant.

The second form, **semi-strong form market efficiency,** proposes that share prices are a reflection of publicly available information. Since market prices already reflect public information, investors are unable to gain abnormal returns without accessing and then acting upon private information. An act which would likely be illegal in most jurisdictions. In a world of semi-strong market efficiency, an investor who consistently outperformed would either be very lucky or have access to private information. In the semi-strong form, market efficiency suggests that analysing public available information will not lead to an investing edge and that Fundamental Analysis won't lead to excess return.

Lastly, **weak form market efficiency** implies that there is some value to some forms of research. It in its weak form EMH claims that past price movements and volume data do not affect current stock prices. In a market that is subject to weak form efficiency, fundamental analysis could still be used to identify undervalued and overvalued stocks. So, there is still hope for some professional investors. In this context, asset managers looking for profitable opportunities can still earn excess returns by detailed analysis of financial statements, meeting corporate management teams, and building financial models amongst other forms of fundamental research. However, to the disappointment of chartists and prospective chartists weak form efficiency proposes that technical analysis won't lead to an investing edge.

In a world where even professional fund managers will struggle to generate excess return, it may seem appropriate to avoid paying asset management firms for their stock picking services. Indeed, many individual investors and advisors will now seek to minimise the cost of an investment rather trying to identify likely winners.

Indeed, if we consider the total investment return of a portfolio to be:

Total Return = Σ Total Return due to market exposures + Σ Manager

Outperformance − Σ Total Costs

Believers in the Efficient Market Hypothesis would look at how total returns are calculated and, realising that manager outperformance is unlikely if not impossible under EMH, would realise that:

Expected (Σ Manager Outperformance) = 0

This simplifies the optimisation problem for those investors who accept the Efficient Market Hypothesis to:

Total Return = Σ Total Return due to market exposures – Σ Total Costs

And, with the total return due to market exposure being a function of the amount of risk taken, optimising for risk adjusted returns leaves the much simpler issue of minimising total costs.

Investors believing in EMH should hence look for the cheapest way of replicating a benchmark or index. For most asset classes and risk exposures, this will typically be done through the use of Exchange Traded Funds or ETFs. The cost advantages of these highly liquid vehicles can often be staggering. For example, the Vanguard S & P 500 ETF (which tracks the S &P 500 with 0.99 correlation) at the time of writing has an ongoing charge of just seven basis points (bp), or seven hundredths of one per cent. This compares to typical charges for active funds of between 75 and 100 bps. The effect of this cost saving is dramatic over time and for many investors could make the difference between a comfortable and uncomfortable retirement. Or an extra five to ten years in the office.

The drag on returns from higher costs are demonstrated in Table 4.1. Where we are assuming an average seven percent investment return from an asset portfolio, which matches historical returns for a medium risk portfolio. These returns are before fund management costs and we start with an initial capital sum of £100,000.

Then we compare the value of an active and passive portfolio overtime, assuming that the managerial skill input is zero as predicted under EMH.

It can be seen that for the longer-term investor, or those at the start of their investing journey, the drag on returns from the larger fees can be significant and could easily account for a twenty per cent loss in portfolio value.

So Why Use Active Managers?

Given the stated and observed benefits of passive funds. Why have regulators not insisted that end users are placed into passive products given the likely higher returns? Or why have consumers not done this of their own volition?

TABLE 4.1   The drag on returns from higher costs

Years	Passive	Active	Cost Advantage	As a Percentage
0	£ 100,000	£ 100,000	£ -	0%
5	£ 139,797	£ 135,408	£ 4,389	3.24%
10	£ 195,432	£ 183,354	£ 12,078	6.59%
20	£ 381,937	£ 336,185	£ 45,751	13.61%
30	£ 746,426	£ 616,408	£ 130,019	21.09%
40	£ 1,458,756	£ 1,130,206	£ 328,550	29.07%
50	£ 2,850,876	£ 2,072,273	£ 778,603	37.57%

It's important to ask: Why should we as investors choose to engage with active managers?; Are there arguments in favour of more expensive investment styles?

1. An expectation of Excess Returns or Alpha

A desired for increased performance or superior risk management is the most obvious response. The search for excess returns, known as alpha in Capital Markets jargon, is an industry in its own right. Every single fund of funds operator, as well as most financial advisors and investment consultants will market 'manager selection' or the similar term 'fund selection' as a value add. There is a whole body of professionals that exists to chase 'alpha' and find those excess returns. Intelligent manager selection and the ability to source skilled fund managers who will be able to consistently outperform their benchmarks on a risk-adjusted basis is a valuable skill, although in practice it may be elusive.

In addition, consultants will often offer access to these managers funds (some of which will be capacity constrained) at attractive and sometimes heavily discounted rates. Many investors will have a target excess return due to manager skill, as part of their investment policy and an expectation of alpha to meet (possibly) optimistic return objectives or needs.

Conversely, a passive fund in many ways locks in underperformance. Whilst a passive fund is aimed at tracking an index as accurately as possible, it still attracts costs, both from management and relatively frequent re-balancing requiring frequent trading. In essence a passive strategy can be said to guarantee subpar performance due to these costs. At least, relative to most indices. However, returns relative to a benchmark inclusive of costs are of course a different story. Active managers and distribution networks argue that with active investing, you could potentially be able to receive returns in excess of the market. Some investors look at accepting passive returns as an admission of defeat and prefer the possibility of significant outperformance to the certainty of minor underperformance.

2. The Possibility of a Superior Customer Experience

The investment industry is above all a service industry and many (admittedly conflicted) financial advisors argue that higher fees can be justified if a superior customer experience can be achieved. By curating and backing a selection of funds and managers, advisors may allow end users to feel more engaged in the investment process and this in turn may feel more rewarding in the short term than backing a faceless and impersonal package of ETFs. Individual investors may relate to a fund manager or firm and enjoy a relationship with them and their ideas, but are unlikely to feel a similar emotional attachment to an index or benchmark. The mass affluent who are the largest consumer of financial services will often choose to pay for luxury in most areas of consumption. Arguably, the savings industry should be no different, and given the vast choice in investment services it would not be surprising if many consumers opted to choose a more interesting and 'luxurious' range of products than rather dull index trackers and government bonds. Certainly, in dinner party conversations a niche EM manager is likely to be more interesting than a FTSE tracker. Frequently in client satisfaction surveys – the higher fee advisors score highest, and they do this by providing a full and personal service.

For example, in the United Kingdom, the large IFA network St James Place has historically scored very highly with its customers, most of whom would recommend the service to friends or family. Yet charges here typically add up to 5–6 per cent per annum, and by recommending a restricted portfolio and sometimes single stocks and private placements it is likely that the firm's clients could achieve more 'efficient' (in the MPT sense) portfolios at considerably lower cost, by utilising a different service. A cynic would argue that, given the luxurious experience of full service personal advice may be illusory, and the ability to speak to an advisor at will, whilst a nice extra, would lead to an inferior customer experience if a pension pot was 50 per cent smaller at retirement due to the extra cost, or if this was known and understood by the customer at the time.

N.B. The higher cost financial advice agencies often argue that their higher costs are justified not just by the superior customer service, but the value created by their tax minimisation services. It is in fact true that for most investors the benefit of a well implemented tax strategy can outweigh the benefits of a well implemented investment strategy. But, whether this outweighs the cost of higher fees and the moral correctness of avoiding tax are interesting topics for a different book.

3. Downside protection

Although managers will often have their performance assessed versus a benchmark, for the end investor this may not be the most appropriate metric. To anyone saving for the future, a few percentage points' difference in capital value, in comparison to a relatively arbitrary index, is virtually irrelevant compared to the size of the total pot when that pot is needed. As such, for many the biggest risk is not that of investment underperformance but the risk of permanent capital loss. It is argued that an effective active portfolio manager can reduce this risk by limiting the magnitude and length of drawdowns in the absolute value of the funds. In other words, an active manager would have the discretion to sell riskier securities to prevent permanent capital loss.

There are unfortunately some weaknesses in this argument, whilst there has been some evidence of active managers (marginally) outperforming in a market downturn, this is in my view more due to technical reasons relating to cash management than because of managerial skill. For operational reasons, a portion of most investment portfolios will need to be kept in cash or near cash assets. This is due to the need to actively manage redemption requests and cope with inflows of new capital, as well as anticipating new trade opportunities. Active managers generally keep a much larger cash balance than Index Trackers, who will always remain nearly fully invested to optimise tracking error minimisation. For an active manager with a large cash balance it can be seen that a severe market downturn would lead to significant outperformance as the cash balance would be unaffected. In an overnight 20 per cent down move it could be seen that a manager with 3 per cent in cash would outperform by:

$$20\% * 3\% = 3\%/5 = 0.6\% \text{ or } 60 \text{ basis points.}$$

Due to the large cash balances many active fund managers will show marginal outperformance in a bear market. This feature of their return profile is described as superior risk management but may in fact reflect inferior operational efficiency and a slight underinvestment in equities.

In fact, the need for greater need for active cash management may be a driver of underperformance for the active sector as a whole. Many historic studies assessing cash levels with market performance have shown that the average excess return to market timing for active managers is negative. With numerous papers demonstrating marginal either under or over performance, the ones indicating outperformance often receive better distribution as the message better suits the financial services industry.

In general, the data will show that average cash level is negatively correlated with the level of the stock market. Managers tend to have lower cash levels at the peak of a market and times of low market volatility. Conversely, they raise cash levels during times of high volatility which are typically associated with lower stock markets or times of financial stress. It seems harsh to draw the conclusion that managers are timing the market consistently badly, but it seems that the need to cope with withdrawals at times of crisis is forcing fund managers to buy high and sell low for technical reasons.

4. Bespoke Risk Management

An active manager can provide a bespoke risk management solution. Indeed, many Liability Driven Investment mandates are examples of this approach. If a pension trust or endowment has known or predictable long-term cash flow needs, it makes sense to hedge these liabilities on an individual granular level instead of simply purchasing a set of funds or indices with less control and predictability of cash flows.

Similarly, to LDI schemes, many firms or individuals may have bespoke needs relevant to their situation. It may be that simply assessing a beneficiary's risk tolerance and risk capacity (alongside their maturity and cash flow profile for more sophisticated LDI and ALM schemes) may not be optimal if other information is not taken into consideration. For example, financial service professionals may wish to avoid investing in Banks and similar institutions to diversify the risks of their human and financial capital.

The Sovereign Wealth Funds of commodity-producing nations may wish to diversify away from equities in the raw materials sector as their income is strongly correlated to these securities.

5. Alignment of Values or Values Based Investment

Whilst most of our financial risk management models rely on risk and return and finding equivalencies between these variables. It is likely that to many investors risk and return are not the only factors which may sway personal investment decisions. It does indeed seem reasonable that humans function on more than two dimensions affecting their behaviour. The rise of ethical investing and ESG (Environmental Social and Governance based) and SRI (Socially Responsible Investment) funds shows that for many end users there are factors other than the purely financial which influence their decision making. The rise of responsible investing has been aided by increasing evidence of sub-par performance from active managers chasing alpha, creating a need for investment firms specialising in active management to look at others ways of creating or demonstrating value. The current growth areas in the active sector are bespoke risk management (LDI) and bespoke more socially responsible or ethical investing strategies as firms look to find more intangible performance metrics – as evidence of outperformance from the 'tangible' has so far been rather poor.

There exists a new class of investment funds that are constructed to include securities and corporations that encompass similar values to an end user's ethics and values whilst simultaneously avoiding sectors of the economy that the investor either feels less comfortable supporting or morally objects to.

There are various ways of achieving this:

The security selection can be done via 'screening' whereby certain sectors are excluded from an end user's investment universe. Certain sectors like oil or tobacco for example, may be excluded by the fund manager and thus unavailable as investments to an end user who objects to these industries on moral grounds. Proponents of this approach argue that over time this will increase the cost of capital for companies in those sectors and people are thus putting their money to work to advance their values (or achieve a moral return), while at the same time earning a financial return. The fund manager can incorporate a client's values into the investment process and incorporate stringent risk-management principles to allay the end user's concerns about a possible sacrifice in financial returns. Although it should be noted that the investment universe will resultantly be smaller which naturally results in less 'efficient' portfolios under MPT.

The disagreements against this approach can be summarised as the 'blunt instrument' argument and the 'efficient market' argument. In essence, the former maintains that if you disagree with what a company is doing you have more chance of influencing their direction by being actively engaged with that company and influencing senior management rather than selling your position and thus trying to affect change from the outside in. The latter argument is that, in an efficient market, if the price were to decrease, the price of the stock would be more attractive to others in the market who are not following the screening approach. If the price falls enough to become attractive to those non-screeners then they may well look to buy and thus the share price will be unaffected by the marginal ethical investor.

An alternative approach is 'responsible investment' whereby an organisation's Environmental, Social and Governance data are taken into account, as well as their financial data, in order to get a more complete picture of the companies being examined. This more granular approach allows for the investment manager to compare peers within an industry to understand better their operational model and how they control costs (Environmental – e.g. water use, electricity use etc.), how they treat their employees (Social – health and safety, employee relations, working conditions etc.), and how they are run (Governance – executive pay, board diversity etc.). This offers the interested investor more data which they can include in their investment allocation process. There is some data indicating that strong corporate governance is correlated positively with risk-adjusted outperformance, however the data is still limited. Plus, it is of course difficult to define 'strong governance'.

The main issues at present with socially responsible investing are that the morals and values of all stakeholders are never certain and that it is unclear how to measure and define them. End users may be unsure of what their ethical stance on investment may be and choose an ethical fund without fully aligning with the values of the fund manager.

Standards in the sector are, however, evolving and improving. This is caused both by demand – end-users responding to the message of creating a better world – but also practicality. Environmental considerations are part of the political discourse and regulators globally are looking at integrating environmental and sustainability reports and detailed ESG risk factor analysis into the data they require from the financial markets.

It can be difficult for the novice ESG analyst to accurately compare different companies within certain sectors at present, as preferred metrics have yet to emerge and data sets are often not directly comparable. That is not to say that it is not a worthwhile approach for those end users who are interested in it. It is important to note, however, that an active investment manager with a thorough understanding of the main ESG issues, standards bodies, and regulatory drivers can help an end user avoid drowning in data – sifting through multiple Corporate Social Responsibility reports. It is also important to note that an active manager can also represent more than just one end user's assets and thus can have more influence on – and better engage with – invested companies. The industry and ESG specialists argue that sharing best practices in ESG policies and procedures can thus enhance an invested company's long-term performance. As responsible corporations can lower their cost of capital as they reduce their environmental costs, enhance social conditions and improve governance in tandem.

SO, PASSIVE OR ACTIVE?

Ultimately, it seems, the main argument in favour of passive investing styles is cost. William Sharpe (famous in academic finance and the hedge fund industry for the Sharpe Ratio) expressed this argument in a 1991 paper 'The Arithmetic of Active Management'. He used simple logic to argue that the total return of all actively managed funds for a particular benchmark or index must equal the return on the index itself. Returns versus an index like this represent a zero-sum game, and for every manager that outperforms there will exist a similar manager with a similarly sized loss.

He states that:

Before costs the return on the average actively managed dollar will equal the return on the average passively managed dollar.

After costs the return on the average actively managed dollar will be less than the return on the average passively managed dollar.

Although we should note that this is an argument against high fees rather than the management style.

With Passive investment gaining acceptance globally it is like to continue increasing market share. Regulatory pressure increasing transparency and revealing the many hidden costs of investment is likely to accelerate the switch to passive.

If you do decide to invest in actively managed funds, you will always have the hope of outperformance. Unfortunately, the evidence demonstrates that odds of success are so low that it could be unwise to try. Advocates of passive investing equate choosing an active manager to going to the races. You may win significantly but you can expect to lose in the long term. The active fund manager and the bookmaker have a lot in common, but the financier is (usually) in a more expensive suit.

For some asset classes, it is of course difficult to gain exposure within a passive structure. Typical examples being Frontier Markets which are not yet large enough to sustain liquid ETFs or similar, or forms of PE or Venture Capital Investing where the small trade sizes ensure that investment products are not readily scalable. However, the market constantly innovates and firms are creating products to mimic the returns of these risk factors. Although usually with limited liquidity or the expectation of a large tracking error.

SUMMARY

- The creation of Investment Portfolios can be divided into three discrete processes. Security Selection, Fund Selection, and Portfolio Construction. LDI is concerned with the last stage, finding the right composition of funds to best manage investors' risk.
- Single Security Analysts or stock-pickers were traditionally divided into two camps. Fundamental Analysts (think economists) and Technical Analysts (think traders).
- Better Technology and the greater availability of data mean that these two camps have been joined by Quantitative Analysts. Quantitative Strategies are now responsible for a significant and growing share of Assets Under Management.
- Investors can use either Active or Passive strategies to gain exposure to risk factors, passive strategies are growing in popularity but are not always available for every asset class, or risk exposure.
- There is growing academic evidence that Active Management offers no extra return over Passive Strategies, but the effect of higher costs will weigh on portfolio return.
- Investors still use active strategies for a number of reasons. Such as, access to bespoke investment styles, bespoke risk management, or alignment of values.
- Values-led investing (ESG and SRI) will become a growth area for the industry.

CHAPTER 5

Building Investment Portfolios

Part 2: Fund Selection

A tremendous amount of literature exists on fund and manager selection, even though as noted in the prior debate on the merits of *passive versus active* investment; some investors and academics are sceptical of the value generated by picking an active manager. Many studies have shown that simply passively tracking an index or benchmark will likely lead to similar returns at lower cost and with better liquidity. However, there are a broad array of assets where low-cost trackers do not exist and there exist a great number of specialist managers with track records demonstrating outperformance and managerial skill in differing market conditions.

In a world where many types of investor are unable or unwilling to directly invest in individual securities, fund managers or fund instruments must be selected to create investment portfolios. Funds also have the advantage that they allow investors to diversify portfolios easily and at low cost. A small investor investing directly into multiple stocks would often have to choose between high transaction costs to diversify their portfolio, or overly concentrated positions leading to higher volatility than the expected return can justify. Because of this, the existence of funds is vital in providing low cost diversification to investors large and small. But it can be seen that when an investor decides not to invest directly in securities, they simply replace one decision with another. Instead of choosing stocks, we must pick indices and managers. How do we then decide which asset classes to purchase, and which investment firms and asset managers to engage with?

The process of manager evaluation can be very challenging in itself due to the limited data available on relative performance for individual managers and the time taken for individual managers to build a track record. It is rarer still for that manager to be able to demonstrate this skill over varied market conditions. It has also been shown that outperforming managers will rarely persist in their outperformance, and what may pass as skill today could look like luck tomorrow.

Manager choice can thus be a difficult and time-consuming exercise, with no guarantee or (potentially even expectation) of financial gain. Recent years have illuminated this, as it has been a period where poor performance has been the expectation for the majority of managers, with many star names losing their lustre and the majority of managers failing to beat the markets or their appropriate benchmark.

But for those who believe in, or are mandated to pick, active funds, the choice of manager is an interesting challenge.

To start the process, the fund analyst will usually perform 'investment due diligence' on the prospective managers in the relevant asset class to create a selection of investable funds or investment universe. This process may involve interviewing portfolio managers or traders in an attempt to understand their backgrounds, values and approach to the markets. The key questions regarding the manager would be does he or she have an advantage or investing edge, is this advantage likely to persist, and are sufficient risk controls in place if market conditions change?

1. The Advantage (Alpha)

In general, when engaging with external managers and paying a fee premium for active management, investors are looking for an excess return. Or more specifically an excess risk-adjusted return. This is commonly known as Alpha.

Questions on the origin of potential alpha.

Has the manager a special edge in their stock selection techniques? How does this edge arise? Is their edge due to an information advantage from more thorough in-depth research or use of better and more esoteric data sources? Is the edge not from the data, but from the analytics, has the manager found ways of using limited data more effectively? After all, many effective investment managers will practically use little more than a Bloomberg terminal, a set of corporate accounts and an FT subscription. If the analyst believes that an edge may exist and hopefully persist, he or she will then ask: Is the investment process to lead to outperformance in all market conditions (unlikely)? In what environments is underperformance likely, and is it likely to be severe?

An interesting and frequent question is: What was your biggest loss and the rationale for that position? Understanding this can lead into insights into both previous failings in risk management and evidence of process iteration and evolution.

For those fund managers deemed appropriate and investable after passing the investment process screen. The consultant will then follow with 'operational due diligence' to ensure that these managers claims are valid and that importantly they meet minimum standards of regulatory compliance, risk management and operational stability.

In today's markets a key part of the 'value add' or 'value proposition' for advisors, whether Independent Financial Advisors (IFAs) interacting with retail customers or Investment Consultants such as Willis Towers Watson, Aon Hewitt, XPS or Redington interacting with the largest Financial Institutions, can be understanding the investment proposition and operational processes of asset managers and then identifying the likely winners and avoiding the likely losers. Sadly, career risk mitigation consultants are often more concerned with avoiding losers, which means many non-conventional managers may be over-looked. Spotting the next Warren Buffett or George Soros early in their career may have a negligible effect on discretionary compensation or career progression for an investment consultant. Whereas investing in the next Madoff could have terminal consequences for a nascent consulting career.

Some advisors can be restricted to a range of funds offered by an employer or platform provider or selected by trustees; others will have a much wider range of managers to choose from. For the broader mandates, the investor / advisor will seek to find potential sources of excess return and look for evidence of managerial skill (the all-important Alpha). In these cases, it is important to spot any extra risks that may exist, and understand where any excess returns are generated.

These days much of this analysis will be template based or automated. Typically, data analytics, risk–return-based filtering systems and peer group analyses will be used to create an investment shortlist from a large opportunity set of available funds. In the last twenty years Manager Selection has become both a quantitative data-driven process as well as qualitative relationship-driven business as more and more data on managers becomes available. Different advisory firms will have differing approaches, many of which will be proprietary, but selection metrics for investment managers may include: diversification within strategies, tracking error, the educational quality and background of the key personnel, their investment philosophy and ethos, their investment process, their perceived operational stability, their systems and controls, their risk control and evidence of potential outperformance or superior risk management.

CHOOSING THE MANAGER

For the analyst concerned with investment processes. Firms and managers come together in many flavours, each requiring a different framework. Fortunately, despite the almost limitless number of available investments, firms and products can generally be split into three broad categories:

- Traditional Long Only managers
- Alternatives
- Private equity or Venture Capital funds

Investors – particularly those using screens or relying on automation – will often find screening traditional long only investment management the easiest process. The data here is usually readily available. Comparative statistics to other managers are also frequently available and much of it without expensive subscriptions, and portfolios of listed securities generate significant amounts of data that can easily be quantified and reviewed. For example, a manager's Sharpe or Sortino Ratio can be computed with ease. Resultantly the search for long only managers will often be data-led due to the availability of information, data and comparative statistics.

Alternative funds can be much harder to analyse due to a paucity of information. Although a number of consultants (such as Cambridge Associates) and data providers (such as Preqin) can provide information on the many Alternative fund managers, the range and breadth of the industry ensure that they cannot cover the entire investment universe. In addition, managers of alternatives will be protective of their underlying algorithms and risk management frameworks, which can make validating the investment process and understanding strategies difficult if not impossible. Depending on the fund or strategy the investment consultant will have to choose a mixture of qualitative and quantitative metrics to find the most appropriate invest-ments for their clients.

For Private Equity, Venture Capital and similar investments the paucity of data is often even greater. There is limited publicly available information for these asset classes, and sometimes even risk expectations can be difficult to gauge. Although a great deal of data is available, it is often incomplete and frequently contains survivorship bias and other flaws leading to expectations led by overstated returns and understated risk. The return data for PE funds can be difficult to analyse, this is as private equity funds are both contributed to and drawn down in a non-consistent and non-predictable way. The investment consultant will have to choose a mixture of qualitative and quantitative metrics to find the most appropriate investments for their clients, taking particular care to communicate to their clients (trustees or investors) the subjective nature of some the quantitative data.

The typical measure used by PE firms is the Internal Rate of Return or IRR

IRR definition:

The internal rate of return for an investment is the rate of return that sets the net present value of all cash flows (both positive and negative) from the investment equal to zero.

Which is equivalent to:

The discount rate at which the net present value of future cash flows is equal to the initial investment.

The main issue here is that the IRR refers only to the periods when the capital is 'working'. IRRs are not compounded returns for the entire time period. Result-antly there may be large differences between an internal rate of return (IRR) for a project and the compounded rate of return for the capital allocated to the project. IRRs will give a picture of the return the manager did with the capital they employed, but not when they employed the capital or what proportion of the capital was utilised.

The implication being that while investors may see outsized returns as achievable for PE investments, these calculations may not take into account the proportion of cap-ital sitting idle and proportion of time that capital has not been called. A more realistic expectation of results might be significantly lower. This strongly implies that the key metric used is: an inappropriate number / not fit for purpose!

Due to these issues, and likely deliberate obfuscation by the industry, no consistent standards have emerged among investment consultants to account for private equity returns in a portfolio, despite the ubiquity of the asset class. Compounded returns for the life of a fund would likely underestimate potential returns, while the standard methodology of Internal Rates of Return is likely to lead to excessive estimates of per-formance. The numbers from most PE firms and institutional investors should be taken with a pinch of salt. It can be difficult to compare performance data between PE funds particularly given issues of cash flow timings and differing valuation methodologies. Whilst the funds tend towards transparency with their positions, the lack of an agreed methodology for performance can make analysis or comparisons between managers' performance difficult.

MOVING ON TO OPERATIONAL DUE DILIGENCE

The advisory firm will also be expected to perform rigorous operational due diligence on the selected few that meet or exceed their criteria. This is important as most end users will not have the resources to perform this process in-house, and outsourcing this process avoids multiple duplication of work.

After the initial process excludes many potential managers and funds from the investment universe, a smaller number of asset managers will then be selected for Operational Due Diligence or ODD. This ODD will include basic checks on the firm: Are the Senior Managers and investment staff of the firm 'Fit and Proper' as defined by the regulator? Does the fund manager pass KYC checks and is their educational and professional background as claimed? This step of the process can often be quite laborious and can become project based rather than automated. Typically, there will be many steps including extended operational due diligence questionnaires and the submission of internal operational documents and compliance manuals, as well as a detailed study of IT systems and back-office controls and processes. An example checklist for the ODD tester is included below.

A SAMPLE (NON-EXHAUSTIVE) LIST OF OPERATIONAL CHECKS

i. Research process – is the investment thesis valid? Are the methods sufficiently rigorous? What methodology is dominant? Does the methodology match the investment mandates and the skills of the investment team?

ii. Data validity – including the track record and historical risk measures. Where is the data sourced from? Has it been audited? Can it be replicated with external data sources? Are they any missing data points, and if so, why?

iii. Trading compliance – Are reporting obligations and fiduciary obligations understood and matched?

iv. Trading process – dealer relationships, portfolio management systems, exchange links, trading systems, record keeping.

v. Outsourcing – Outsourcing policies and relationships with external service providers should ensure quality and cost-efficiency (custodians, prime brokers, auditors, systems integrators, compliance consultants, etc). What the important outsourced functions, are the agreements appropriate? Does the manager have contingency plans for the non-fulfillment of outsourcing agreements?

vi. Asset valuation – particularly important for illiquid assets. Areas of interest might include: What percentage of the fund's assets are exchange traded and marked to market via exchange prices versus model prices or non-tradable broker quotes? Who takes ultimate responsibility for pricing, and is there a formal dispute mechanism with stringent safeguards? Have the valuation methodologies used been consistent through time? Have any changes in models or valuation methodology been documented and explained? Is there a sufficient degree of independence between the manager and a third-party valuer?

vii. Compliance with current guidelines – with regulatory fines becoming an increasingly large cost for many financial institutions, on-going compliance is more important than ever. Compliance costs have risen rapidly since the Global Financial Crisis and are predicted to continue rising. Does the compliance team have an understanding of the regulatory hierarchy and a positive working relationship with the relevant regulators?

viii. Systems and Procedures to deal with regulatory change – Is the manager ready to deal with frequently changing regulations. For example, the impact of GDPR (The EU General Data Protection Regulation) or MiFiD II (the second Markets in Financial Instruments Directive) which is possibly the most complex set of Financial regulations the industry has dealt with.

ix. Fund Structure and Domicile: Some domiciles and regulatory regimes will present extra risks. The full structure of the fund's structure and regime should be understood; e.g., in Europe the appropriateness of UCITS vs AIFMD structures.

x. Remuneration Policies and Human Resources Procedures; Are investor and staff incentives aligned? Are the investment staff discouraged from significant risk taking?

xi. Conflicts of Interest Policies – Are they detailed, unambiguous and fair? Is there likely to be the risk of investor detriment due to ill thought out or non-enforced policies and processes? Does the manager have examples of situations where they have dealt with Conflicts of Interest that have arisen, if so, What was the outcome?

xii. Business continuity / disaster recovery – is a sufficiently detailed contingency plan in place? Are these recovery plans tested regularly and without prior warning to the relevant teams?

xiii. IT and physical security – Firstly, physical security. Are access to buildings, and staff controlled appropriately? Is Information and Cybersecurity at acceptable standards. Tests may need to be carried out on outsourced relationships, software providers and trading partners. Penetration and stress testing of IT systems is also likely a necessity particularly if the firm deals directly with retail clients.

xiv. Diversity – Diversity has shown to breed innovation, and helps investment teams avoid groupthink. This is particularly relevant in finance where Groupthink can lead to 'herding' and crowded positioning. An asset manager who embraces diversity is likely to attract a wider range of candidates to fill their vacancies, as well as creating an increase positive culture. Likely benefiting from increased employee performance.

xv. Data – With the General Data Protection Regulation (GDPR) in place from May 2018, Data storage and usage policies are more relevant and important than ever. The GDPR is probably the most important change in how we store and process data ever. In the UK it replaces the Data Protection Act (DPA) of 1998, which had become outdated and was not appropriate in a period where information has become so important. The GDPR now has much stronger requirements for all companies using personal data. Does the firm have a data policy in place; Does it match the standards recommended by the Information Commissioner's Office (ICO)? Has a GDPR or Data Audit been carried out? Again, this test is particularly relevant for firms facing non institutional clients.

xvi. CyberSecurity – Are CyberSecurity protocols at an acceptable standard? Tests may need to be carried out on outsourced relationships, software providers alongside security procedures. Penetration and stress testing is also likely a necessity, particularly if the firm deals directly with retail clients. In the event of a Data Breach or Security lapse, are the processes in place to inform the regulator and other stakeholders as well as acting against the breach?

After clearing the first set of quantitative screens a diligent consultant will seek to check every aspect of the manager's claims. Inquiries will be made as to whether the track record is comparable to similar strategies, whether the data has been professionally audited. Who performed this audit and for which periods? (Any missing periods would be a cause for concern and a possible red flag.) The investor will also ask: Are there enough data points for statistical evaluation and inference? Is the team responsible for the historical track record still in place today, or have small changes been made that could hinder future returns or reduce alpha?

The modern investor may also wish to simplify the fund selection process by simply choosing 'passive' investments. Although we should note that passive exposure to all asset classes is not yet available. For example, Venture Capital returns are difficult to emulate in a passive structure, and I know of no passive specialised art or collectables fund.

Many pension funds are now moving towards passive strategies, typically taken with liquid low-cost products, such as ETFs, and then adding an LDI or asset-liability management overlay.

QUICK ASIDE: Replicating Private Equity and a Passive Venture Capital Fund

Until recently it has been difficult for smaller investors to gain access to the return profile or factor exposure of private-equity and venture capital funds. Large minimum investment sizes and regulatory protections due to smaller investors have meant that both PE and VC firms have neither targeted or been targeted by retail savers. Hence historically these investments have been reserved for institutional investors and the very wealthy.

(This exclusion may not be a bad outcome as a great deal of existing academic and quantitative research has indicated that the Private Equity industry may not provide the diversification benefits promised, and that leveraged exposure to the public markets could in theory provide superior returns at lower cost and with significantly greater liquidity.)

However, in financial services there is always a desire to innovate, and the hunt for a competitive edge is continuous. Resultantly many asset managers are currently developing products that are designed to mimic PE returns but at significantly lower cost. One practical method developed by these innovators is to purchase a liquid portfolio of Exchange Traded Funds alongside developing a process to manipulate the portfolio leverage to obtain the desired risk profile. As an example, State Street, the US asset manager, has created a private-equity risk-and-return profile fund with a basket of public assets. The investment team first matches the sector weights of a typical private equity portfolio with what they deem to be equivalent public companies, and some clients then add leverage (typically between 20 per cent to 40 per cent) to both increase expected returns and more accurately represent the higher risk within Private Equity products. Use of this product synthetically replicates the risk and returns of PE investments but at a fraction of the cost and early returns have been encouraging.

Even more interestingly: Venture capital instruments have historically also been considered hard if not impossible to replicate until recently, and as a result many investors have been under-exposed to this asset class. However, continued financial innovation is now leading to products that would have been unimaginable even a few years ago. A passive venture capital fund now exists and is open to UK investors (with generous tax breaks to UK taxpayers). It was created by Syndicate Room, which is a leading 'FinTech' and crowdfunding platform based in Cambridge, UK. The management team at Syndicate Room have developed a passive fund that contains a diverse set of venture capital style investments. (Although it may not track VC indices particularly well.) Known as Fund Twenty8 the fund invests alongside Business Angels, Venture Capitalists and the 'Crowd'. The investment managers of the fund use the Syndicate Room crowdfunding platform to source equity investments in startups and SMEs investing automatically alongside the crowd and professional investors with pre-ordained amounts committed to each pitch according to a matching algorithm. Whilst the funds invested remain small at sub £10m (as of Jan 2018) the proof of concept indicates that more passive instruments are likely to be developed in this area.

These developments show that there may be no limit to the passive methodology. We hope to see similar funds enter other asset classes in the near future.

For newer managers in particular – trustees and fiduciaries will also want to investigate operational stability.

Historically, running an asset management firm has required little capital and garnered high profit margins. There were low barriers to entry, and with little competition on fees and often even lower barriers to success, this caused a boom in financial services. Which ultimately led to the sector over expanding and indirectly led to the Global Financial Crisis (GFC) and the need for the industry to contract from the bloated mess it had become.

Today, post-GFC, there are much higher barriers to entry for those developing investment management propositions, be they new managers establishing funds or existing managers changing markets or asset classes. There is now increased regulatory scrutiny and significantly more extensive costs in compliance, both in terms of monitoring and operating. The cost of meeting regulatory minimums, or meeting the *'regulatory burden'* is now a significant part of revenue for firms operating in financial services. These difficulties compounded by continuously decreasing fees and margins has led to operational strain for many managers.

As a sign of the times, in the last ten years, the number of fund failures has exceeded the number of fund launches, and this trend is not expected to reverse anytime soon. As the industry continues to contract after a period of over expansion. This has interesting implications to investors searching for new or smaller managers, with operational failure potentially a high risk for many of these firms. As such, dealing with new managers can represent a source of uncompensated risk that should be avoided because a fund that fails will need to be liquidated. Unfortunately, capital or asset withdrawals at this time could become difficult if not impossible. In extreme cases, there may be litigation and prolonged exposure to the manager and assets controlled by them, which may last for years. This creates additional reputational risk for the pension trustee, investment team or the consultant responsible.

In the UK the shuttering of Woodford Equity Income has shown the dangers of buying into star managers and having overconcentrated positions in new firms.

When assessing startup asset managers, it should be remembered that most investment professionals are not entrepreneurs and the assumption of entrepreneurial nous can create difficulties. Managing capital is not the same as running a business and many financial service professionals underestimate this. A manager's ability to control costs and predict revenues is important for long term viability, but isn't necessarily evident from their investing performance or their Sharpe Ratio.

It is possible to find brilliant investment managers with a flawless track record, who nonetheless are un-investable, as their operational processes and lack of knowledge of the regulatory environment create a recognisable and unnecessary risk for advisors.

By contrast, established firms with significant assets, a diverse client base and multiple revenue streams, have less business model risk and offer trustees and advisors a safe haven and reduced need for extensive oversight. The financial equivalent of *'Nobody gets fired for buying IBM'* sadly exists and is an important factor when observing how and why capital gets allocated.

The phrase *'Nobody gets fired for selecting JP Morgan'* has a ring of truth to it and may help explain why institutional inertia exists. A cynical or cautious trustee or fund-of-funds manager may be unwilling to take the career risk associated with finding overlooked but brilliant bespoke boutique managers and take the safe option of simply selecting a basket of well-known names.

The established firms, however, can also have performance challenges or scaling issues. So, whilst choosing a smaller boutique manager presents a risk committee with an operational headache, by operating small nimble strategies these managers, in the eyes of many, are a potential source of extra return. Indeed, many investment consultants / advisors see manager selection and finding new or boutique managers as an important part of their proposition. And although selecting a smaller asset management firm can't guarantee better performance, and in many cases adds new forms of risk, these firms offer the potential for superior risk adjusted return. So, it is important for investment consultants to understand their proposition and match them with investors who would benefit from their expertise.

One advantage of small boutique firms may be related to the alignment of incentives. Typically, boutiques are owned by the investment staff and key employees. These stakeholders are often solely responsible for asset management as well as being co-invested in the funds. Some owner-managers will also have a significant portion of their personal assets invested in the portfolios they manage. This 'skin in the game' would certainly sharpen their focus. Conversely the failure of a high percentage of managers at larger firms to invest in either their own or their employers' portfolios would seem to indicate a lack of belief in their ability to outperform or generate Alpha. Anecdotally, a large number of active managers in my professional network use Vanguard's passive product range for at least some of their personal accounts. They often see cost-minimisation as more important than the hunt for Alpha, when they are paying the costs themselves.

Due to the strange incentives that can arise at large and bureaucratic organisations investment staff at the largest asset managers are often rewarded for stability rather than growth. In reality, employees at large institutions are often more worried about managing their career than their fiduciary duties. Fund Managers at MegaBank or GigaInsurer will often see little upside from significant outperformance but their careers can suffer severely in the event of even minor underperformance or small deviations from their benchmark. This encourages herd like behaviour, with none of these managers wishing to stand out from the crowd. Ultimately these incentives can lead to index style performance throughout large asset managers.

Many sceptics consider engaging with a large active manager to be an expensive way of guaranteeing market performance (minus costs).

Indeed, in the United Kingdom, the Financial Conduct Authority (the FCA), the UK financial services regulator, has sought to take action against firms that have simply sought to mimic market performance whilst charging end users for fully active management. The FCA has dubbed these funds *'closet trackers'* and helpfully defined them:

> *'Closet trackers and closet constrained funds look like and charge fees similar to active funds. Yet they are managed in a way that is similar to passive funds which traditionally charge a much lower fee. Closet constrained funds make active decisions. However their investment strategy is constrained to making restricted decisions around their respective benchmarks. Closet trackers are passive but look and charge like they are active.'*

As part of its consumer protection remit the FCA investigated whether firms were simply allocating funds in a near passive way but charging for a more active approach. They used a mixture of quantitative and qualitative analysis to define a fund's investment approach, and compared with marketing materials and investor communications, to see whether strategies had been communicated in a way that was *'clear, fair and not misleading'*. They reviewed a total of 84 funds in 2017 that had been marketed as active. This market examination took place across multiple funds, managers and asset classes including a mix of equity, government, credit and multi-asset funds. Strangely the regulator did not name the funds or firms under investigation. An action that led to some criticism as naming the guilty looked to be an appropriate additional punishment.

The regulator had found that less than a quarter of the sample, just twenty of the funds investigated, were accurately describing their investment process. The remainder were found to be lacking in either the manner of investment process or the manner of communication. As of March 2018, the FCA demanded that £34m in compensation be paid to funds and investors. Showing that 'closet tracking' at the largest firms is an issue that has been recognised by the industry. Because of behaviour such as this, some of the largest firms are pejoratively described as 'asset gatherers' rather than asset managers. This is because they seek to collect asset and fees through franchise value and allocating resources to business development rather than focusing on investment process and superior risk management. See Table 5.1.

TABLE 5.1 A Comparison: The Asset Managers and The Asset Gatherers

Compared	Asset Manager	Asset Gatherer
Objective	A pure focus on Risk-Adjusted return. Performance is the raison d'etre of the true asset manager. Pure asset managers will often have capacity constraints in place and turn away business so as not to compromise their returns.	The asset gather will focus on maximising asset under management (AUM). The key here is the satisfying the goals of senior management and the investment staff. Investors needs are often secondary to managerial and staff utility
Specialty	An asset manager will specialise and usually (but not always) have deep product expertise in a very narrow area.	The asset gatherer will launch a range of funds, irrespective of whether it has the internal expertise as its core objective is maximising AUM.
Alignment	An asset manager will have strong convictions in their own ideas and may have significant wealth tied up in the fund or similar investments. Investor and investee are in alignment.	The asset gatherer will likely not have significant capital tied up in their strategies. Over time they are likely to emerge as closet trackers, as the investment staff prefer not to stand out from the crowd.
Marketing	A true asset management firm will be run by its investment staff. It will have little in the way of marketing expenses as investors are naturally attracted by its superior performance and focus. Any marketing or recognition is likely to be inclusive of the investment staff rather than focused on the firm.	An asset gatherer will have a large marketing and business development team. It will typically try and offer a full range of products so as to minimise the chance of missing business. It will also have a large advertising budget and rely on name recognition of the franchise rather than individual performers.
Scaling	An asset manager will close their fund to outside investment when it reaches optimal size. They recognise that excess capital in a strategy can diminish return, and that not all all strategies are scalable.	An asset gatherer will allow capital to accumulate even as risk premiums diminish as its objective is always to maximise AUM and of course fees.
Independence	An asset manager is often independent of the larger institutions and has one product not wishing to cross sell multiple financial services.	An asset gather will seek to maximise the benefit of all client relationships. They will seek to cross or up sell other financial services to what they hope is a captive client base.

PART 3 PORTFOLIO SELECTION

After creating an investable universe by choosing a selection of appropriate assets, be they favoured stocks, favoured managers, structured products or index tracking funds, the investment consultant, asset manager, trustee or investor must blend these assets to create a risk – return profile that matches the objectives. Here the problem becomes one of mathematical optimisation using Linear Algebra.

Some investment assumptions

1. Investors see financial instruments as being represented by a probability distribution of returns that is measured over a defined time frame (this is known as the holding period).
2. Investors' units of risk are proportional to the variability of the returns (as measured by the standard deviation, or equivalently, the variance of returns).
3. Investors are willing to base their decisions on only the expected return and risk statistics. That is, investors' utility of returns function, U (r), is solely a function of variability of return (σ) and expected return [E(r)]. Or U (r) = f [σ, E(r)].
4. For any given level of risk, investors prefer higher returns to lower returns.

Or stated differently, for any given level of rate of return, investors prefer less risk over more risk.

Portfolio Selection requires that an investor has the following estimates for every security to be considered:

i. The expected return μ
$$\mu(x):= E[RP] = E[X\ i\ x_iR_i] = X\ i\ E[x_iR_i] = X\ i\ x_iE[R_i].$$

ii. The expected volatility of returns σ
Where $\bar{R}_i := E[R_i]$
$$Var[R_i] := E(R_i - \bar{R}_i)\ 2 = E[R\ 2\ i] - (\bar{R}_i)\ 2$$
$$\sigma_i := sqrt\ Var[R_i]$$

iii. The expected correlation between the chosen securities
Where the covariance between two random variables X and Y is defined as:
$$Cov(X, Y) = \sigma XY := E[(X - E[X])(Y - E[Y])] = E[XY] - E[X]E[Y],$$
and the correlation between two random variables X and Y is defined as:
$$Corr(X, Y) = \rho XY := Cov(X, Y)\ \sigma X \sigma Y$$

It is usually possible to obtain the security correlations from available historical data. However, we should remember that correlations are unlikely to be constant, so sometimes a more subjective approach may be necessary as the risk profile of all securities is likely to change over time.

If the historical data are both accurate and extensive and market conditions in the future are expected to resemble those from the sample period, then using historical data is likely to be appropriate and the best estimate of future conditions. However frequently, some market data may be missing or inappropriate. All of these estimates are also likely to change depending on the time-period used and the frequency of observation.

But if the security analyst is an expert with a specialist insight or the market is thought to be changing, subjective estimates may be preferable to historical data. The portfolio analyst must consider many securities at once when constructing an optimal portfolio, and in practical terms accurate data is unlikely to be available for all securities at all time points.

It is worth noting that a lot of these data points can only be estimates, as many asset classes trade infrequently, if at all. Volatility is constantly changing and not necessarily observable and of course correlations between many assets are not constant and change frequently if not constantly.

When working with large portfolios, the computation involved in representing the asset class expected returns and correlation becomes difficult to manage. The use of matrix (linear) algebra can greatly simplify many of the computations. Matrix algebra formulations have many uses in science but have also found uses in economics and finance. The matrix algebra formulas we use are easy to manipulate in many statistical packages such as R or Python. However, in practice, the bulk of this modelling work is still done with Microsoft Excel, which often forms the backbone of a consultant's analysis.

Typically, a Linear Optimisation problem will be run on a selection of asset classes, with estimates of Risk and Return generated either from historical data or a more subjective framework. The optimisation would typically include the boundary condition that no assets can have negative weight, and some riskier assets may be capped at sometimes arbitrary weights; i.e., a quantitative research firm would be unlikely to recommend more than 10% in a speculative asset such as commodities no matter what their model output is.

This would give a series of idealised model weights

An example of a conservative portfolio might be:

Equity 25%

Government bonds 30%

Fixed Income – Non Gov 30%

Alternatives – 15%

Once these asset class weights are known, the process of fund or manager selection can begin.

Figure 5.1 is a real-world example of a large institutional portfolio that is using an LDI framework.

Asset allocation

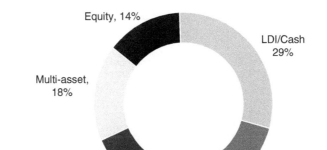

FIGURE 5.1   Asset Allocation

CHAPTER 6

Moving Towards Liability Driven Investing

THE TIME VALUE OF MONEY

'A dollar today is worth more than a dollar tomorrow.'

Saving and investing is a complex process and really the first step to understanding its mechanics is the 'time value of money' which is outlined here for clarity. This key economic concept involves calculating the present value (PV or value today) of a payment to be made in the future. Calculating the 'time value of money' helps us assess the equivalency of differing cash flow streams across time and makes cashflows at different times directly comparable.

The time value of money allows us to know or estimate:

– The value today (PV) of a payment to be received in the future
– The PV of a stream of equally sized cash flows to be received at uniform increments of time in the future (payments or an annuity, similar to the demands of a pension fund or a retiree saving the future)
– The PV of a stream of unequally sized and/or timed cash flows in the future (CF)
– The future values of the above
– The annuitised values of the above

For an individual saving for a goal, be it house ownership, education, or retirement, the effect of time on the value of the nest egg is clearly important. Similarly, for the trustee of a pension fund or someone approaching retirement, it is necessary to work out the size of any obligation or desired lump sum or annuity and then discount back to find an appropriate amount to save. For a pension fund, an actuary will look at the size and time profile of the likely obligations. For each member, the actuary estimates what benefits that member is expected to receive in the future and the likely time of payment and then aggregates to develop a likely pay-off profile for the fund.

Say for example that the pension fund predicts or has identified a cash flow need of £1,000, and that the fund has invested in a UK government Bond or Gilt to hedge this exposure. (Gilts, short for Gilt-edged securities, is the usual way of referring to UK Government Debt). Assume also that a Gilt of exactly the same maturity exists and has a yield of 1% and that this payment is to be made in ten years.

In this example to calculate the present value. We have:

£1,000 / 1.01 / 1.01 / 1.01 / 1.01 / 1.01 / 1.01 / 1.01 / 1.01 / 1.01 / 1.01 or
£1,000 / (1.01) ^ 10 = £905.29

Now here is where it gets interesting. If we invest £905.29 in gilts, we would be certain to meet the payment, as gilts are considered risk-free. A conservative investor may choose exactly this approach. But as we can see this may not be the optimal approach for all stakeholders.

Historically, it has been observed that you can take on higher risk to receive a higher return. There exist many risk premia across asset classes, and long-term investors will seek to earn an extra return by moving into riskier assets.

What if we do decide to take on more risk to earn a higher return? There are many ways of doing this. For example, an investment team in a similar position to ours, might have the option of purchasing an investment grade corporate bond (or a basket of investment grade corporate bonds) of the same maturity paying 2 per cent. Changing the investment to these higher yielding securities would change the expected return on investment and hence the amount of capital needed to be set-aside. If the team were comfortable with / allowed to take the extra risk.

In this scenario a pension fund sponsor would only need to set aside:

£1,000 / 1.02 / 1.02 / 1.02 / 1.02 / 1.02 / 1.02 / 1.02 / 1.02 / 1.02 / 1.02 or
£1,000 / (1.02) ^10 = £820.35.

The higher expected return implies that we would need to set aside less capital today.

£1,000 / (1.01) ^ 10 – £1,000/ (1.02) ^10 = £85.14

So, in our basic example, investing in Corporate Debt which is still very low risk, rather than 'boring' government debt looks to be more than 10 per cent capital efficient!

Looking at this, you could reasonably ask why would any long-term investor buy gilts? But this is potentially misguided. Developed Market Governments issuing in their own currency are considered as default-risk free. There is a risk that this basket of corporate bonds could fall in value, or that some of the issuers will default and not be able to meet their future payments or obligations. Gilts have inflation and market risk, whereas the lower (but still high) quality corporate bonds also contain Credit Risk and extra liquidity risk, as they less liquid. This could negatively impact return if the portfolio needed to be unwound or altered as circumstances change.

This is where we as investors are forced to balance higher expected returns with higher expected risks. We can also see the conflicting interests of the stakeholders. The beneficiaries would prefer that £905.29 was invested to guarantee the cashflow, the sponsor would presumably prefer the, still low-risk but riskier, corporate bonds to lower their capital contribution to £820.35.

Clearly finding appropriate discount rates for Fixed Cash flows in the future is a matter of finding the market price of an *appropriate* bond, calculating the yield and then adjusting for likely credit losses. Although there may be some debate on which are the most appropriate instruments to discount with. However, the bulk of many institutional portfolios is invested in equities or similar securities which do not so readily offer their expected returns. For the riskier assets in the portfolio, projections must be made for the likely period of investments.

It is reasonable in the first instance to look at historical returns for guidance, we would then be likely to see the return on risk assets as the return on less risky assets plus a risk premium. Typically, the size of the equity risk premium (ERP) is quoted as an excess return over cash, government bonds or inflation.

Here in the United Kingdom the historical data shows that the stock market might be expected to return inflation plus four per cent over the long term. Using the Monetary Policy Committee (MPC)'s inflation target of 2 per cent this gives us expected returns of 6 per cent per annum and suggests a discount rate of 1.06 might be appropriate when discounting potential stock market returns for our purposes.

The FCA (as of September 2017) suggests:

'In relation to equities, our analysis suggests that expected real returns have declined from a range of 4 per cent to 5.5 per cent in 2012, to a range of 3 per cent to 5 per cent at present.'

But by some measures, the stock market could be expected to return nine per cent over the next ten years. An optimist might say, that if the portfolio was 100 per cent invested in equities, it could be reasoned that you would only need to set aside:

£1,000 /1.09/1.09/1.09/1.09/1.09/1.09/1.09/1.09/1.09/1.09 or
£1,000 /(1.09) ^ 10 = £422.41.

This is a substantially smaller outlay, which could potentially obtain the same outcome! But equities are inherently riskier than fixed income products and here there is a significant risk we might not be able to meet the future payment (conversely, if equities do better than expected, we may have more than £1,000 at the end of the period).

In some cases, the actuary, investment consultant or trustee has a great deal of freedom to make assumptions about the expected performance of the underlying asset classes and to choose an appropriate discount rate. The return projections are usually based on the portfolio composition and the historical performance of the underlying asset classes.

Taking the case of the previously mentioned 70 / 30 portfolio, which is a simplified reference portfolio of 70 per cent stocks and 30 per cent fixed income. If the portfolio allocation is 70 per cent in equities, and these securities are expected to return 6 per cent, and the remaining 30 per cent in Fixed Income which is expected to yield 2 per cent. Then the investor could reasonably argue that the appropriate rate to discount future payments is a weighted average of these results; i.e.,

(6 per cent x 0.7 + 2 per cent x 0.3) = 4.8 per cent.

Indeed, in all jurisdictions and for most defined benefit schemes the riskiness of the asset classes must be taken into account. For example, under IAS 19 or the International Accounting Standard 19 rule concerning employee benefits there are broad prescriptive rules for discounting liabilities. In general, all future liability cash flows must be discounted using the rate that could be earned on high-quality (AA-rated) corporate bonds or a derivative thereof. In the UK this is often modeled as Gilts plus a spread.

As we've seen above a lower discount rate, reflecting a low-risk investment strategy, would lead to a larger present value of liabilities and in the case of pension funds; larger deficits. With the size of the deficit equalling value of assets minus value of liabilities.

In the pensions industry there has been an ongoing debate between the optimists and the pessimists (or the aggressive versus the cautious) on the appropriate interest rate. The extremes positions expressed are – purely Gilts based discounting with zero spread for the cautious, although this would typically be done only on a fully 'immunized' portfolio. The adventurous or optimistic position would be to suggest discounting using projected long-term equity return. This is to properly account for the accepted existence of the equity risk premium for long term holdings.

LDI practitioners are generally sceptical of overly high discount rates, they draw an analogy between having a mortgage whilst also holding a portfolio of stock market investments. For an individual with both of these financial products, when assessing their personal balance sheet, it would seem clear that discounting payments due from an individual mortgage with expected profits from equity holdings would not give an appropriate measurement of wealth. The analogy would imply that the value of your mortgage is a function of projected equity returns rather than a contractual agreement with the bank!

More Extreme than the Extreme

The Gilts minus model: Although not yet seriously discussed in the academic or regulatory debate on appropriate discounting, possibly due to the strain on deficits if enacted. There is a school of thought that suggests a lower discount factor than purely gilt based discounting could be appropriate. It could be said that not even gilt returns are guaranteed. This argument can be broken into two parts.

Costs: The first argument is due to the fact that, whilst Gilt returns may for practical purposes be considered risk free, there are costs associated with accessing these returns. Trustees or investors will need to pay both fixed and variable costs on their investment portfolios. The long list of costs varies from custody charges for storing assets, fund managements charges on the gilt portfolios, and on-going monitoring from actuaries and investment consultants, as well as the cost of meeting regulatory obligations, even of communicating risks and returns to stakeholders. Over time these costs add up and then compound. Clearly for a Pension fund with the bulk of obligations payable over a timeframe longer than thirty years, these incidental expenses could easily consume five to ten per cent of assets.

Uncertainties within Liabilities: The liabilities modelled by actuaries are usually only estimates of likely cash flows. In many cases unknown variables will make cash flows impossible to know precisely. For example, Defined Benefit schemes: for precise knowledge of obligations an actuary would need to know the date of retirement of each beneficiary and, perhaps more worryingly, the date of death of each pensioner. To our knowledge, no actuary claims to have this skill.

The calculations will often also require detailed knowledge of inflation and the historical time path of inflation over time. This is as most DB schemes have caps and floors on the rate of inflation payable by the sponsor. In the United Kingdom these limits are often 0% and 5%. It is possible, if not a near certainty across the universe of trusts, that some actuarial estimates of future cash flows are insufficient and that more capital will need to be found to pay future liabilities, for this reason a more conservative discounting rate may be appropriate if it encourages a greater saving rate.

THE BASICS CONTINUED: REAL VERSUS NOMINAL DISCOUNTING

Some investors may prefer to look at expected returns and liabilities in terms of 'real' liabilities: i.e., instead of using the discounting rates outlined previously they are concerned only with real or inflation-adjusted returns. This could be for a variety of reasons personal or technical. In many real world cases liability structures will have a fixed or nominal component and a component linked to the rate of inflation or a defined inflationary index. In addition, the returns of many asset classes are more stable when examined in reference to inflation than on a standard alone basis, which can make for simpler analysis and risk management. Intuitively the price level at each point in the investment life cycle is crucial when assessing the cost of a liability; indeed, for all Defined Contribution investment it is reasonable to assume that the price level is important. So, if we compare cash flows over time, it is important to consider the effects of inflation. This is why as investors we should be comfortable moving between two different types of interest rates; the nominal interest rate and the real interest rate.

Nominal Interest Rate

The nominal interest rate is the headline rate and describes the interest rate with no correction for the effects of inflation. The quoted interest rates seen on bonds, mortgages or credit card/ credit accounts are usually nominal. The rate shows you the actual rate you receive (or pay) if you lend (or borrow) funds.

Real Interest Rate

The real interest rate refers to the interest rate adjusted to remove the eroding effects of inflation. This rate shows you by how much the actual purchasing power of the money you have in your bank account decreases over time.

How to calculate real interest rate

To demonstrate, let's create a simple example.

Say that we have £100 and are investing it for a period of one year at a nominal interest rate of 3%. Clearly at the end of the year we will have £103.

Now, let's say during the same period, the overall price level in the economy has increased by 2%, which matches the Bank of England's inflation target. In this case, the buying power of £1 has decreased, and you will now need more money to buy the same basket of goods.

Hence, we need to adjust for the effects of inflation.

In this example, we can approximate:

Real Interest Rate (R) = Nominal Interest Rate (r) − Rate of Inflation (i)

So, we take 2 per cent (the inflation rate) from 3 per cent (the nominal interest rate), which results in a real interest rate of 1%.

And, our purchasing power would have increased by only 1 per cent.

However, this is only an approximation; the precise formula is:

$$(1 + R) = (1 + r) / (1 + i)$$

Which gives,

$(1 + R) = (1 + 3\%)/(1 + 2\%) = (1.03)/(1.02) = 0.98\%$

In low interest rate environments, the approximation will give reasonable results, however as we demonstrate below it is less effective in highly inflationary regimes.

Take a scenario of 10 per cent interest rates and 6 per cent inflation.

Here the approximate formula gives:

Real Interest Rate (R) = Nominal Interest Rate (r) − Rate of Inflation (i)

$R = 10\% - 6\% = 4\%$

But the precise figure is

$R = (1 + r)/(1 + i) - 1$

$So \ R = (1 + 10\%)/(1 + 6\%) - 1 = 1.1 / 1.06 - 1 = 3.77\%$

NB Real Interest rates are likely to be higher in inflationary environments as investors will seek extra return to compensate for the extra risk, although this is not always the case.

A SIMPLE AND BRIEF LOOK AT BONDS

Fixed Income or bond investing is often seen as equity investment's boring cousin. However, there are a host of benefits to bonds that make them important, if not crucial instruments for nearly all investment portfolios. The certainty and the predictability of cash flows ensures that as an asset class they are of particular interest to LDI or ALM investors.

Bonds, alongside equities, are the most important asset class in the standard investor toolkit. The fixed income market is also significantly larger than the equity market: by far the largest securities market in the world, this despite the equity market generating more headlines. As an asset class, bonds are considered less risky than equities, but riskier than cash. They constitute a residual claim for a corporation's assets in the event of liquidation or an obligation for a government issuer. High Grade Bonds can be used to provide a secure income from an investment portfolio with minimal risk to capital and as such are ideal for hedging long dated income needs.

When a bond is created, the issuer promises to make regular interest payments to the investor at a specified rate (known as the coupon rate) on the amount borrowed (known as the principal) until a specified date (the maturity date). Upon the date the bond redeems, the interest payments will stop and the issuer repays the face amount of the principal to the investor.

Coupon rates are generally fixed – ie the payment stays constant throughout the life of the bond. Hence why bonds have become known as fixed income securities. The income is typically fixed. However, some bonds may have variable or floating coupon rates (payments that change from coupon to coupon based on a pre-determined schedule or benchmark rate). A further class of bonds known as zero-coupon securities make no payments until the return of the principal at maturity.

In the UK the largest issuer of fixed income securities is the UK government. Bonds issued by the UK government debt are known as Gilts. This is an abbreviation of Gilt-Edged securities, and is a reference to how historically the paper ownership certificates were gilded.

For a GBP investor; gilts can be viewed as risk free from the point of view of default. The price of the securities will fluctuate in the market, depending on the outlook for interest rates but investors buying risk free debt, and holding the bonds to maturity can be certain that interest and principal will be repaid in full.

The gilt market is split into four main parts.

- **Shorts** – *five years or less until they are redeemed by the Government*
- **Mediums** – *five to fifteen years until they are redeemed by the Government*
- **Longs** – *over 15 years until they are redeemed by the Government*
- **Index-linked Gilts** – *the return paid out is linked to changes in inflation with a lag*
- *Also* **Undated Gilts** – *these types of Gilt have no set redemption date; they are less actively traded and not important for our purposes. Trading in these securities represents less than a tenth of one per cent of market turnover. The most well-known of the undated gilts was the UK 3.5% War Loan.*

The key features of a typical bond are:

- Maturity – the date the principal is to be repaid
- Coupon – the interest rate paid by the issuer
- Coupon Type – are the coupons fixed or floating, what is the payment frequency?
- Credit Rating – Rating agency assessment of credit quality, for LDI strategies we generally use government bonds which are AAA and considered to be credit risk free. For the growing field of CDI (Cash Flow Driven Investing) investors are moving to more speculative credits to lower their capital requirements, and to get better cash flow matching.

Some Other Types of Bonds

Floating rate bonds: These are bonds where the coupon is not fixed, but based on a reference rate, typically LIBOR with a positive spread (this spread is to compensate for credit risk). Floating rate bonds, often abbreviated to floaters, will not exhibit the same degree of interest rate sensitivity as conventional bonds, but will have interest rate exposure limited to the date of the next coupon. Floating issues are generally a credit product and the majority are issued with maturities between two and ten years.

Convertible bonds: These are bonds where the holder may convert his redemption proceeds into the equity of the issuing company. As such they are considered a hybrid asset class, mixing the defensive qualities of fixed income with the potentially uncapped upside of equities. Sometimes they are known as 'equity convertibles' and can offer a combination of a secure income and growth for investors. These instruments can see their price driven higher by a rise in a company's share price (or even by a rise in earnings' volatility). Volatility, however, is generally higher and the coupon lower than standard bond from the issuers.

Subordinated bonds: The majority of bonds issued and traded are 'senior debt'. Entitling the holder to a priority claim on the company's assets, ahead of the shareholders. However, some bonds are issued with 'subordinated' status. This means that the buyer of the bonds accepts a lower claim on the company's assets, below the senior debt holders, but above the equity holders. Because of the additional risk, these bonds offer a higher return.

How to Price a Bond

A bond's price is a function of its coupon rate compared to the current level of interest, its remaining term to maturity, its credit or default risk and any other features it may have.

Newly issued bonds are normally priced at or around par. The price of the issue then fluctuates throughout the bond's lifetime and the bond may be trading at a price greater than (at a premium to), less than (at a discount to) or at its face value (known as par). Frequently, bonds are priced (or valued) against a benchmark. This means that an individual security is compared to a similar-term bond (usually a Government Security) and priced as a function of that issue. For example, in the UK corporate market, issues are traded as a spread over Gilts and the market maker will often take delivery of the gilt at the same time. (When trading a Package such as this the counterparties gain access to the credit exposure but have no interest rate exposure.)

The main risk for all but the lowest quality fixed rate bonds (which often trade like equities) are Interest Rates. Fluctuations in interest rates directly affect the price of bonds. Bond prices move inversely to interest rates because the coupon rate remains constant through the life of the bond. If current interest rates move higher than the coupon rate, the bond is less attractive to investors and its price will fall, as investors would be unwilling to pay as much for a series of lower coupon payments than available elsewhere and vice versa. Bond prices increase when the coupon rate is higher than current interest rate levels.

Key Terms

The Yield

The **running yield** is the annual return on the cash amount paid for the bond. It is calculated by simply dividing the dollar amount of the coupon rate by the purchase price.

For example, a bond with a £100 face value and a 3 per cent coupon, purchased at par, has a running yield of 3 per cent (annual interest of £3 divided by £100 purchase price).

If the same were to be bought at £110 then the current yield would be 2.73 per cent (annual interest of £3 divided by £110 purchase price). Of more practical interest is **the yield to maturity or YTM**. This calculation will give the total return received by holding the bond until maturity. YTM takes into account all the interest payments the investor will receive. (It is often assumed that the investor reinvests these interest payments at the same rate as the payments from the security, but this does not need to be the case.) In addition to the difference between the purchase price and par.

Confusingly, the market convention for gilts (and most other markets) is to quote annualised yields with semi-annual compounding. So, for example, a YTM of 2.00% would be quoted as 1.99%, this is as $1.0199 \times 1.0199 = 1.02$.

The YTM in addition to the coupon rate will also tell us whether the bond is trading at a premium or discount.

The Coupon with Yield To Maturity

If a bond's coupon rate is less than its YTM, then the bond is selling at a discount.

If a bond's coupon rate is more than its YTM, then the bond is selling at a premium.

If a bond's coupon rate is equal to its YTM, then the bond is selling at par.
And both these terms relate to the running yield like so:
For a bond selling at a discount
Coupon Rate < Current Yield < YTM
For a bond selling at a Premium
Coupon Rate > Current Yield > YTM
For a bond selling at Par
Coupon Rate = Current Yield = YTM

Basis point. A basis point is a unit of measurement equalling 1/100th of one per cent. Alternatively, we may think of one hundred basis points as being equal to one per cent.

Duration. Duration has two related but different meanings in Fixed Income and it is important to be clear on the two.

Macaulay duration. Which is the name given to the weighted average time until cash flows are received, and is measured in years. The Macaulay duration in years is always less than the time to maturity, with the exception of a zero coupon bond when it is the same.

Modified duration. Which is a measure of risk and is the name given to the price sensitivity of a bond and is the percentage change in price for a unit change in yield.

Bonds are a powerful if not perfect hedge for Liability Driven Investment as changes in interest rates will affect the value of the instrument in the same manner that they affect the value of the liabilities. A fall in interest rates will increase the present value of a scheme's liabilities, but the bond will also increase in value as the future cash flows are being discounted by the correspondingly lower rate. The perfect hedge comes at the price of lower expected return. In the absence of leverage, to implement an appropriate fixed income portfolio a pension scheme would needs to raise capital by moving out of assets with higher expected return (stocks, private equity, venture capital, emerging markets, property, etc). All of these assets are expected to provide higher returns over the long-term and the pension scheme may even be guaranteeing performance lower than inflation. These lower expected returns may require a capital infusion from the sponsor to have an expectation of meeting obligations. This will often be resisted.

IMMUNISATION THEORY AND FRANK REDINGTON

Many of the concepts involved in Liability Driven Investment are actuarial in nature and the modelling of Liabilities (be they defined benefit pension obligations or A.N.Other) as fixed payments similar to fixed income instruments allowed the developers of LDI strategies to use frameworks from the world of Fixed Income. Much has been written on Fixed Income hedging and of particular interest to us was the work of Frank Redington who was a noted British actuary working in the middle of the last century.

Frank Redington was a First Class Mathematics graduate from Cambridge University (Magdalen College, 1928) who joined the Prudential straight after university and never left. Mr Redington rose to become the Chief Actuary of the Prudential Life Insurance company from 1951 and remained so until his retirement in 1968. He was also voted the 'the Greatest British Actuary ever' by Actuary magazine, and had a reputation for thought provoking and insightful work.

Redington was an advocate of the advantages of applied mathematics and the use of statistics to improve investment outcomes and made a significant number of contributions to the life insurance industry. In multiple areas ranging from pension planning to mortality statistics, but it is his contribution and development of immunisation theory that is important to us when looking at Liability hedging. His 1952 Paper (the same year as Markowitz') on the Principles of Life Office Valuation looked in detail at the relationships between assets and liabilities in a life office and considered how to manage the risks within. Frank is considered the father of Fixed Income immunisation. Immunisation is a risk management tool used to minimise the interest rate risk of bond investments by adjusting the portfolio duration to match the investor's investment time horizon. It does this by locking in a fixed rate of return during the amount of time an investor plans to keep the investment.

Interest Rates are the main risk factor affecting bond prices (and by association, liabilities), the vast majority of bond price returns can be explained by changes in Interest Rates. Interest rates affect bond prices inversely. When interest rates go up, bond prices go down and vice versa. But when a bond portfolio is immunised, the investor receives a specific rate of return over a given time period regardless of what happens to interest rates during that time. In other words, the portfolio becomes 'immune' to changes in the prevailing interest rates.

To protect a portfolio from fluctuations in the yield curve, an investor needs to know the duration of the instruments in the portfolio and then adjust the portfolio so that the portfolio's duration matches the investment time horizon.

As an example, consider an institution that requires £100 million in five years' time for a new factory. A triple A rated fixed income portfolio would allow them certainty over this cash flow, and they could immunise the effect of interest rates by selecting High quality bonds whose payments will equal exactly the target amount in five years regardless of changes in the market. The closest hedge would be a government issued zero coupon bond with the same maturity, but in practice this is unlikely to exist. Practical possibilities for investment would include, an investment in a government bond with a similar maturity, or a selection of bonds at or around the target date, that allow a small yield pick-up. Other possibilities would include bespoke derivative contracts, that whilst they can allow more accurate date targeting can be expensive to design and implement. They will often expose the corporation to unnecessary credit risk from their counterparty.

Advisors will often caution against over precise hedging. In this example, the institution has expressed a desire to spend an amount (£100 million) at a certain time (five years in the future) but the amount, timing and need are not guaranteed. Depending on the success of the underlying business the factory may be needed sooner rather than later, or possibly not at all, and the amount is an estimated liability which depends on many unknown variables such as future property values and costs of construction. In this example a precise and expensive hedge would likely be inappropriate.

AN INTRODUCTION TO INTEREST RATE SWAPS

Alongside government bonds and credit products one of the most important tools for an LDI practitioner is the Interest Rate Swap. Interest Rate Swaps are bespoke OTC (over-the-counter) products than can allow more accurate hedging of cash flows and can be used to match liabilities with a great deal of precision.

Unlike most securities which have origins shrouded in the mists of time. The birth of the interest rate swap is well documented. Whilst, for example government debt goes back centuries if not millennia, and even more exotic products such as inflation backed bonds can be dated back to 1780. We can say with precision when and how the interest rate swap markets developed with the development evolving from the parallel loan market between London and New York. Back in 1981 perhaps the most famous IR swap was conducted between the World Bank and IBM. At this time the relevant interest rate in the U.S. was 17 per cent, near the peak of anti-inflation tight monetary policy of Paul Volcker. In West Germany the interest rate was 12 per cent and Switzerland 8 per cent. The World Bank was subject to borrowing restrictions in both Switzerland and Germany. IBM had outstanding debt in both Swiss francs and German deutsche marks and had to make payments in both currencies. The World Bank received dollar payments in return for paying IBM's Swiss franc and deutsche mark obligations.

What Is an Interest Rate Swap?

A swap is an agreement between two parties to exchange one set of payments for another over a defined time period agreed at the outset. For an interest rate swap the parties exchange fixed coupons – similar to bond coupons – for floating payments – which represent the short-term funding costs. In the GBP market, which is the third largest in the world, the conventions are for fixed payments to be exchanged semi-annually against six-month LIBOR. The party that pays fixed is known as the 'payer' and the party that receives fixed payments is known as the 'receiver'. At the start of the swap the value of the swap for each party should be zero (or negligible).

Receiving fixed is equivalent to receiving a set of bond coupons and is hence equivalent to owning a bond. Conversely paying fixed is equivalent to a short-fixed income position.

The Mechanics

Say two parties are entering into a swap. For practical purposes one of the counterparties is always a market-maker and he / she will respond to their client's exact request. Take the example of a corporate Treasurer who wishes to gain exposure to 10y interest rates but does not wish to buy a bond as they lack the funding for the position.

Suppose that 10y swap rates in the UK = 2.00% and that 6m Libor is 1%. In this example the payer would pay out 1% of the notionally agreed amount annually. In the UK, the convention is for semi-annual payments, hence assuming that 6-month Libor doesn't change the payer would pay 0.5 per cent every 6 months. It can be seen that the receiver has a risk exposure similar to being Long high-quality fixed income securities.

If interest rates fall or move lower, the receiver would make money as their payments are fixed, but their obligations will move lower with interest rates. The market value of the swap will typically move in the same direction and at the same magnitude as a position in a Gilt or Treasury with the same notional.

Some Terms Used in the Market

Long Position: an interest rate swap being long refers to the counterparty in the receiving fixed position.

Short Position: an interest rate swap being short refers to the counterparty in the paying fixed position.

Notional: The principal value of a swap transaction, which is not exchanged but is used as a scale factor to calculate cash settlement payments.

Swap Spread: The difference between the fixed rate on a swap and the government yield of equivalent maturity.

LIBOR: The London Interbank Offered Rate, which is used to calculate the floating payment. See Table 6.1.

A Quick Aside: Forward Rate Agreements (FRAs)

A swap can be thought of as a series of forward rate agreements also known as FRAs. A FRA is an obligation to exchange a pre-specified fixed rate for a floating reference rate, in the GBP markets this is usually 3 month LIBOR, at a pre-specified date in the future for a pre-determined period of time and notional amount. In other words, a FRA can be used as a way of ensuring a rate of interest on the trade date for borrowing/lending that is to take place at some time in the future. Market convention is that the buyer of the FRA pays the fixed rate, while the seller receives the fixed rate. The interest rate level is a combination of market expectations of forward rates alongside risk premia that exist in the rates markets.

Differences between swaps and FRAs

Whilst there are many similarities and a series of FRAs could be used to broadly replicate a swap there are important differences between the two instruments.

FRAs settle at the beginning of the forward period. For a swap the cash flows are at the end of each period.

FRAs generate a single net cash flow from buyer to seller or vice versa, A swap has multiple cash flows with two for each period (one fixed, one floating) – although these payments will be netted if in the same currency.

Discounting – A FRA will be discounted using the agreed rate in the derivative. For swap agreements, the rate in the instrument may not reflect the funding costs of the position for either counterparty and adjustments would need to be made. These

TABLE 6.1   LIBOR

	Floating Leg	Fixed Leg
Currency		
USD		
USD less than 1yr		
EUR		
EUR less than 1 yr		
GBP		
GBP less than 1yr		
JPY		

adjustments will depend on whether the derivative positions are collateralised or uncollateralised. If they are collateralised the valuation will be a function of overnight funding costs. Known as SONIA (for Sterling Overnight Interbank Average Rate) in the UK and the Fed funds rate in the US. If uncollateralised the discount rate will be a function of the creditworthness of each party as well as general market rates.

AN INTRODUCTION TO INFLATION-LINKED SECURITIES

The presence or threat of inflation is one of the key risks for savers. Inflation clearly demonstrates the risk of under-investment as cash will slowly be eroded away in an inflationary environment. High or volatile inflation rates will have negative conse-quences for the real value of most traditional investment portfolios, causing a number of assets to lose value in terms of purchasing power. The overall capital loss will vary according to the portfolio composition. But conventional bonds will often be the worst affected asset class, despite being considered less risky than other potential invest-ments, they are not a natural hedge for inflation. Many assets are likely to increase in value due to increases in the price of money, but asset classes that can potentially offer some protection against inflation. Such as equity, real estate, infrastructure and commodities offer only an indirect hedge at best, and correlations between these asset classes and inflation is neither stable or constant. As a result, there is a natural demand for high grade instruments that both protect against inflationary pressures and can offer a return enhancement or capital gain for investors. To meet this demand many governments now issue debt that is explicitly linked to inflation. The practical features of this debt can both aid the issuer with balancing their books, as tax revenues will go up in the short term due to inflation matching the increase in payments needed and gives domestic investors an instrument which can hedge their long-term cash flow needs. As such inflation-linked bonds and securities have become increasingly impor-tant in the capital markets particularly in nations with advanced debt markets. Indeed, in many countries these inflation derivatives now form a significant proportion of bond issuance. The global volume of inflation linked securities (often known simply as linkers) has risen to match increased demand for reliable inflation hedges across many developed markets as well as to diversify funding sources for both government and corporate issuers. The market for Linkers is particularly well developed in the United States and the United Kingdom, and institutional portfolios in these markets are likely to contain an allocation of inflation linked bonds and potentially other inflation linked securities and hedges.

   Inflation-linked government securities are incredibly useful to those managing lia-bility driven portfolios as they provide a default risk free hedge to inflation linked liabilities (such as an index linked defined benefit pension plan). Not only this, they provide this hedge while also having a low correlation to other risk assets. Linkers hence provide significant diversification benefits for multi-asset class investment port-folio mandates; in addition, they can act as a reliable hedge for many obligations and long dated cash flows and as such are an ideal security for LDI / ALM managers.

   However, these instruments may have drawbacks when compared to the better understood nominal bond asset class. For example, linkers are nearly always less liquid than other fixed income asset classes. The lack of liquidity is an increasingly important concern as Post-GFC market-makers have been withdrawing liquidity from many asset classes, as for most liquidity providers the cost of balance sheet utilisation as has risen significantly. Resultantly, the ability to execute large trades in inflation products cannot be guaranteed and in some cases even expected. This lack of liquidity can even apply in the largest sovereign debt markets. The withdrawal of the large investment banks from Fixed Income market–making since the crisis has compounded this issue as the market-makers have reduced the balance sheet available for inventory of fixed income products for clients. This reflects a decision from the central bankers to decrease liquidity but also decrease systemic risk.

The market for credit linked inflation products has also yet to take off and the market for corporate issuance is still small. This is despite inflation-based funding making sense for a lot of corporate treasuries. To this day sovereign issuers continue to dominate the market. It's also important to note that credit issues can be more of a concern for inflation linked government bonds than the more established nominal government securities. This is because there is a positive correlation between government credit risk and inflation. Governments can print money to pay off liabilities or they can control the money supply and hence control inflation, in times of crisis they are unable to do both.

The relation between printing money (more properly the money supply) and inflation is formalised in the Fischer Equation:

Quantity Theory of Money
MV = PY
Where
M = Money Supply
V = Velocity of circulation
P = Price Level and
Y = National Income

In the words of the late Milton Friedman of the University of Chicago, and a Nobel Prize-winning monetarist economist and well-known inflation hawk:

'*Inflation is always and everywhere a monetary phenomenon in the sense that it is and can be produced only by a more rapid increase in the quantity of money than in output.*'

Inflation-linked securities have a surprisingly long history and have been used in many markets.

In fact, inflation-linked bonds arguably have centuries of history behind them. A bond whose principal and interest were explicitly linked to the price of a basket of goods was issued by the Commonwealth of Massachusetts as far back as the eighteenth century as a result of inflationary pressure caused by the Civil War.

Early examples of governments issuing bonds with an inflation component include:

  i. The Finnish Government as far back as 1945
 ii. The Swedish Government in 1952
iii. The Israeli Government in 1955

The larger inflation markets began trading significantly later; the United Kingdom in 1981 and the United States in 1997, Germany entered the fray as late as 2006.

Why Do Governments Issue Inflation-Linked Bonds?

There are numerous advantages for governments opting to issue linkers, here are some of the most important.

1. Diversification of funding sources: Diversification creates stability for both borrowers and investors. Any government issuer will have both outgoings that are fixed and outgoings that vary with inflation. As a result, it makes sense to diversify funding sources across both cash flow types if this funding is available. Many governments in both developed and developing markets have as a result supported the development of inflation markets. In theory a total liability consisting of multiple securities with multiple different characteristics will help reduce volatility in the cost of funding and the price of government debt. This can also aid fiscal policy as more stable funding can lead to greater allocation of capital. So, the less concentrated funding profile can contribute to more stable interest rates on government debt, reducing the risk of unpredictable and erratic but necessary tax changes to fund outgoings.

2. To widen the investor universe: Diversification of funding types also opens up new sets of investors and can lower funding costs (as well as funding risk). It does this by widening the universe of potential lenders. This has been particularly true in emerging markets where governments have created inflation linked securities to gain access to the funds of international investors. Many of these investors have large amounts of capital mandated to buy inflation-based products. Interestingly International fixed income investors in many cases prefer inflation linked bonds. Particularly if they are worried about domestic inflation in the countries of issuance. This is because the rate of inflation and the strength of the currency are negatively correlated. By buying EM inflation linked debt instead of nominal denominations investors still gain access to the credit risk premium (from the bond) but will have naturally offset some of their FX risk (due to the inflation component).

3. To meet demand: Government debt issuers will often listen to their end-users. In the United Kingdom, the Debt Management Office or DMO (which is the government agency responsible for managing the national debt) takes frequent soundings from investors and will choose the maturity profile, timing of new issuances and the nominal / inflation ratio in conjunction with multiple stakeholders. Of whom the buyers are paramount. In the Gilt market, Liability Driven Investment has led to strong demand for long dated debt, and this demand is across both nominal and inflation linked paper. It is calculated that total inflation-linked liabilities of all kinds for UK pension trusts are significantly greater than £1 trillion, this compares to outstanding linker issuance worth approximately £300bn and shows a supply demand imbalance which the DMO is mandated to take into account. And it has done so by frequent issuance of inflation linked Gilts. Given the need for issuance of both short dated and nominal paper – it seems that the demand for long dated government debt surpasses supply and can continue to do even in the face of persistent government spending deficits. Recent years have seen more focus on issuing long dated linkers both in response to the demand from pension funds, much of which has been caused by an increase in LDI mandates, and as government issuers themselves have sought to lock in low long-term funding costs.

4. Removal of a risk premium: It is argued that issuing Linkers can save the issuer money by eliminating the inflation risk premium that is in many theoretical pricing models for fixed income securities. This risk premium is considered part of the yield on nominal bonds. It exists as investors will naturally seek to be rewarded for bearing uncertainty due to risk-aversion. In a world where risk-aversion exists issuers of safer assets will be rewarded with lower funding costs as investors no longer need to be compensated for taking on the additional risk.

   An example of a similar risk premium within fixed income is the credit risk premium. It can be observed that Corporate securities have higher coupons than comparable gilts with the same maturity date. This is because, even the highest grade corporate bonds contain default risk and Gilts are considered default risk free. Similarly, as conventional nominal bonds expose contain inflation risk part of their return could be considered due to an inflation risk premium.

   Decomposing the nominal yield on a conventional government bond:

   y, the real yield,
   r, the expected average inflation rate until maturity,
   p, the inflation risk premium.

   As linkers are free of inflation risk, their yields need not contain an inflation risk premium ($i = r + p$). Hence lowering the cost of funding.

   There is a counter argument to this, and it is possible that, issuing inflation-linked bonds either in place of or as well as nominal debt, could result in market segmentation of the instruments into a larger number of less liquid categories. This could actually raise the cost of financing for the government due to the existence of a liquidity risk premium. It is possible to imagine scenarios in which the effect on liquidity could be greater than the gains made from the decrease in the inflation risk premium.

5. Demonstration of Commitment to Stable Monetary Policy: Many governments have a policy of low and stable inflation. Since an inflation linked borrowing cannot simply be inflated away, there is considered less likelihood of political leaders generating inflation to reduce their cost of interest and national debt burden. Signalling can have a powerful effect on markets and a commitment or desire to issue more inflation linked paper shows a belief in lower inflation which should lower risk premia for domestic or fixed income products, both nominal and real.

The Basic Mechanics

Conventional bonds are issued with a fixed nominal coupon and a redemption value known in advance. These conditions take account of inflation expectations at the time of issuance but are fixed at the outset. The same is not true of linkers. Linkers are designed to protect the purchasing power of the capital invested and as such must rise in value in line with inflation. This generally happens through the appreciation of the principal, the idea being that the cash value of the investment will be protected and that a real return will be earned throughout the lifetime of the instrument. The nominal coupons and the nominal principle are calculated by increasing the real quantities based on the rate of inflation. More precisely an index ratio is calculated to account for the difference in purchasing power between the present day and the date of issuance.

Index Ratio = Price Index (t = now)/Price Index (t = Issuance Date)

When considering the index ratio, it should be noted that for practical reasons official inflation indices are not calculated on a daily basis. Instead they are generally calculated monthly and released with a time lag. Depending on the specific index, the consumer price for a specific month may not be published until one to three months later, for many indices are also subject to frequent revision. It is therefore important to check the specific rules for each issuer regarding the calculation of the index ratio for non-complete reference periods and data which may be subject to frequent revision.

The coupons and principal payments can be calculated thus:

Coupon n = Fixed Rate * Principal n

Where,

Principal n = Principal 0 * (1 + Total Inflation between year 0 and year n)

The difficulty in frequent and accurate inflation measurement leads to another issue. For perfect inflation protection, any cash flows would have to be adjusted in line with realised inflation. However, this is impractical in practice because the difficulty of compiling and checking data means that official inflation rates are always published with a delay, and often subject to revision. There is hence a short period at the end of an inflation-linked life where the inflation risk is not hedged. The difference between the time at which inflation-linked bonds' cash flows are made and the reference point for the underlying inflation index is known as the 'indexation lag'. For most global inflation-linked bond markets the indexation lag is three months (meaning that interest and principal payments are calculated on the basis of the inflation index from three months earlier). Index-Linked Gilts are currently issued with a three month lag, but those issued before 2005 have an indexation lag of eight months.

The UK has two sets of linkers with differing lags – this is for historical reasons. When the UK issued its first linker in 1981 no convention had emerged on the size of the lag, although one was necessary for practical reasons. The US treasury launched its first linker (known as a Treasury Inflation Protected Security (TIPs)) as late as 1997, with a three-month delay. This became a global convention across global markets and the UK felt obliged to follow suit. It should be said that this has had repercussions on liquidity.

Inflation-Linked Swaps

Whilst there is still a dearth of inflation linked credit products, government securities are not the only option for hedging portfolios against inflation. Inflation swaps make it possible to obtain synthetic inflation protection for inflation linked cash flows. A swap contract involves two parties exchanging future cash flows (Figure 6.1).

The use of Inflation Swaps can have advantages over government bonds. The derivatives can be specifically tailored to meet the needs of the end user. In our case, to exactly match an inflation linked liability in the future. Due to their bespoke nature,

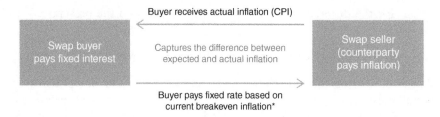

FIGURE 6.1   The mechanics of an inflation swap

they are not traded on an exchange, but instead are traded 'over the counter' (OTC). It should be noted, that just like the cash market, the inflation-rate swap market is not as liquid as the interest-rate swap market. Whilst pricing is available from a number of counterparties, this liquidity may not be guaranteed in the long term, and in the extreme could vanish overnight. There will also be credit issues with long dated swap contracts and margining agreements and credit agreements will part of a standard swap contract. When the value of a swap becomes non-zero, then one party of the swap will have credit-risk exposure to their counterpart. The counterparty risk being the positive value of the swap. In practice these risks are mitigated by:

1. Selection of the counterparty; usually relying on Credit Rating Agencies;
2. Margining agreements; constant exchange of cash flows or assets to reduce credit exposure.

The Global Market

The inflation swaps or inflation derivatives market (Table 6.2) focuses on the same indices as the inflation-linked government market, as the underlying government bond issues bring liquidity and support to the market. In Europe the most important swap contracts are the HICPxT index from Eurostat, the FRCPI index from INSEE, and for GBP derivatives the RPI index from the ONS. One strength of the derivatives market is that it is not restricted to the indices for which Government Issuers choose to back,

TABLE 6.2   The Inflation Swap Market

The Inflation Swap Market		
Inflation Payers	Payers & Receivers	Inflation receivers
Sovereigns	Market-makers	Pension funds
Agencies	Proprietary desks	Insurance
Utilities	Hedge funds	Corporate ALM
Asset Finance	Relative Value funds	Inflation fixed income
Real Estate		
Asset Swaps		
Corporates		

but can be tailored to the bespoke needs of the end user. Indeed market-makers will provide prices in a variety of inflation swaps for the main currencies, currently EUR, USD and GBP. They will even provide swap contracts linked to indices for which there exists no sizable cash market. However, liquidity in swaps such as this is likely to be low and bid offer costs will often render them uneconomic to potential users.

Payers vs Receivers

The exists are a number of natural payers and receivers of inflation in the market, currently there is a natural imbalance between supply and demand with there being a greater number of natural receiving interest than paying. This is due to the large demand from pension funds and insurers to mitigate long dated cash flow needs (ALM and LDI). Indeed, it has been calculated that the natural receiving (or long) interest from pension funds is greater than the total supply of government debt.

In previous years, there had been willingness from Hedge Funds and Relative Value players to pay inflation and extract various risk premia from the inflation market, however a continued tightening (lowering) of real yields meant that these positions generally lost money more or less consistently. As a result, these participants withdrew from the market.

The Zero-Coupon Swap

Unlike the nominal markets, where the notional size of the swap is generally fixed at the outset. In the inflation market it makes more sense for the notional to increase in size with the rate of inflation. This is both to act as a better inflationary hedge, and to better match the underlying government securities that drive the market. Hence the zero-coupon inflation swap has become the standard inflation derivative and is much more liquid and widely used than fixed notional swaps. The inflation buyer or receiver will pay a predetermined fixed rate, and in return will receive from the inflation seller or payer payments linked to inflation. The name zero-coupon comes from the fact that there is only one cash flow at the maturity of the swap, without no intermediate payments.

Although to reduce counterparty risk – there may be frequent changes in collateral provision as the swap changes value over its lifetime. Due to the general long-dated nature of the inflation market these payments can become significant as the swaps can accrue significant value over time.

CHAPTER 7

The Defined Benefit Pension Plan and Explicit Liabilities

'They thought we were bonkers'

– John Ralfe. Boots Pension Scheme 2001

The attitude of investors towards asset allocation and multi-asset investing has evolved considerably since the turn of the century when balanced mandates were the norm and little credence was given to liabilities. Historically, the asset allocation decision was delegated to a fund manager who followed a balanced investment strategy investing across a range of asset classes, with the benchmark being the median or average return on a peer group of pension schemes with similar objectives. Unfortunately, this led to a misalignment of incentives between the manager and the managed. Investment managers were simply (cynically?) over-investing in equities in an attempt to beat their peers by taking more risk. This strategy worked when stocks were rising, creating surpluses, which allowed contribution holidays for the plan sponsors. Unfortunately, as a strategy this was far from optimal for pensioners who were exposed to underperformance but didn't benefit from the contribution holidays.

In the United Kingdom successive changes in legislation have forced trustees and managers to change this approach. The Pensions Act 1995 and The Myners (2001) Report on Institutional Investment asked trustees not to look at assets or deficits in isolation and to set an asset allocation with reference to their liabilities with less concern on relative performance. Further, plan sponsors were asked to demonstrate their *'willingness to accept underperformance'* if this led to superior risk management. This focus on understanding the needs of the beneficiaries, rather than the sponsor, and risk mitigation rather than maximising the 'surplus' or assets naturally leads to a Liability Driven solution.

Due to changes in the regulatory environment such as the Myners Report, Liability Driven investing has for many become the default approach for portfolio construction. Particularly, at least at first, for the larger more sophisticated investors. To understand LDI it is useful to look at its origins in the pensions industry where LDI has been steadily growing in popularity since its inception in the UK at the turn of the millennium.

At first these innovative risk management strategies were only available to the largest schemes. The Corporate Finance team at Boots led by John Ralfe were thought to be responsible for the first implementation. The move was considered revolutionary at the time and the trustees at the Boots Pension Scheme were initially wary of both the strategy and even of making an official announcement of their investment approach. They were, with some reason, fearful of a condescending reaction from the City, opposing experts, and a sceptical press.

The cult of equity was still strong at this time and the rationales for proceeding with LDI were not well understood. Particularly as in this period most investment trustees' projections of equity outperformance and market risk premia were far too high.

Several elements of the new LDI – Style strategy defied conventional beliefs:

Belief 1: Equities are the best for the long term. But here the Boots Pension Scheme had gone totally into Fixed Income.

Belief 2: Diversification is considered the best way to mitigate risk. But here the Boots Pension Scheme was again 100% into Fixed Income. But worse still, a small subset of this asset class. AAA-Rated Long Dated Bonds.

Belief 3: Equities and risk assets are the best, if not the only, way to beat inflation. Interestingly – the long-dated inflation bonds purchased on behalf of Mr Ralfe and his team, comfortably outperformed equities since the trade was initiated. Although this is in many ways just icing on the cake. The aim at inception was risk mitigation rather than investment performance.

Belief 4: Identifying and then selecting the right composition of Active Managers is important. But here the team had moved to passive framework after identifying (or more accurately estimating) the liabilities inherent in the scheme.

The Boots Pension Scheme was the original and is still arguably the most famous use of Liability Driven Investment – the trustees and advisors were the first to announce the move to an LDI framework as far back as 2001. But in the UK at least LDI had started to gain traction and understanding. Other large schemes, such as the Rolls Royce Pension Scheme and the ICI Pension Scheme, soon followed. At the time these LDI solutions were only available to those who had the resources to develop bespoke solutions to match the unique profile of their liabilities. As a result, for the first few years only the largest corporate schemes with tens of thousands of members were able to implement Liability Driven Investment strategies. Indeed, until fairly recently, there has been a gap in the market for smaller schemes, which is now being addressed through the development of LDI pooled funds. Although sadly the main variable in whether LDI is used for pensioners/investors in the UK is the size of the corporate sponsor not the needs of the beneficiary.

Strange Footnote: John Ralfe left Boots in 2002 soon after completing the transition of the corporate pension scheme to an LDI framework. There was some speculation that the board of directors were unhappy with their position as Pension Mavericks. He is now a successful consultant.

THE BOOTS EXAMPLE

Boots was one of the first large pension schemes to go public with the implementation of an LDI investment strategy back in July 2001.

Market Cap of Sponsor: £5.8 bn
Assets of Scheme: £2.3 bn
No. of member: 72,000
<u>Original Composition</u>
75% Equities
20% Short Dated Fixed Income
5% Cash or Cash Equivalents
Then followed a 15-month transition and execution period.
Final Composition
75% AAA – Rated Long Dated Sovereigns
25% AAA – Rate Inflation-Linked

The scheme exited the stock market with the FTSE 100 at approximately 6,000, a level that with hindsight looks very good indeed.

The bonds purchased had a weighted average maturity of 30 years, similar to the maturity and indexation of the accrued pension liabilities.

The trustees reasoning was;

- A reluctance to embrace significant credit risk over the very long term
- The availability of fixed income securities with long maturities
- Identification and capture of a significant (and mispriced risk premium)
- In 2001 supranational bonds offered a 1% premium (close to 100bps) over equivalent Government bonds.

With hindsight, a significant amount of the value created seems to be in the timing on the market. With the scheme avoiding an underperforming stock market and ten years of flat returns whilst at the same time hedging liabilities before the global collapse in yields.

However, market timing was not an objective and risk mitigation was at the forefront of both trustee and sponsor thinking.

In 2004, the fund moved away from a total fixed income strategy, and invested 15% of assets in equities and other 'risky' assets. This was for two reasons:

i. A shortage of appropriate sterling denominated bonds of sufficient duration and credit quality in issue to cover the fund's liabilities.
ii. Changing estimates of longevity meant the hedge was no longer ideal. Increasing life expectancy of the scheme's members meant that liabilities had increased. The trustees saw this as a reason to increase the allocation to risk assets.

The need for higher returns in the current world of low yields and significantly longer retirement periods has led to large pension fund deficits and resultantly a much greater need for the understanding of risk. The importance of risk management having been underlined by collapses in world equity markets and the Global Financial Crisis (GFC). Instead of focusing on maximising expected returns with a risk constraint LDI asks the question. Where does the investor need money and how can we maximise the likelihood of successfully fulfilling these obligations?

Funding Position = Assets – Liabilities

By viewing the liabilities as just a large, negative, bond-like asset, this negative asset can be brought together with the scheme's asset holdings to give regular view of not only the value of the liabilities but the risks contained in the investment approach.

Multiple Asset Class investing consists of splitting the portfolio into a number of parts and investing each part in a separate asset class with the historic returns of the asset classes so chosen having as little correlation with each other as possible. By introducing the concept of multiple risk premia, it expands on Modern Portfolio Theory; however, in its basic form it only focuses on one side of the balance sheet which is why for many investors an LDI approach would be preferred.

In the UK current legislation mandates nearly all employers to provide a pension plan to workers. For most companies the only offer is for a defined contribution scheme, which places investment risk in the hands of the employee. The previous generation had benefited from Defined Benefit Schemes where the corporate sponsor took the investment risk, and the workforce was guaranteed a set income (often inflation linked, in retirement). The funds allocated for workers' futures are ring-fenced from the employer and paid through a pension fund managed by a board of trustees, who are (in theory anyway) independent from the sponsoring company itself. Contributions are made into the pension fund by future by the company, which is often referred to as the sponsor. In the case of a Defined Benefit trust this guarantee will introduce a considerable amount of risk to the pension fund and the sponsor, the main exposures being:

   i. Interest Rates; Both short-dated for re-investing new cash flows, and long-dated to match the future needs of pensioners
  ii. Global Asset Prices; Domestic and Global equity, Property, etc
 iii. Inflation; for some schemes, cash flows are explicitly linked to inflation.
  iv. Longevity; An increase in life expectancy for beneficiaries will increase the funding requirement for the plan sponsor.

The goal of the trustee is simply to achieve sufficient performance to match the guaranteed pension without placing financial strain on the sponsor and the need for limited contributions from the sponsoring company. The trustee's ultimate responsibility is to the future pensioners, and in most cases the pensioners will not benefit from extra stock return or extra contributions from the sponsor. For this reason, Asset-Liability Management (ALM) and liability-driven investment (LDI) have come to dominate, ie the trustees' aim is to pay all obligations rather than outperformance. To develop an LDI strategy we therefore need a holistic picture of beneficiaries' needs rather than aiming for a simple risk–return optimisation on the asset side of the balance sheet. To start we compare the pension fund's asset value with our best estimate of the fund's liabilities. Then with this more detailed picture we can assess funding sensitivities of the assets and liabilities with the risks implicit in the portfolio. This leads to designing investment portfolios that will match the estimated cash flow needs with the least amount of risk.

THE STAKEHOLDERS IN A TYPICAL PLAN

A typical plan will have many stakeholders all with competing objectives. It is the job of the trustee to match their obligations with all stakeholders with the need of the pensioners (both active and future) ultimately being paramount.

- The Trustee. Whose objective is to meet the obligations of the fund. For defined benefit schemes this is often a binary process. Are the obligations met?
- The Sponsor. Usually a corporation. The sponsor's objective could be to minimise contributions which would place them at loggerheads with both the trustees and the beneficiaries.
- Active members, who are employees of the company, and are currently contributing to the pension plan.
- Deferred pensioners, those who are not employed by the company anymore, but are not retired yet. They do not contribute currently, but will receive future payments.
- Pensioners. Those who are currently receiving pension payments.
- Asset Managers who are delegated by the trustees to perform day-to-day portfolio and risk management.
- Investment Consultants, who supply the expertise needed for the trustees to perform their duties. As well as importing higher standards of governance and risk management.
- The Regulator and Government. In most developed nations, a government agency will guarantee a partial or total payment of obligations to members in the event that both the sponsor and the pension fund become insolvent. These agencies are typically financed through levies, defined by a given set of rules, on every pension fund in that nation. In the United Kingdom the Pension Protection Fund fulfils this role.

A Checklist for Trustees

Having identified the stakeholders, it is necessary for the trustees to implement or refine a framework for investment, operations and governance.

The trustees are responsible for deciding the investment strategy to be adopted. (Only trustees of fully insured schemes will not have to worry about investment policies.)

1. Trustee appropriateness: As a trustee, do you and your colleagues have the appropriate skills, knowledge and experience to perform your duties? Are potential areas of weakness with the team identified and addressed? Do the trustees have credibility with other stakeholders?
2. Investment Objectives: Are these both practical and reasonable? Are the return objectives likely given historical returns? Do these calculations take account of all weights on portfolio performance, ie fees, both implicit and explicit? Do the investment objectives reflect the need of all the beneficiaries? Is there a fair balance between the growth required for future beneficiaries and the stability necessary to meet upcoming obligations due to those currently receiving payments? Is there agreement on the process or policy in place for reviewing and changing the objectives as and if circumstances dictate?

3. Risk Management: Are there policies and processes in place, detailing how to cope with sudden changes in risk exposures or portfolio values? Is there a risk framework, identifying and quantifying potential sources of risk, are the risks understood? Is the technology used suitable and does it provide accurate, consistent and useful risk information as and when required? Is there a risk committee with stakeholder input, does this team have the appropriate experience? Have the advisory team performed scenario analysis and stress-testing on the liabilities?

4. Operational Effectiveness: Are the means of management cost effective, particularly given the scale, scope and complexity of the tasks required? Have operational processes capable of coping with a changing environment or a significant change in inputs? Are policies, processes and functions benchmarked against accepted standards.

5. Communications Strategy: Do the trustees have a communications strategy in place? Have stakeholder groups been identified and engaged with? Is there a dialogue between stakeholders? Is the effectiveness of communications tested, and if so: How?

6. Compliance: Post-GFC there has been a great deal of focus on compliance and regulation, possibly at the expense of other areas of risk management. The trustees should ask: Is there understanding within the group on which regulations and statutes are relevant and the regulatory hierarchy in place? Is there a detailed compliance plan or manual? Are their frameworks in place to cope with: i) breaches, and ii) regulatory change? Is there an individual ultimately in charge with Regulatory Compliance, and are their responsibilities understood and monitored by the other trustees?

WHAT ARE THE LIABILITIES?

The liability structure of a pension fund can be broken down into a long series of uncertain cash flows, these cash flows can be modelled as fixed income payments. It can be seen that there are two sides to the story.

On the asset side of the balance sheet, are past contributions are made to the fund by the sponsor and its employees, alongside investment returns, and future contributions.

On the other side are the pension payments and future obligations. They are often indexed to inflation by using, for example, the retail price index as a reference.

It should be stated that the liabilities are in many cases only estimates. Pension cash flows typically occur over very long time periods, potentially as many as sixty years or more, and investment time frames can be measured in decades rather than years, meaning small differences in compounding can lead to vast differences in outcome.

Table 7.1 shows the amount needed to hedge a £1 million pound cash flow given different holding periods and discount rates.

For example, an investor anticipating the need for £1 million in 50 years' time would need £371k assuming a 2 per cent discount rate but only £228k at a 3 per cent

TABLE 7.1 The cost of a long dated cashflow

Discount Rate	10 years	20 Years	30 years	40 years	50 years
0.00%	1,000,000	1,000,000	1,000,000	1,000,000	1,000,000
0.50%	951,348	905,063	861,030	819,139	779,286
1.00%	905,287	819,544	741,923	671,653	608,039
1.50%	861,997	742,470	639,762	551,262	475,005
2.00%	820,348	672,971	552,071	452,431	371,528
2.50	781,198	610,271	476,743	372,431	290,942
3.00%	744,094	553,676	411,987	306,557	228,107
3.50%	708,919	502,566	356,278	252,572	179,053
4.00%	675,564	456,387	308,319	208,289	140,7134
4.50%	643,928	414,643	267,00	171,929	110,710
5.00%	613,913	376,889	231,377	142,046	87,204

discount rate. This is a 63 per cent difference (371 / 228), and shows the importance of choosing the correct discount rate.

Nevertheless, to understand our risk, it is necessary to estimate the present value of these cash flows. This is generally a process of sophisticated estimation using accepted actuarial and accounting methods, or potentially using market prices where available.

Unfortunately, the vast majority of asset classes lack similar payment structures to pension fund obligations. This makes the task of hedging non-trivial. High quality bonds which represent long dated (near certain) payments are the best proxy, but Fixed Income products often lack the depth and liquidity required at long dated tenors, and a portfolio consisting solely of such securities may not be capital efficient.

In most G20 nations the fixed income or bond markets have an average duration of less than ten years. Even in the United Kingdom, which has the most developed market place for Liability Driven Investment in the world, there is a supply–demand imbalance. Here, the government bond or gilt curve still only has an average duration of fifteen years for its nominal debt despite the demand for longer dated paper. A lack of available hedging instruments and the fact that liabilities are often only estimates can make hedging more of an art than a science. Hence, despite the dull actuarial nature of fixed income risk management, many practitioners could describe themselves as artists!

In the United Kingdom a 'typical' pension fund may have the bulk of its liabilities or expected cash flows with a maturity of around 20–25 years, but as these are typically estimate rather than guarantees, these ongoing obligations could last significantly longer. The LDI strategies that can be developed to mitigate these maturity mismatches can include automatic re-balancing and complex swap arrangements.

The most important factors driving the value of these liabilities are:

i. Interest Rates: Particularly long end interest rates, which are used to discount the cash flows or liabilities.
ii. Longevity: It is difficult to know precisely the life expectancy of all beneficiaries to a scheme. Increases in longevity lead to ongoing obligations for trustees to

match. Changes in mortality or longevity assumptions will have significant effects on funding ratios but are difficult to predict and can be expensive to hedge. The longevity assumptions tell us how many cash flows to expect.

iii. Inflation: Depending on the nature of the scheme, some schemes are indexed to inflation whereas some are not. But in all cases inflation will have an effect on the interest rate environment. Inflation is positively correlated to Interest Rates and hence discount rates.

iv. Regulation: The basis for valuing assets and for discounting liabilities is ultimately decided as a matter for the pensions regulator. A change in the regulatory landscape can have a significant impact on the risk capacity as well as the risk tolerance of even the lowest risk schemes.

CHAPTER 8

ESG, Governance
and the Pensions Industry

For pension fund trustees operating today, purely financial decisions and the need to make payments, and meet obligations when they are due, are not 100 per cent of the picture. There has been an increase in the demands on trustees as regulations change to meet the needs of an ageing population. Changes in the standards of pension scheme governance encouraged by an increase in regulation in the sector mean that many other factors are at play.

In the UK more detailed risk reporting has become a requirement as more and more data become available and more risks are identified and understood. From October 2019 all UK pension schemes with more than 100 members have been required to disclose in more detail the nature of their investments, including the risks arising from environmental, social and governance (ESG) concern.

Previously, a statement concerning ESG factors needed to be incorporated into the statement of investment principles. Now for both defined benefit (DB) and defined contribution (DC) schemes it is necessary to have an investment policy taking account of 'financially material' considerations, which include ESG factors.

Just like any corporation the governance of a pension scheme can be crucial if it is to meet its goals. It's clear that whilst good governance alone is not enough to guarantee success, that it is good start. As well as possibly a necessary addition to good risk management and financial decision making. In many cases there is a clear correlation between the quality of the governance and the quality of the financial decision making, and often the two will work in tandem. Governance is ultimately the responsibility of the trustees and their advisers and there is a clear link between good governance and ensuring positive outcomes. Without a strong governance framework and understanding the trustees are likely to compromise the chance of beneficial outcomes for their members.

In the last few years regulations requiring pension scheme trustees to disclose their ESG policies have been added to the list of requirements for trustees to consider, and this coincides with an increase in interest in ESG factors in the modern economy.

As we have seen investing is not simply a matter of risk and return. Clearly when looking at investment opportunities the concept of positive and negative externalities will be of concern to any investment manager. Whilst Modern Portfolio Theory and its most simple derivations look at investment as a crude linear algebra optimisation problem across multiple variables, the decisions made by investors are rarely as simple. They will include qualitative factors that are hard to calibrate to numerical models. Some investors will have a natural discomfort with investing in sectors of the economy they dislike. Sectors that can arouse disquiet include Tobacco or Defence for some, but others may feel unease in supporting industries such as Meat or Fossil Fuels, and their unease may be caused by different reasons. The sectors which are disliked by one set of investors may also not match the investment preferences of a different set of investors, this ensures that fitting an ethical dimension to investing on top of risk and return does not naturally allow a one size fits all solution.

Over the last few years, with LDI saturation in many markets and Active Management suffering from underperformance and oversupply, there has been a marked increase in offerings from the fund management industry addressing ethical concerns. It's notable at trade shows and conferences now that all major exhibitors will have a suite of ESG enhanced products and be visibly promoting them, whereas a few years ago. ESG and values were more an interesting but growing niche. Originally most ESG funds were concentrated on listed equity investments, but now a broad range of instruments can be accessed in an 'ethical' way including Fixed Income, Private Equity and Infrastructure.

The current terminology is moving from SRI (Socially Responsible Investing) to ESG. Both frameworks are similar and often used interchangeably, but we are seeing ESG become more dominant with an increased focus on environmental concerns, either through limiting carbon emissions or greater support of the circular economy. The reasons behind the recent uptake in ESG vary from institution to institution, but for some there is a belief in the financial value (ie ESG can outperform or be a source of alpha) of investing ethically. Talk of investment alpha however rarely dominates moral motivations and the perceived need for reputational risk management by being seen to engage with ESG issues.

Investors don't always act as rationally as the character *'homo economicus'* found in all good economics textbooks. Instead they will behave as human beings and (hopefully) responsible members of society. As such they have a natural desire to support ethical projects and create positive impacts where possible. They may also have a natural aversion to investing or supporting sectors they find immoral.

Modern Portfolio Theory and its many offshoots however do very little to accommodate this reality. The traditional marketing narratives for Asset Managers and Asset Gatherers have either been aspirational, when directed at end users, or risk return based when targeting institutions. Rather than addressing the role of positive and negative impacts on society when investing in individual projects. However, the last few years have shown that there is support for ESG-focused investments from both institutions and retail savers. With a significant minority of investors keen to invest in both products they believe in and dis-invest from products which they object to. In tandem with the growth in retail demand, corporations are more openly looking at ethical concerns and seeking to support the values of all their stakeholders when making investment decisions rather than pure PnL. All of these factors have been encouraging the take up of ESG frameworks.

With a global push to incorporate environmental concerns into the investment process as a means of lessening the likelihood of climate change we are seeing increasing regulatory demands on investors to consider ESG issues. Hence there is a growing interest, fuelled by need from pension trustees in incorporating ESG concerns into the asset allocation process. A broad consensus of investment consultants now believes that ESG factors are likely material to long-term returns. With the potential for better risk management as ESG awareness can be helpful in avoiding the key risks associated with Climate Change. But also, in the hunt for 'alpha' as fund managers chase extra returns from finding firms and industry sectors with strong governance which many academic studies have shown to potentially outperform.

In the UK, when asked many savers have expressed an interest in Ethical Investments. As a result, we have seen Product Providers large and small rush to provide solutions. For example, Legal & General, the UK's largest fund manager, has launched a range of ETFs and actively managed funds that provide investment solutions that are either 'broadly ethical' or seek to positively invest in issues that savers believe in, whilst a range of small startups seek to provide ESG first investment strategies. The last few years have also seen FinTech Digital Advice firms such as Nutmeg and Wealthify launch Ethical Portfolios in addition to their broader more traditional offerings, showing that demand can be led by the desire of retail market, not simply forced by regulation. Many UK pension funds would suggest that they have always integrated ESG factors into their investment decision-making framework, however funds and complete investment solutions that explicitly integrate ethical concerns into their investment decisions are a relatively new and important part of the market.

THE UN PRI

The United Nations Principles for Responsible Investment are perhaps the best-known guidelines for Ethical Investment currently. With backing from the United Nations and a wide array of signatories including some of the world's largest asset managers, they provide a set of principles which help define Responsible Investing:

> *'The six Principles for Responsible Investment are a voluntary and aspirational set of investment principles that offer a menu of possible actions for incorporating ESG issues into investment practice.'*

With 7,000 and counting corporate signatories in over 100 countries, the UNPRI has become the world's largest voluntary corporate sustainability initiative. Since its formation in 2006 with 100 signatories, it has worked to understand the investment implications of ESG factors and to support its investor signatories in incorporating these factors into their investment and ownership decisions. It works to both increase awareness of ESG products and to improve the quality of the products offered through a better understanding of the processes involved and active engagement with stakeholders.

The Principles are listed below.

Principle 1: **We will incorporate ESG issues into investment analysis and decision-making processes.**

Possible actions:

- Address ESG issues in investment policy statements.
- Support development of ESG-related tools, metrics, and analyses.
- Assess the capabilities of internal investment managers to incorporate ESG issues.
- Assess the capabilities of external investment managers to incorporate ESG issues.
- Ask investment service providers (such as financial analysts, consultants, brokers, research firms, or rating companies) to integrate ESG factors into evolving research and analysis.
- Encourage academic and other research on this theme.
- Advocate ESG training for investment professionals.

Principle 2: **We will be active owners and incorporate ESG issues into our ownership policies and practices.**

Possible actions:

- Develop and disclose an active ownership policy consistent with the Principles.
- Exercise voting rights or monitor compliance with voting policy (if outsourced).
- Develop an engagement capability (either directly or through outsourcing).
- Participate in the development of policy, regulation, and standard setting (such as promoting and protecting shareholder rights).
- File shareholder resolutions consistent with long-term ESG considerations.
- Engage with companies on ESG issues.
- Participate in collaborative engagement initiatives.
- Ask investment managers to undertake and report on ESG-related engagement.

Principle 3: **We will seek appropriate disclosure on ESG issues by the entities in which we invest.**

Possible actions:

- Ask for standardised reporting on ESG issues (using tools such as the Global Reporting Initiative).
- Ask for ESG issues to be integrated within annual financial reports.
- Ask for information from companies regarding adoption of/adherence to relevant norms, standards, codes of conduct or international initiatives (such as the UN Global Compact).
- Support shareholder initiatives and resolutions promoting ESG disclosure.

Principle 4: **We will promote acceptance and implementation of the Principles within the investment industry.**

Possible actions:

- Include Principles-related requirements in requests for proposals (RFPs).
- Align investment mandates, monitoring procedures, performance indicators and incentive structures accordingly (for example, ensure investment management processes reflect long-term time horizons when appropriate).
- Communicate ESG expectations to investment service providers.

- Revisit relationships with service providers that fail to meet ESG expectations.
- Support the development of tools for benchmarking ESG integration.
- Support regulatory or policy developments that enable implementation of the Principles.

Principle 5: We will work together to enhance our effectiveness in implementing the Principles.
Possible actions:

- Support/participate in networks and information platforms to share tools, pool resources, and make use of investor reporting as a source of learning.
- Collectively address relevant emerging issues.
- Develop or support appropriate collaborative initiatives.

Principle 6: We will each report on our activities and progress towards implementing the Principles.
Possible actions:

- Disclose how ESG issues are integrated within investment practices.
- Disclose active ownership activities (voting, engagement, and/or policy dialogue).
- Disclose what is required from service providers in relation to the Principles.
- Communicate with beneficiaries about ESG issues and the Principles.
- Report on progress and/or achievements relating to the Principles using a comply-or-explain approach.
- Seek to determine the impact of the Principles.
- Make use of reporting to raise awareness among a broader group of stakeholders.

THE INCREASING IMPORTANCE OF ESG

The wealth management industry is continuously changing, as we have seen over the last few years active management is falling out of fashion, and has become less 'fashionable' with asset allocators every year this millennium. In the last decade, since the Global Financial Crisis, we have seen the relentless expansion of the passive management industry and a consumer base that is more cost aware than ever before. The King of Passive Management, Vanguard, is now the largest Asset Manager in the world and its relentless growth and outperformance of its peers (both in attracting Assets under Management and in investment Returns) continues. The firm has always been the parent of both passive and low-cost solutions in asset management and this has had dramatic effects on the industry. As it looks to defray cost pressure, areas of asset management where cost pressures are weaker are of note to the industry.

There is indeed one area of active management that is expanding dramatically, and with less pressure on fees, and this is Ethical or Values-led Investing. In financial jargon ethical investing is often known as ESG or SRI. ESG has now become the most used term to represent an investment methodology that incorporates risk, return and social outcomes replacing the previously popular SRI. ESG is predicted to grow at 15% / year for the next few years and how ESG frameworks develop should be of interest to anyone who is concerned about the environment or interested in the investment industry.

What Does ESG Represent?

- The E in ESG represents the environment, including the externalities both negative and positive that an investment decision can create. For example, the energy and waste used by an investment, the resources it needs, and the environmental consequences. Of particular note, environmental criteria include carbon emissions, with reference to likely effects to climate change. Depending on the evaluation methodology, carbon emissions are sometimes considered as negative, in other frameworks the marginal change in carbon usage is more important. Underlying every investment decision every allocation of capital uses energy and resources, and this in turn affects the world we live in.
- The S represents social factors. The social definition can often be a bit loose, but generally it looks to factors relating to an underlying investment's impact on society and the broader community. For a firm this could refer to working conditions, health and safety, human rights, diversity and inclusion.
- The G represents corporate governance, and principally relates to oversight and stakeholder management. In a well-run business stakeholder incentives will align with the business's success. Governance describes the controls and procedures by which a firm is managed and meets the needs of stakeholders. Often with particular reference to the interests of investors / owners vs the executive class and the broader workforce. All organisations can benefit from strong governance. It is hoped by ESG-focused investors that by finding well run companies you can create better social outcomes as well as enjoying superior returns.

Slowly but surely all the largest investment houses are creating and expanding their ESG teams, and they are doing this hand in hand with regulatory support. With Global regulators looking to 'nudge' investments into socially superior outcomes, and in addition regulators are requiring additional detailed reporting to better analyse the environmental consequences of investment manager's capital allocation.

Here in Europe the EU has created a legislative programme to make ESG issues more prominent in the regulation of the financial services industry. The EU initiative will apply to all asset managers, even those without an explicit ESG mandate, which ultimately means that all investors will have to consider ESG factors when constructing their portfolios. This is going to require new systems, teams and ideas at investment firms large and small.

The largest active asset manager in the world, BlackRock, looks to be embracing ESG throughout its portfolios, as well as making social concerns a key part of its culture. From his recent statement to investors:

> 'Our investment conviction is that sustainability- and climate-integrated portfolios can provide better risk adjusted returns to investors. And with the impact of sustainability on investment returns increasing, we believe that sustainable investing is the strongest foundation for client portfolios going forward.'

Larry Fink, Chairman and CEO, January 2020

We can see that ESG is becoming more and more important. These words are being met with actions. BlackRock tends to both bark and bite, with the result that the firm often ends up dominating fields it enters. The changes represent both a commitment to a different way of investing as well as a sea change in corporate behaviour.

Previously at the firm semi-autonomous investment teams sought to seek advantage as independent units, this created a culture that was often able to outperform. In the new culture, the majority of asset allocators will have to look to their higher corporate principles before investing. This will require more than a tweaking of spreadsheets but an incorporation of new frameworks in the investment process.

All of the larger asset managers are now seeking to position themselves in ESG investing, after criticism from investors, regulators and politicians that the industry has failed to use its influence to act against corporate mis-behaviour and mitigate the effect of consumption on the environment.

The steps being taken at BlackRock:

Positive: Doubling the number of Ethical ETFs it offers to more than 100.

Positive: Accumulating assets of over $1trn in ESG focused funds within the next ten years. However, a cynic might suggest that this is not as all-encompassing a cultural change as BlackRock are making out as it will still only represent 10% of assets.

Negative screening: It will also cut companies that derive a quarter or more of their revenues from thermal coal from its actively managed portfolios, as it aims to increase its sustainable assets ten-fold from $90bn today to $1tn within a decade.

Across the industry as a whole, ESG is one area where we can see vacant roles advertised in an industry that is contracting, and anecdotally in the last few years we have seen ESG moving from an interesting niche to a core offering at trade shows, conferences and investment companies.

Now in 2020 developing and expanding ESG teams is a priority for investment funds, pension trusts and corporate investors and throughout the financial services sector. The hope is that investors can lead to better social outcomes without compromising returns. With ethical investment teams screening potential investment assets for human rights abuses, strong workers' rights, corruption avoidance and pollution mitigation positive change is possible and can be driven by the oft-derided financial services industry.

THE MAIN APPROACHES TO ETHICAL INVESTING

Screening and Beyond

Previously we've looked at defining ethical or values-led investing, explaining the rationale behind its growth and looking at how practitioners are describing and implementing their new responsible practices. Ethics means different things to different folk so the area is naturally an environment for differences of opinion, process and outcome. But we hope that by diving into the finance industry's love of jargon and explaining the weird and wacky terminology that has developed – ESG, SRI, CSG, etc – we can begin to understand the way that asset management is changing to actively incorporate ethical decisions into the investment process. As well as adding more TLAs and acronyms to our knowledge bank.

Writing in 2020, how to approach and integrate ethical investing criteria into the risk management process is now more important than ever. The largest asset management firms are now forced to consider ESG as a regulatory obligation. Whereas previously many just paid lip service to a small (but growing) minority of investors and their desire for ethical capitalism. New legislation requires institutional investors and asset managers to disclose at least annually their engagement and voting policies and voting records and to explain how they have implemented those policies. Which means that in the years to come environmental and ethical concerns must be understood and mitigated as part of the investment process; in some cases it requires a whole new approach to risk management. Understanding these differing approaches is crucial to any long-term investor whether they are using MPT, LDI, CDI or A.N.Other framework for capital allocation.

Institutional investors in the European Union must now include disclosure of how they monitor investee companies on ESG criteria. The process of monitoring for ESG Factors inevitably leads to their inclusion in the investment decision process as very few asset managers are likely to completely ignore a risk report or data which could be useful. Adjusting for these new reports could have profound effects on how pension portfolios and other investment vehicles others are constructed. More capital allocated to responsible investment can and will have effects throughout the entire economy, changing the cost of capital for different industries and altering the distribution of resources, potentially profoundly.

Simplistically there are four main approaches to putting ESG assessments into practice within an investment framework. Although in practical terms practitioners may use a mixture of them to achieve the desired result. Also, we should note some of the more cynical 'greenwashing' investment firms may use none of them and simply stamp the term on their product.

The main approaches are broadly:

- Screening
- Thematic investing
- Integration
- and Engagement

Here we will look at each in turn, each methodology will have its advantages and none is perfect. The first step towards implementing ESG has historically been investment screening. With decades of experience in the industry and widely accessible data and results being generated by this approach.

ESG: A SCREENING APPROACH

A simple way of avoiding investments in securities or firms associated with poor ethical standards from a savings portfolio is by excluding firms with poor governance or by excluding investments in particular sectors. Ethical investing began with the concept of negative screening. Indeed, the concept goes back hundreds of years, to when faith-based organisations refused to support projects that were involved in the slave trade.

Perhaps due to its simplicity and transparent focus, exclusion is still the most widely known and widely used ESG framework for institutional investors today. Its simplicity is also reflected in the growing divestment movement. Divestment being when an investor excludes certain investments from a portfolio that previously contained them. Whilst most people would now associate the divestment movement, in the UK at least, with students against fossil fuels, ie a number of Cambridge University students demanding college funds are not invested in BP, the driver has been more organic.

It is possible that faith-based investors led the change to modern negative screening. Arguably, large scale and public negative screening was first publicly demonstrated in the United States equity markets by Christian foundations, they created the now common concept of 'sin stocks' and directed their investment managers not to invest in them. Sin stocks were defined as stocks that received all or a significant (or sometimes a non-zero) proportion of revenue from various sins. With weapons, alcohol, cigarettes and gambling becoming popular sins for ethical folk to avoid. Ex post this may have been particularly annoying for some of the more virtuous investment managers as Tobacco Stocks were some of the best performing in the entire stock market after these changes were implemented. Tobacco as a sector outperforming the broader market index by nearly 100% over a decade in some cases. In the United Kingdom over-weighting Tobacco Stocks accounted for a large part of the excess returns of a certain investor, then employed by Invesco, known as Neil Woodford. Mr Woodford is now mainly known for one of the largest fund blow-ups in British investment history. In the early part of this century at least, vice outperformed virtue, as well as providing diversification.

Previous to institutional and sector-based divestment campaigns. A policy of investment exclusion had been directed at South Africa during Apartheid. Along with political pressure, sovereign wealth funds, institutional investors, and particularly corporates under consumer pressure, disinvested or refused to invested in the South African regime. It is possible that a lack of investment in the nation helped accelerate the end of apartheid. Although sanctions such as these are best thought of as a catalyst rather than a cause for positive change.

When looking for the highest ethical scandals and avoiding the lowest, the filters used vary from firm to firm, investor to investor, and increasingly data provider to data provider. Most screens have focused on sector avoidance – with the Defence, Alcohol, Tobacco and Gambling industries that were originally avoided in the early noughties before being joined by fossil fuel extractors recently.

But defining what is 'good', 'bad' and 'just about fine', and the degree of acceptance and resistance to individual sectors and stocks, varies a great deal. As can the reasoning behind an exclusion. For example, currently some ethical investment funds are avoiding investment in Telecoms, this as a significant proportion of data transported on data networks is related to pornography. Whereas other funds, also 'ethical', have happily invested in a range of telecom assets with no such filter in place, the benefits of freely available data outweighing the negatives associated with morally dubious data or poor corporate governance. Some funds avoid investments relating to nuclear power for ethical reasons. Some funds seek investments in nuclear power as it's greater efficiency will likely lead to lower carbon emissions and make 'positive' ESG investment decisions regarding the nuclear industry as a socially positive sector. So we can different filters / investors will have different processes sometimes leading to directly adverse decisions.

Many pension funds see divestment as a way to create positive change and a way of changing the behaviours of those who've been divested from. Their argument being; that by removing a source of funding from corporations you raise the firm's cost of capital and this in turn leads to a change in practice as firms actively seek to lower their funding costs. This argument, whilst arguably sound, misses the point that the secondary markets for shares are just that – secondary; most firms, particularly in the established 'sin sectors', are not seeking primary capital, and indeed most return money to their investors every year through dividends. A marginal change in the price of their equity is unlikely to have much effect on management decision making and operational strategy. Indeed, most firms subject to such disinvestment in their equity are actively buying back shares and not issuing equity – perversely in this situation divestment could lower their cost of capital. The avoidance of primary consumption is a far more efficient way of enacting positive change, but for many investors consumption decisions and investment decisions coincide and are two sides of the same coin.

For example, those seeking to disinvest from fossil fuel suppliers are presumably avoiding flying and wearing an extra jumper in winter (obviously not always the case).

One issue, frequently raised with Negative Screening, is it is usually completely Binary in nature, and this can sometimes lead to arbitrary decisions. For example, an investment in a hospitality firm receiving 50% of its revenue from alcohol could be allowed on some systems, the stock being classified as a hospitality firm, but divested from others as an Alcohol stock. A Beverage manufacturer which actually earns most of its revenue from Hotels in its portfolio could be invested, partially invested, or dis-invested by investment managers aiming for the same goals but using different screens, and depending on which sector the screen allocates it to.

Although most screens are designed to place little impact on investment performance, the existence of an additional optimisation constraint causes problems for investment managers. Many managers will have an ethical screen but a market benchmark, which can lead to a hard life when aiming to replicate market returns as substituting assets is often more of an art than a science. Removing stocks and securities from any manager's investment universe will naturally lead to a greater tracking error and implies worse risk / return metrics in efficient markets. (ESG strategists and salespeople will of course argue that the ESG factor drives excess return, but that is of course a different story.) Many managers will use quantitative models to synthetically create sin portfolios from assets that have similar market behaviours but act in different industries. Some managers have multi-record returns of implementing these quantitative replicative strategies in markets with a great deal of success. However, these strategies cannot guarantee future success and correlations between assets are not constant and can change in unpredictable ways over time. Tracking error is a source of concern which for some managers is more important than performance. Which is to say, some investors will accept a small degree of underperformance if volatility relative to their benchmark is low.

Implementing a Screen

In practice, there are two main ways of implementing an exclusionary screen:

- Sector Classification
- Sector Exposure

Sector Classification: Creating an 'avoid' list based solely on sector classification is the easiest method for starting an ESG portfolio but is perhaps not the best way of creating positive change or the most appropriate investment portfolio. Avoiding entire sectors of the market may lead to large tracking errors for mandates charged with matching overall market performance. There are techniques to mitigate this but differences in risk and return are inevitable with a different investment universe. This approach can lead to inconsistencies, and companies with diverse or changing business interests can easily be mis-categorised.

Sector Exposure: This takes a more detailed look at the underlying actions of a security, typically by looking at share of revenue generated by an activity. This can still lead to difficult decision making and sometimes arbitrary choice. For example, where firms with a small exposure to a 'sin' industry, or indirectly associated with 'sin' revenues (say, telecoms and pornography), will be included in some portfolios and not in others. Small exposures to sin are generally ignored, although the actual exposure may depend on the mandate or the strength of the investor's beliefs.

Negative screening is a good first step when developing a framework for Responsible investment and there is growing support for divestment from controversial industries by many stakeholders. But for ESG providers and stakeholders the ideas developed are now more complex and more impactful solutions are available.

ESG: AN INTEGRATION-BASED APPROACH

Moving on from screening, integrating ESG factors in a holistic way is a necessary next step in developing a more complex ESG framework.

Rather than simply reducing the investment universe as one would in a pure negative screening method. Using an ESG integration framework allows us to take a more positive approach looking for reasons of inclusion rather than exclusion. An integrationist approach typically identifying factors, such as emissions or diversity, relating to responsible investing styles and then selecting securities based on these. To many this looks like Factor Analysis or Smart Beta. Factor analysis is often used to identify components of investment portfolios that can generate excess return and as such some argue ESG integration can be used as a potential source of Alpha or is a responsible twist on Smart Beta.

The exact nature of the ESG integration will depend on the mandate and the values articulated by the end investors or their representatives. But there are many potential ESG factors to consider. Factors to be potentially analysed include diversity (from the composition of senior management, to the members of the board, to the composition of the entire workforce), financial governance (accounting standards, leverage, audit quality etc) pollution (carbon emissions, etc), energy efficiency and waste management, labour relations (representation, diversity, inequality) and, of course, many many more. Researching and analysing ESG factors allows investors to create many more metrics, other than simple financial ratios on which to base an investment decision. It has also been noted by risk managers that running ESG screens can find potential warning signals or 'red flags' which would be of interest to non-ESG investors. For example, academic studies have shown that weak corporate governance is strongly correlated with later bankruptcy and an ESG factor screen could provide an early warning of impending doom. A sophisticated corporate governance filter such as the one described could work well across the different forms of capital markets, for example in both equity markets, avoiding lower stock prices, and bond markets, avoiding default.

Responsible investment practitioners can create their own factor screens and data sets to create their investment frameworks / algorithms and as each practitioner will adjust each metric differently an almost infinite array of possible allocation decision can develop for the same set of defined values. Modern investment techniques often rely on automation and the quantitative analysis of large data sets, ESG is no different, and the addition of new risk / return factors creates more data to manipulate and creates in turn more potential trading decisions and investment ideas. The quantitative analysis of Environmental data and its inclusion in the investment process is often known as **Systematic ESG Integration**. Using systematic techniques, analysts can create scores or metrics, for firms, individual instruments and entire portfolios. Mathematically, we could look at the portfolio construction challenge as a Linear Optimisation Problem with an extra constraint i.e., a minimum ESG score or a reduced investment universe.

Integration of non-negative factors also allows the development of positive screening, the best-known family of screens are 'Best in Class'.

Best in Class Positive Screening

A common approach used to integrate environmental issues whilst also incorporating environmental considerations is best in class filtering. The technique allows investors to gain exposure to every sector and industry. This ensures that the ESG portfolio can broadly track the overall market minimising tracking error and lowering underperformance risk for the responsibly investing end-user. Utilising the best in class approach means investing in companies that score highest in their sector or industry in terms of meeting ESG metrics.

A responsible investor who uses a best in class methodology would not exclude entire sectors or industries, such as defence, fossil fuels or aviation, but instead invests in those companies that have the best policies in place to meet the ESG criteria that are relevant for their respective industries, or have shown the best past performance in dealing with ESG issues.

By investing in what may be considered problematic industries, it is hoped that investors can act to modify their behaviour through engagement with management and in extreme cases direct control of operations. For many investors, there is a belief that engagement is the only way of creating lasting change. The existence alone of investors following these principles is enough to create change in management behaviour as executives wish to make their firms attractive to this growing investor base, and of course for their firms to be included in indices and benchmarks that are attracting Responsible Capital.

An example of an index or family of indices following the best in class approach that attracts large capital allocations are the Dow Jones Sustainability Indices. For large listed firms to be included, they are assessed and selected based on their ESG plans and the top 10% of firms in each industry are selected for inclusion. The Indices are updated yearly and companies and performance metrics are monitored throughout the year, meaning that for selected firms ESG is constantly assessed.

As we have seen, given the large number of possible techniques, the design and implementation of positive screens can vary from provider to provider. Typically, a best in class methodology will be sector agnostic and seek to replicate the broader stock market indices with as little disruption as possible. A small as possible tracking error to broader market indices is very attractive to decision makers as it lowers the risk of significant underperformance and helps limit their career risk.

By selecting firms across the entire stock market and by investing in every sector, performance will (nearly always) be similar to non-ESG portfolios and this is a practical positive as investment managers are always keen to avoid explaining underperformance to disappointed investors. Indeed, many ESG mandates will seek to replicate the performance of traditional portfolios but with an allowed small increase in risk to account for i) the difficulty of duplicating returns without access to all of the assets and ii) the smaller investment universe.

Investors may choose to generate their own filters or to rely on outside data providers. For reasons of cost many investment managers must rely on outside data to create their ESG portfolios, this in itself can cause further issues as different data providers can create different results for the same mandate which means that the investment selection process may lack rigour.

As an example, the correlation of ESG scores between two large and respected providers FTSE indices and MSCI is positive but still low and has been measured at approximately 30% (this correlation will change depending on the sample set and weighting of recent data). A large and growing number of criteria for investment benchmark inclusion now rely on businesses' ESG metrics. Some banks are now offering lower interest rates to firms with positive ESG scores and refusing loans to more controversial industries.

In the future greater standardisation of data between providers will reduce the lack of consistency in current ESG approaches and end users should be able to rely on a robust process, but as the industry is relatively nascent and constantly evolving this may be some time away. Currently the industry for providing ESG data is unregulated (unlike for example, credit ratings) and regulation which is probably inevitable may encourage a more transparent and obvious process.

ESG integration is now common at investment firms: what started as a 'fringe' technique in developed market equities now exists across multiple asset classes. It is now common to see environmental concerns embedded into global investments in fields as diverse as Emerging Market Equity to Venture Capital to Corporate Loans

---

RATINGS MOMENTUM

Another integration approach that is gaining popularity is not just to consider an ESG score, but also the first derivative of that ESG score: i.e., ratings momentum or the rate of ratings change.

An investor may wish to include securities in their portfolio that are likely to have positive ESG ratings increases. An investor could use a time series of such ratings to indicate likely further improvements in an asset leading to further buying. Or potentially use positive momentum as a predictor of further increasing scores and a need to include in a portfolio.

Similarly, negative ratings momentum could indicate trouble ahead and act as a sell signal to any investor, not just an ESG investor.

and Government Debt. With some investment firms now talking of environmental concerns impacting every investment decision, we may in the future see ESG factors enter the investment process for the bulk of actively managed funds even if it is not explicitly mentioned. Regulatory standards requiring the disclosure of climate specific risks will make this inevitable, so even those non-concerned with ethical issues will have their risk management process impacted by changes in ESG factors.

IMPACT-BASED ESG INVESTING

Impact investing is perhaps the fastest growing segment of the ESG sector. The asset management industry is showing increased interest in this field as it expands its ESG capabilities into ever more complex areas. High fees and a difficulty scaling mean that impact is a small part of the ESG ecosystem but it is gaining importance and relevance.

When discussing definitions or defining terms, it is still not clear where ESG engagement-based investing ends and impact investing begins and there is clearly some overlap between the two fields. Many firms are offering impact portfolios, which to my eyes at least, are simply portfolios offering ESG integration but charging the higher fees that true impact investing would earn. ESG integration tends to be easier to implement, but it is much harder to create meaningful engagement in a way that typifies genuine impact investing.

Generally, like its sibling ESG – integration, impact investing has the explicit intention to generate not just a financial return but positive social and environmental outcomes. Impact investing will look at specific investments or projects and have visible and defined social goals at the start of the project.

Due to its project-based nature impact investment unescapably has higher costs and a smaller capital allocation than other ESG approaches. Think of the difficulty of allocating £1bn across hundreds if not thousands of individuals projects, compared to the simplicity of buying £1bn of ESG friendly large cap equities in developed world stock markets. Then consider this difficulty on an even larger scale. The world's largest asset managers now manage trillions of dollars and moving a significant proportion to ESG assets is challenging. Moving a significant proportion to impact investment funds would in the short-term at least be impossible.

Impact based investing involves examining individual projects or securities to assess the impact that an investment would have on certain issues. Impact investing is currently considered a small sub-set of ESG. Similarly to ESG, 'impact' can represent a broad range of activity, and will often span multiple asset classes. From micro-loans to Seed Capital, to Infrastructure and Debt. An impact fund seeks to generate financial returns for investors while investing in assets that can generate visible positive social or environmental change. Impact investors will often expect and accept a lower return in exchange for positive externalities related to the project or investment.

The large listed securities associated with institutional investing are not necessarily readily available to impact investors. Some potential investment types are used by those investors hoping for an impact are:

Seed or Venture Capital: Small illiquid investments (often in emerging markets and charity supported) that support innovation and social development in areas of poverty or high inequality, often technology based (intermediate technology in some areas) as technology can provide the greatest positive externalities.

Growth Capital or Private Equity: Larger but still illiquid investments to scale activities with traction and proven benefits.

Working capital loans: Often provided by philanthropic organisations to help cashflow issues and payment issues in smaller social impact ventures.

Secured Fixed Income: Providing loans to organisations that generate positive social equities to purchase assets and infrastructure that aid them delivering positive outcomes.

Impact investing is often seen as a bridge between pure philanthropy and responsible investment, and for some impact investors the financial returns are secondary to creating sustainable capital that can create positive impacts. The need to repay a loan rather than a direct grant is thought to instil financial and operational discipline in the recipient and create lasting value.

The impact investing trade body, The Global Impact Investing Network defines impact investments as investments made with the intention to generate positive, measurable social and environmental impact alongside a financial return. It also defines what it considers to be the four key elements behind each impact investment.

- INTENTIONALITY: *'Impact investments intentionally contribute to social and environmental solutions. This differentiates them from other strategies such as ESG investing, Responsible Investing, and screening strategies.'*
- FINANCIAL RETURNS: *'Impact investments seek a financial return on capital that can range from below market rate to risk-adjusted market rate. This distinguishes them from philanthropy.'*
- RANGE OF ASSET CLASSES: *'Impact investments can be made across asset classes.'*
- IMPACT MEASUREMENT: *'A hallmark of impact investing is the commitment of the investor to measure and report the social and environmental performance of underlying investments.'*

Impact investing naturally leads to an engaged ownership structure where the investor is concerned with not just risk and return but also output. Expected or desired returns can be below, at or even above market rate (although above market rate returns are more often a desire than a reality for all investors). An example of an investor accepting a below risk-expected return or a concessionary return would be the expansion of credit to those unserved by traditional means at a non-usurious rate. The 'investor' achieves a below market risk-adjusted return but creates a product that otherwise could not exist and creates positive outcomes in society.

Whilst we can apply standard techniques of financial analysis and risk management to impact investment portfolios, the quantification of 'impact' can be tricky. Identifying measurement points or creating metrics and monitoring them can difficult and time consuming, the sheer number of available 'impact scores' can easily lead to confusion, and as with any financial framework opaque processes can lead to sub-optimal decision making and poor performance analysis. There is no consistent and homogenous 'impact' rating metric that can be used in every case. Nor could there be as the range of possible projects is so vast. Stakeholders will have to rely on data but be aware of and understand its implicit limitations. Impact measurement just like financial risk management can be more of an art than a science.

Performance analysis and comparison between projects is clearly difficult if success cannot be measured at outset. We believe that standardisation of reporting will over time help to change this, and thankfully the industry does look to be moving towards this. At the present time the Impact Reporting and Investment Standards (IRIS), published by the 'Global Impact Investment Network' is widely used and is gaining acceptance among some, but not all, asset managers. IRIS provides a template which is increasingly popular among practitioners and can provide some much-needed homogeneity between reports from different investment managers. There is a long way to go, but standardisation of reporting will become important in the future when Responsible Investors seek to select managers or validate their investment choices.

The IRIS template breaks 'impact' into five separate dimensions:

WHAT: *'Understanding the outcomes the enterprise is contributing to and how important the outcomes are to stakeholders.'*

WHO: *'Understanding which stakeholders are experiencing the effect and how underserved they were prior to the enterprise's effect.'*

HOW MUCH: *'Understanding how many stakeholders experienced the outcome, what degree of change they experienced, and how long they experienced the outcome for.'*

CONTRIBUTION: *'Assessing whether an enterprise's and/or investor's efforts resulted in outcomes that were likely better than what would have occurred otherwise.'*

RISK: *'Assessing the likelihood that impact will be different than expected.'*

The bulk of the reporting concerns the first three dimensions: What, Who and How much? But identifying key metrics in each dimension is necessary to understand the validity and externalities of an investment. After identifying metrics, reporting can be instigated, and a project's success can be determined.

Impact investing due to its project-based nature and high cost of implementation can never replace ESG in its entirety but might be considered a 'gold standard' by those investors wishing to make a difference.

In the words of Tim Fright, Director of Investments at Responsible Asset Manager Plenitude.io:

'In my view, ESG is simply a stepping stone to impact investing. ESG derives its metrics and decisions from the operations of the underlying investment. Impact goes further. Impact adds scrutiny to the products and services that capital is producing. The firm will be eligible for ESG portfolios if it has good environmental, social and governance practices. But to qualify as a true impact investment, it has to be creating products and services that benefit society.'

The objective of impact investing is to receive a return on capital whilst accomplishing specific goals that are beneficial to society or the environment. As impact investing is often project based it is hard to either benchmark or to carry out at large scale. But as discussed, as such it is likely to remain a small part of Responsible Investment Portfolios for the time being.

Impact investing also presents an opportunity for the industry with retail investors increasingly wanting to know how and why their savings are invested. Asset managers are looking at impact reporting as not only a way of creating social value, but also increasing customer engagement. Modern investors are often concerned with the ethical implications of their actions, detailed 'impact reporting' can be a way of creating a dialogue between the industry and its clients.

This style of investing merged with philanthropy can service a wider base of capital providers than ESG investment as it looks to include new forms of capital from the public sector and philanthropists. Stronger and more consistent standards are need for impact measurement, to help popularise impact investing. The growing number of measurement metrics and the emergence of templates such as IRIS will help this. As the sector develops demonstrating success both financially and socially will become a key method for a stronger message leading to more capital and even greater impact. Case studies, a track record of success and transparency will become crucial for building confidence in this nascent sector as it becomes an ever more important part of not just ESG investment but philanthropy and public sector resource allocation. A larger impact investment sector would improve the availability and quality of services that improve day to day conditions for people and households living in poverty. This can only be a good thing.

ENGAGEMENT-BASED ESG INVESTING

Engagement can be enacted alongside screens and integration. It is not necessarily a replacement for other techniques but can work in tandem with them. A fully engaged strategy involves more than just investing blindly but also creates lasting relationships with underlying firms and managers, and like impact investing, engagement moves beyond simply allocating capital towards creating a dialogue with the agents of capital. The relationships should go beyond investor and investee, a fully engaged ESG framework would involve interactions with all stakeholders in a firm's operations from its employees, contractors, suppliers and more, even including the consumers of its products.

As an asset management professional, it is clear that by engaging with firms in an investment portfolio, you can begin to understand them better and then through dialogue each party can develop a greater understanding of each other's long-term goals. For the ESG manager this could be encouraging a business to take an approach to ESG issues more in tune with the values of the end investors. For the firm a better understanding of investor goals should lead to a lower cost of capital and potentially a competitive advantage. Engagement can also educate the investment team of the industries in which it operates, which will again aid the investment process creating a virtuous circle. The investment team benefit as knowledge gained from this process directly leads to new insights on operational issues affecting the underlying investments and information resulting from the process can feed back into any future investment decisions potentially leading to better risk management.

An engagement strategy is not just about picking virtuous organisations and backing them, it could involve investing in 'bad' or less than virtuous players and then enacting behaviours that force positive change or greater alignment of values. Whereas simple divestment would not allow any interaction with many sections of the economy that impact investors' lives and hence curtail the ability to create change. Engagement is a key element of Stewardship as it involves exercising shareholder power on behalf of members to work with companies on improving their attitudes towards subjects such as diversity or climate change.

A practical engagement approach will create an ongoing dialogue between investors and investees. Raising awareness on issues that move simply beyond PnL and identify the needs of all stakeholders and the responsibilities of operational managers and the stewards of capital. Responsible investors can help firms identify potential ESG risk factors and track changes in the identified risk profiles of operations.

Direct engagement is a powerful tool to aid understanding of business processes and reduce the ESG risk of a portfolio. ESG can form a natural part of the dialogue between the investment team and firm management and this is consistent with the prevailing view that governance issues should be an integrated part of the investment process as we discussed in the section on ESG integration.

Engaged investing is by definition active investing. The relentless rise of passive investing is in some people's eyes a threat to the advent of concentrated ESG investing and engagement. In others it could be an advantage, as ESG integration could come from the end investors giving mandates to benchmark providers to incorporate their values; although this would likely be more useful for simple screens and systematic integration than for engagement or impact-based projects. The modern institutional investor has a broad toolkit of low-cost solutions such as ETFs and Trackers to help investees save for retirement and other financial goals. With many institutions simply looking for the cheapest way of matching their liabilities there is little thought of the operating companies that each fund can represent or any thought of engaging with them. However, modern corporate and social responsibility (CSR) at the largest asset managers are beginning to change this. Asset managers are now approaching engagement as a source of investment advantage as well as marketing point. And this engagement will often begin by discussing ESG issues.

A key form of engagement is acting on shareholder resolutions and utilising the voting rights conferred with ownership. Although it sometimes feels like an abstract concept; as pensioners, small savers and general investors, either directly or through the funds we own. We are the ultimate owners of the firms on the stock market. Whilst we delegate the management of an enterprise to the executive and directors, as shareholders collectively we guide the strategy, financing and operations of the firm. Arguably, we are responsible for the actions and mistakes of the management. Responsible Investors look at this power as a responsibility not an unnecessary side effect of investment.

Engagement can occur at any part of the process. Not just between manager and underlying corporation. A programme of engagements and monitoring of asset managers by investors or their advisors can create stronger forces for change. The investment managers will maintain control over investments and monitor to identify any instances where a potential breach of values has occurred, but ultimate responsibility lies with the investor. And understanding of the engagement between investors and the Engaged ESG manager is important to both sides. The manner and form of the engagement required or desired should be outlined in both the Investment Management Agreement (IMA) and the Statement of Investment Principles (SIP).

ESG IN HISTORY

The Case of Cowan vs Scargill

Developments in pension administration can be weird and wonderful, and for anyone old enough to remember Arthur Scargill's battles with Mrs Thatcher in the 1980s they may find it surprising to know that he is also an interesting footnote in the history of pensions reform. The case of Cowan vs Scargill is quoted today, and looks at the responsibilities of trustees and their ability to impose their values on beneficiaries.

Historically the fidicuary duty of trustees meant it was unclear whether the ethics of stakeholders could be taken into account when investing. This lack of clarity had been reinforced by British case law, that meant that anything other than considering an investment on its own merits and risk / return guidelines could be a breach of the minimum requirements for investment analysis and allocation. For many practitioners it is still not clear the extent to which the legislation requires trustees of occupational pension schemes to take ethical factors and the values of beneficiaries into account when allocating capital. However, for the industry as a whole, and stakeholders in aggregate, ESG factors can give rise to material financial risks. Hence these risks should be identified and modelled by investors and would hence affect the capital allocation process. Adding any extra requirement or constraint to an optimisation problem naturally leads to more complexity. Hence ESG can become more opaque (which many consider inherently a bad thing) whilst seeming more virtuous, so it is important to identify and clearly explain what these values are.

The key case law for the appropriateness of ESG investing in UK pensions is now over three decades old and comes from the judgment in **Cowan v Scargill***, which required financial concerns to be paramount.

*Yes – that Scargill.

From the judgement:

'When the purpose of the trust is to provide financial benefits for the beneficiaries, as is usually the case, the best interests of the beneficiaries are normally their best financial interests.'

The case took place all the way back in 1984 and has had a long-term effect on pension investment and been an impediment on the rise of Responsible Investing. The case of Cowan vs. Scargill rather ironically given its later relevance to ESG and climate focused investing concerned the pension investments of the National Coal Board. The National Union of Mineworkers (NUM) led by Arthur Scargill had sought to gradually re-allocate the National Coal Board's pension fund from investments that competed directly with the U.K. coal industry. This was thought to be more in line with the values of the NUM rather than the end-user. The British courts considered that investment in line with Union policy was not considered a legitimate basis to enact the trustee's fiduciary duty to act in members' best interests. The judgement implies that trustees should not take their own ESG factors into account if these conflict with the financial interests of the beneficiaries even if they coincide with the beliefs of the beneficiaries. In this framework even simplistic ESG analysis such as negative screening would be inappropriate unless it was explicitly aimed at generating the highest possible risk adjusted return. For trustees of a pension fund in the UK it is implied that risks associated with climate change are a secondary consideration and should only be taken into account in a financial context. Although the case acknowledged that trustees could in principle choose lower return investments due to ethical concerns whilst performing their duties, such circumstances are rare and it would fall to the trustees to justify the investment particularly with concern for the benefit of the beneficiaries.

However, it is now argued that the conventional view of the law is unnecessarily restrictive. This reflects both changing mores. People are more likely to seek ethical investments now, are more aware of the process and seek more engagement. As well as other driving factors, such as integration of ESG factors into the regulatory framework for financial services. But it also reflects the concern that the judgement in Cowan vs Scargill was based on a legal (and fundamental) misunderstanding of investment theory. In particular that profit maximisation of each individual investment as prescribed in the judgement was at odds with Modern Portfolio Theory which argues that investments must be considered in aggregate, and this is of course before we consider high level considerations such as cash-flow matching or LDI.

It is clear that we live in a different world now, with an evolved regulatory system. In 2005, in a report prepared for the UN Environment Programme Finance Initiative Freshfields Bruckhaus Deringer concluded that a court twenty years later could find differently. Freshfields were concerned that the case had generated broad implications for the investment industry in general and pension trustees in particular. However, the case itself was focused on a very narrow set of issues regarding one particular investment plan. This investment plan would likely have very little in common with a modern SRI or ESG strategy, meaning that conclusions should be taken with a pinch of salt.

A further issue, resulting from the particular circumstances of this case, was that Arthur Scargill represented himself. He was not a trained lawyer which meant there was not equality in process or argument between the sides.

The report even argued that it might be a breach of fiduciary duties to not consider relevant ESG considerations given the evidence that ethically conflicted investments can suffer poor returns. In particular, firms with weak corporate governance have a habit of going bust.

Currently the majority of practitioners in ESG space, certainly judging by the marketing material of the leading fund houses, argue that better ESG practices are associated with better returns and sustainability and hence the fidicuary duty of trustees choosing to allocate according to ESG frameworks is trivially met by superior performance. This is due to the fact that there are an increasing number of academic studies available in effect on risk and return of taking ESG / SRI or similar factors into account. The majority of results indicate a positive financial impact on return, both outright and risk-adjusted. We should take some caution over relying on these results though, if we take ESG simply as a factor that is currently showing outperformance, we should not rely on this or take it as permanent. Historical outperformance of any factor tends to zero as the market absorbs the relevant information and includes it in the price. A lack of excess return or even a negative return shouldn't mean the end of ethical investing and a reliance on demonstrating outperformance may be the wrong path for the long term.

It is amazing to think that in the last few decades incorporation of negative externalities into investment management has gone from a breach of fiduciary duty to an obligation. With larger funds now required to have a strategy to mitigate climate risk for their end-users.

INCORPORATING ESG INTO THE SIP

How to incorporate ESG considerations into the Statement of Investment Principles. A Brief Guide.

As discussed previously, as of October 2020 pension trustees are required to update their Statement of Investment Principles, to explain their arrangements with asset managers or to explain their non-compliance: With non-compliance quite likely in smaller schemes in the initial stages.

A new updated SIP will be expected to explain:

- how asset managers are incentivised to create an investment strategy and decisions with the trustees' investment policies, including in relation to ESG matters;
- how asset managers are incentivised to make decisions based on assessments about medium-to-long-term financial and non-financial performance of an issuer of debt or equity and to engage with issuers of debt or equity in order to improve their performance in the medium-to-long-term;
- how the method (and time horizon) of the evaluation of the asset manager's performance and the remuneration for asset management services are in line with the trustees' investment policies;
- how the trustees monitor portfolio turnover costs incurred by asset managers, and how they define and monitor targeted portfolio turnover or turnover range;
- the duration of the arrangement with the asset manager. Trustees must also set out the methods by which they monitor and engage with investee companies and other stakeholders in relation to their capital structure and the management of conflicts of interest.

Where duration and 'Appropriate time horizon' refers to the length of time considered appropriate for the funding of future benefits by the investments of the scheme. This requires trustees to consider risks in the context of a scheme's own profile and maturity. Hence, here the length of time refers to benefits payable by the scheme and not the duration of individual investments, or the risk measure used in analysing fixed income portfolios.

In their white paper the pensions regulator asks us to consider climate related risks as a key part of this new approach to governance and risk:

> 'You should consider the recommendations of the Taskforce on Climate-Related Financial Disclosures (TCFD), which have been endorsed by the UK government, these recommendations provide a global framework for identifying, assessing, and managing climate-related risks.'
>
> 'You can find asset owner guidance to help engage with fund managers on climate-related risks and opportunities at https://www.tcfdhub.org/ The PLSA's climate risk 'guide for trustees' gives an overarching practical framework for schemes on how to consider climate risk for trustees: https://www.plsa.co.uk/Policy-andResearch-Document-library-More-light-less-heat'

A further set of reporting requirements will add further strain on some trustees and this will be particularly onerous for smaller schemes who in many cases will lack the resources to make the necessary changes in a cost-effective way. The Pensions Regulator is aware of this and we can expect enforcement actions where they identify failure to comply with the new governance requirements, with the bulk of these actions likely to be against smaller schemes. It is likely that further consolidation into larger schemes such as master trusts will be likely and this should improve governance.

THE REVISED STATEMENT SHOULD

Describe how the fund's stakeholders defines Environmental, Social and Governance concerns and their relevance to outcomes, performance and risk management, as well as its ability to make investment decisions.

For example: *'The Trustees recognise our responsibility as long term investor to support and encourage good corporate governance practices in the firms and managers in which we invest. Responsible investment encourages openness and stronger corporate governance. The Trustees through the Fund can contribute to better outcomes through greater accountability between management, boards, investors and other stakeholders. It is our belief that this is likely to enhance the value of the Fund's investments over the longer term.'*

Many examples of SIPs exist online and the regulator insists that for larger schemes they are publicly available, it should be noted that whilst many opening statements are somewhat generic, the crux of understanding the philosophy will be throughout the document.

The SIP should also explain the trustees' support or understanding of the relevant ESG-related bodies or associations, such as UKSIF and the UNPRI. Including any relevant memberships and involvement alongside the date the of inception of the relationship with the ESG body.

The SIP should make clear their requirements of investment managers. Do the Trustees require their fund managers in their stewardship of the Fund's assets to pay appropriate regard to relevant corporate governance, social, ethical and environmental considerations when considering the purchase or sale of investments?

The SIP should explain that trustees have asked the investment managers to exercise their voting and rights as shareholders in a manner they believe to be consistent with the SIP and the values of the stakeholders.

The SIP should explain – its use of ESG data, for most funds they will rely on third party data, how this data is selected and monitored should be explained.

The revised SIP will create greater transparency of process particularly concerning non-financial matters, but we are also likely to see a lot of 'greenwashing' in early days as trustees match to meet reporting requirement without changing the underlying investment process. The regulatory and reporting burden will also have a profound effect on smaller schemes the increase in cost will likely lead to further consolidation.

CHAPTER 9

Moving Beyond Liability-Driven Investment

THE WORLD OF CDI

Financial theory and the multiple techniques for Multi Asset Class investing are constantly moving forward and with 'Peak LDI' arguably upon us, investment consultants are always looking for the new new thing to demonstrate their expertise. As even the most bullish consultant knows that LDI is certainly not a perfect hedge for most pension schemes.

The often-used phrase, when things go wrong, is 'the only perfect hedge is in a Japanese garden'. To address any imperfections, finance practitioners are always looking to add overlay strategies to compensate for some of the deficiencies within the basic LDI framework. With a holistic approach to investing now expected for institutional portfolios, the industry has to look for ways of expanding their product suite beyond just long-term risk hedging and to address other identified consumer needs. Indeed, most funds and trustees will quickly identify many risks other than inflation and interest rates which are the main concern of the LDI practitioner.

The development of new products is becoming acutely important as Liability Driven Investment nears market saturation in some developed markets, particularly in the UK. Resultantly LDI practitioners are constantly refining their frameworks and introducing new ideas and concepts, both to closer align end-users' investments with their needs, but also to protect the consultants' value proposition as LDI expertise is becoming increasingly commoditised.

Typical investment overlays currently being developed and utilised in the market for pension scheme strategies include ESG (Environmental, Social and Governance) and CDI. ESG is covered elsewhere in this book and covers Governance and Ethical issues beyond the basic financial considerations that have historically been considered by investment managers. CDI stands for Cash Flow Driven Investment and is a natural overlay to LDI strategies.

CDI aims to change the focus beyond Liability Hedging to ensuring that a pension schemes cash flow and funding needs are met. With half of the larger DB schemes in the UK cashflow negative as schemes move from the accumulation phase to decumulation, treasury management is becoming increasingly important. In essence CDI is a complement to LDI rather than a radically different methodology. As such CDI will usually be used in addition to rather than instead of a standard LDI framework. When developing a CDI strategy or overlay the investment strategist wishes to obtain a low risk investment portfolio, that is complemented with a stable funding position, as in an LDI structure. But they will also seek to meet cash flow needs from income generated internally within the investment portfolio.

The investment team will estimate the cashflows of the scheme, and then find appropriate investments to meet these payments. Hence, just as in an LDI framework, it makes sense to place the assets in a well-diversified, fixed income portfolio. However, with many of the cashflows in the short and medium term, the focus of investment must move away from default free long gilts to other assets. Due to the shorter duration and greater illiquidity of some of the instruments, more risk is introduced to the portfolio, but this can lead to greater capital efficiency and less strain on the plan sponsor. Due to the illiquidity and high transaction costs the non-gilt assets are typically held on a buy and hold basis, leading to more predictable returns (as the cost of future liquidity is difficult to estimate).

When using a standard Liability driven investment approach, the practitioner aims to mitigate any change in the value of liabilities. These liabilities are modelled as payments in the future and represent long term funding needs. The key variables when calculating these 'needs' will be mortality rates and long-term gilt yields. (Or similar risk-free debt.) However, historically immediate term cashflow requirements have not usually been targeted. A cashflow driven investment strategy is hence an evolution of this basic LDI framework. The strategy will select assets that provide cashflows to match the future estimated cashflow requirements of the portfolio alongside LDI style risk management.

There are a large number of income-yielding securities that are available to match liability cashflows as part of a CDI strategy. Typically, when commencing a CDI led approach the investment universe will be widened to increase the precision of cash flow matching, this will be done by adding more credit risk to the portfolio, this can allow CDI schemes to be more capital efficient. Although clearly with more layers of risk in the structure.

Moving away from government debt will cause concerns, particularly for the risk averse. The move into lower quality credit also changes the liquidity of the portfolio as the credit notes and corporate issues selected will be less frequently traded with much wider bid–offer spreads than similar government bonds. Indeed, there is a growing interest in 'illiquid credit' from pension funds and similar institutions as a low interest rate environment makes investors look further and wider for yield.

There is also an issue that is a relative scarcity of high-quality debt linked to inflation, despite many corporate treasuries have funding requirements that would naturally benefit from issuing inflation linked debt. It is difficult if not impossible to obtain a selection of inflation linked credit assets that offers both high credit quality and diversification across sectors for UK pension schemes. However, broadening the investment universe away from solely GBP issuances to EUR and US schemes can negate this. (This solves one problem but creates another, as GBP inflation is strongly correlated to EUR and US inflation, but not an exact match, and that correlation could change at any time.)

Due to this scarcity of credit products explicitly linked to inflation, Cash flow demands linked to inflation will often, due to necessity not desire, be matched with nominal bonds. Nominal bonds being more available at specific required dates. The portfolio will then require an inflation hedge with inflation swaps. This adds a layer of complexity and introduces further risks such as counterparty risk and basis risk. The complexity of inflation swaps is explained elsewhere.

Government and Corporate issuance of inflation linked debt has however been rising in response to this demand. In the UK, the Purple Book* shows nine straight years of an increased allocation to inflation linked assets, as investors have become increasingly comfortable with this asset class, and inflation linked assets have become a more significant part of the investment opportunity set due to increased government issuance.

The Purple Book is produced annually by the Pension Protection Fund provides the most comprehensive data on the UK universe of Defined Benefit (DB) pension schemes in the private sector. In 2018, their analysis covered 5,450 schemes – which is approximately 99% of the pension funds eligible for PPF compensation.

WHAT IS THE DIFFERENCE BETWEEN LDI AND CDI?

For a typical fully or nearly funded pension scheme the trustee's task is to ensure that pension payments, ie the liabilities, are met as they fall due. Obviously, there will be other concerns, but ultimately the success or failure of both the scheme and the trustee will be judged by matching all the appropriate payments as and when they come due.

As most defined benefit pension funds are closed to new members, and the age of their members mean that they are beyond the accumulation stage, the cash flows in a scheme will typically become negative or have become negative as the payments to beneficiaries will be larger than the income generated from the underlying investments. Currently many LDI solutions, particularly pooled funds do not allow for this and schemes are forced to sell down assets over time to meet their obligations. To address this issue, a CDI practitioner will look at shorter dated fixed income assets that can smooth the cash flow requirement. The aim being to select assets that yield income to approximate the future expected cashflow requirements of the pension scheme. A typical LDI scheme would typically invest in UK government debt securities, a typical CDI scheme will have a much more varied portfolio, even if it has a similar risk profile. As the number of gilts in issuance is finite and they have a limited number of payment dates, a gilt-only solution is not really possible for CDI. With only a few gilts maturing each year the payment profiles of pension schemes are impossible to completely match. Clearly, exact cash flow matching requires a greater number of instruments. A CDI strategy would typically include high quality corporate bonds and some private debt. Unlike Government debt, these securities are not considered default risk free. However, high quality debt will still contain little credit risk (typically less than twenty basis points per year) but would generate an increase in income (typically greater than the cost of defaults). Liquidity concerns are somewhat negated by holding the issues to maturity, when all being well the payments generated from the asset will meet an upcoming liability.

CDI can be a good overlay strategy for a well-funded scheme. But for a poorly funded scheme more pressing issues like investment return or the need for additional contributions from the plan sponsor are a greater concern. If a pension were to require investment returns significantly greater than gilts a CDI strategy may not be appropriate, as CDI is implemented on the hedging part of the portfolio, not the growth or risk part. The Fixed Income Securities selected provide relatively secure income but will typically have a lower expected return than traditional risk assets, which means that CDI may not be appropriate for a poorly funded scheme.

The credit instruments used in CDI can provide a yield increase to a hedged portfolio but will lack the liquidity of the gilts they are replacing. Moving into illiquid investments presents its own risks and will also remove some flexibility from the portfolio.

It should be noted that better cash flow management does not negate the need for LDI. Both the short- and long-term obligations of a portfolio are rarely known with certainty. For example, cash flows may be higher than expected if members have decreased mortality or opt out of the scheme. A liquid gilt portfolio representing an LDI allocation allows extra funds to be raised quickly and easily either by selling liquid assets or through increased leverage, this flexibility is not available if the portfolio has been moved into illiquid credit.

Currently only the largest pension schemes are fully utilising CDI strategies. Like all new strategies the trickle-down effect will take time, but it does seem likely that more granular hedging using a greater number of income-producing assets is inevitable. Large schemes are able to implement CDI using bespoke, segregated portfolios, that it would be impractical for smaller vehicles to replicate. However, some parts of the CDI framework can now be mirrored through the use of pooled vehicles specifically designed to meet an increased demand for CDI style solutions from pension trustees. These pooled funds can offer long-dated investment-grade bond credit funds which are managed on a 'buy and maintain' basis and target a specific set of benchmark cashflows which are designed to meet the needs of these clients.

In the world of traditional Liability Driven Investment, LDI pooled funds are readily understood by informed users and have become the default solution for smaller schemes. The available funds provide a strong risk management tool for both interest rate and inflation risks and have been shown to provide significantly less volatility of funding surplus.

Fixed income assets of other durations are also available in packaged forms, and through vehicles such as funds and synthetic structures, a broad array of credit instruments become accessible to smaller pension schemes. Through mixing and matching funds, Cashflow Driven Investment solutions are available to smaller pension schemes, although the hedges will not be as refined as the products available to their larger cousins.

CREDIT WHERE IT'S DUE

Moving into Illiquid Credit

The rise of CDI, alongside the hunt for yield in a low interest rate environment, has led to a search for alternative credit assets by pension schemes. A key compositional difference between an LDI portfolio and a portfolio where CDI has been applied will be the addition of alternative and illiquid credit products. This is as the widening of the investment universe increases the possible number of payment dates and the overall flexibility of the portfolio.

But as there are very few free lunches available in finance, the increase in flexibility will also increase the risk. The returns for an illiquid credit portfolio will likely be higher than a liquid credit portfolio due to the additional risk premia taken on. These additional risk premia increase the return from the underlying assets and can lead to greater capital efficiency. This can make CDI an easy sell to a plan sponsor as it will decrease their contributions. When implementing CDI the trustees will need to be aware of the conflicts between the sponsor and the beneficiaries and act accordingly.

There is no standard definition for illiquid credit, and the numerous assets defined in this way can be varied in nature. The assets can be very long-term eg Freeholds and ground rents, or very short-term eg Bridging Loans. But the commonality is that there is a non-government borrower seeking funds and that there is no ready secondary market for this obligation, and so due to this lack of liquidity in many cases the purchaser will aim to buy and hold the debt until maturity.

Before the Global Financial Crisis, domestic banks were the dominant providers of capital to credits such as these. With the banking sector assuming the credit risk either internally, on their own balance sheet or externally, by packaging and distributing multiple similar credits in the Capital Markets. However, the retrenchment of the banking and finance sector since the crisis has dramatically changed the function of these parts of the capital markets. Weak regulatory controls and high leverage before the credit crunch, alongside a belief in the fungibility of similar rated products led to a liquidity which allowed too much risk into the system and the capacity to provide this risk disappeared when the markets changed.

The believed homogeneity of the banks' packages, encouraged by the ratings' agencies Moody's and S & P, created a demand from borrowers for funding that needed to be replaced when the traditional sources dried up. For the larger institutional investors such as the biggest DB schemes and other long-term investors, the retrenchment of the banks creates an opportunity to replace this risk capital and to diversify and capture more risk premia leading to a better risk return profile.

Many large corporations now go directly to asset management firms negating the need for the banks to act as middlemen and saving substantially on fees. There is of course a downside when purchasing assets in this way, as these securities will suffer a lack of liquidity as the both the sell-side and other potential market-makers have no interest in supporting these assets when they are not earning fees for syndication etc.

With many corporations anxious to lock in long term funding at advantageous rates, pension schemes are natural bedfellows as they have obligations that require a long-term investment horizon, require regular payments and are somewhat predictable. Low risk and predictable cashflows are essential to a pension scheme. But immediate liquidity is rarely desired or needed. In many ways this makes gilts or treasuries an unsuitable asset for these long-term investors, as part of the reason for the low returns generated by high quality fixed income, is that some investors are happy to sacrifice return for liquidity. It seems that for some schemes this would be undesirable. Obviously, illiquid credit instruments will derive their value almost entirely from their cashflows, and so are an appropriate instrument to support a pension scheme's stream of liabilities. See Table 9.1.

TABLE 9.1 The hypothetical return expectations and objectives of an investor in various credit linked asset classes

Credit Instrument	Investor's Objective
Global Bonds	Generate returns and provide stable cashflow to help meet obligations.
Multi-Sector Credit	To achieve a return of 3% to 5% pa net of fees over rolling five-year periods.
Secured Finance	Provide predictable cashflows, but a better risk-return profile than public corporate bonds.
Illiquid Credit	Outperform 3-month LIBOR return by 5 % net of fees over a five-year period.
Real Estate Debt	Target an internal rate of return of 5% to 7.5% net of fees.

CASH FLOW-DRIVEN INVESTMENT IN ACTION

Let's look at a hypothetical scheme which has moved to a CDI framework. These have been drawn up to represent a typical but conservative UK mature pension fund which has embraced LDI and then added a CDI overlay.

Various practitioners have contributed to this study. But particular thanks are due to Ben Gold and the Pensions team at XPS for their invaluable assistance.

The ABC Scheme

For this scheme, we assume:

- Best-estimate of return on the current strategy is 1.25% above gilts.
- For Technical Provisions, assumed (prudent) investment returns are 0.5% above gilts.
- Investment returns under buyout are assumed to be lower than gilts.

A conservative buyout strategy might have the following features:

- All familiar asset classes (avoiding illiquid credit and some of the more esoteric alternatives)
- A focus on lower-risk end of credit spectrum for both greater certainty and liquidity
- Increased liability hedging to protect low-dependency funding position
- Mainly liquid assets that can be sold to transact a buyout when pricing is attractive
- An awareness of the biggest sources of ESG risks facing the companies in which the underlying funds invest, and identifies risk management strategies to help mitigate these concerns.

This strategy would naturally lead us a CDI-based solution. Which would aim to lock in contractual payment flows for the long term. See Table 9.2.

Which would be obtained from a sample investment universe similar to Figure 9.1.

TABLE 9.2   Suggested Portfolio Composition for the Gilts + 125 target

Asset Class	Allocation
Illiquid Credit	13%
Alternative Credit	15%
Corporate Credit	23%
LDI and Cash	49%

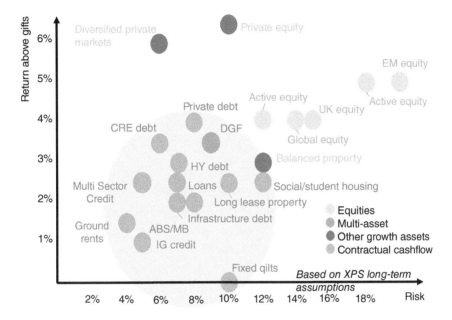

FIGURE 9.1   Sample investment universe

What Are the Objectives of Our Typical CDI Scheme?

The objectives of each scheme, and each stakeholder within a scheme will vary, but at a broad level, they might look similar to this:

1. **Target a suitable level of returns to:**
   at least remain fully funded on the Technical Provisions basis without Sponsor contributions. Ideally, to improve the buy-out funding position over time or reduce the time to buyout.
2. **Reduce Market-to-Market Risk:**
   by controlling funding volatility, so the likelihood of needing additional company funding is minimised.
3. **To ensure there is appropriate liquidity:**
   - to support the LDI portfolio,
   - and pay all member benefits and other Plan outgoings.

CHAPTER 10

The Statement of Investment Principles

The statement of investment principles, or SIP, is a written statement governing decisions about investments for the purposes of a pension fund. It is the responsibility of the trustees to ensure that the SIP is produced, appropriate and abided by. Trustees or more realistically their investment consultants must prepare, maintain and when appropriate revise the SIP. There is a great deal of legislation governing the production of SIPs and professional help is a necessity for all but the most experienced trustee.

Before updating a SIP, trustees need to consult the sponsoring plan sponsor. In the UK a review of the SIP must take place at least every three years, but also without delay after any significant change in the investment policy.

The pensions regulators high level guidelines are clear.

DRAWING UP A STATEMENT OF INVESTMENT PRINCIPLES

The trustees of most schemes must draw up a written SIP. This sets out the principles governing how decisions about investments must be made.

What the SIP must include

The SIP must include your policy on:

- *choosing investments;*
- *the kinds of investments to be held, and the balance between different kinds of investment;*
- *risk, including how risk is to be measured and managed, and the expected return on investments;*
- *realising investments;*
- *the extent, if at all, you take account of social, environmental or ethical considerations when taking investment decisions; and*
- *using the rights (including voting rights) attached to investments if you have them.*

Preparing the SIP

Before the SIP is drawn up, you must:

- *obtain and consider the written advice of a person who you reasonably believe to have the appropriate knowledge and experience of financial matters and investment management; and*
- *consult with the employer.*

A SIP will usually contain the following sections:

    1: Introduction
    2: Governance
    3: Scheme Objectives
    4: Investment Policy
    5: Risk Management
    6: Investment Manager selection and Policy
    7: Additional Voluntary Contributions

A sample SIP is included at the end of this chapter.

A SAMPLE STATEMENT OF INVESTMENT PRINCIPLES

As might be used by a current UK scheme, which is the decumulation phase and moving into buyout. The scheme has previously used an LDI framework but has now added a CDI overlay.

STATEMENT OF INVESTMENT PRINCIPLES FOR THE ABC PLAN

The Trustee of the ABC Plan ('the Plan') has prepared this Statement of Investment Principles ('the SIP') in accordance with the Pensions Act 1995 ('the Act'), as amended, and also the Occupational Pension Scheme (Investment) Regulations 2005, as well as the principles recommended by the Myners Code.

The SIP supersedes any previous SIP and reflects the investment policy agreed by the Trustee in respect of assets covering Defined Benefit liabilities and AVCs.

Before preparing this SIP the Trustee has:

- obtained and considered the written advice from the Plan's Investment Consultant, and the investment consultant is suitably qualified through ability and experience and has appropriate knowledge;
- consulted the employer.

This SIP will be reviewed at least every three years or immediately after any significant change in investment policy.

When Choosing investments

The Trustee will be responsible for the investment strategy and investment policies for the Plan.

The Trustee has considered the both the liabilities of the plan and the strength of employer covenant when creating the investment strategy and policies.

The Trustee relies on Investment Managers for the day-to-day management of the Plan's assets but will retain control over all decisions made about the investments in which the Plan invests.

Where Investment Managers are delegated discretion under Section 34 of the Act, the Investment Manager will exercise their investment powers in accordance with the Act, relevant and subsequent regulations, and this SIP.

The Trustee relies on the Investment Managers to appoint appropriate Custodians for pooled funds who are responsible for the safekeeping of the assets of the Plan.

The Trustee relies on the Investment Managers to appoint appropriate Administrators or Registrars for pooled funds who are responsible for keeping records of the Plan's entitlement within the pooled funds.

Investment Objective and Strategy

Investment objective

The Trustee has set the following objectives:

- To achieve a fully funded position on a Technical Provisions basis.
- To implement an investment strategy targeting a return sufficient to ensure that the liabilities are met as they fall due.
- To achieve the above objective whilst controlling volatility and the long-term costs of the Plan.
- To adhere to the provisions contained within this SIP.

Investment Strategy

The Trustee intends to meet the investment objective by investing in a diversified portfolio of return-seeking and liability-matching assets.

The Trustee can utilise a wide range of passively and actively managed investments, which shall include (but not be limited to):

- Assets or funds primarily utilised to match liability risk (typically movements in long term interest rates and inflation) including gilts, swaps and repurchase agreements and the use of derivatives and leverage.
- Assets or funds primarily used to outperform the liabilities over the long-term, including equity, private markets, hedge funds, commodities, currency, bonds and other forms of credit, property, infrastructure and insurance including the use of derivatives and leverage. Illiquid assets can be used where a higher return or lower risk is expected.
- Assets or funds primarily used to provide immediate liquidity such as cash or cash instruments.
- Assets or funds that combine liability outperformance, liability hedging or liquidity characteristics including the use of derivatives and leverage.
- Annuity or insurance policies designed to match the specific characteristics of the Plan's liabilities or membership.

The intention of the Trustee and the Plan sponsor is to implement a strategy that follows the principles of Cashflow-Driven Investment ('CDI'). Under a CDI approach, the Plan's assets will be fully invested in a portfolio comprised of corporate bonds and other assets that provide a contractual cashflow designed but not guaranteed to cover the outgoings of the plan.

Investment Restrictions

The Trustee intends to adhere to the following restrictions:

- No more than 3% of Plan assets can be held in investments related to the Employer.
- Whilst borrowing on a temporary basis is permitted, this option will only be utilised where absolutely necessary or where it is expected to reduce overall risk (e.g. for very short time periods during an asset transfer).
- Investment in derivative instruments may only be made where they contribute to risk reduction or facilitate efficient portfolio management.
- Stock lending is permitted at the discretion of the Plan's Investment Managers in line with their overall investment objectives, policies and procedures.

Investment Risk

The Trustee has identified a number of risks including (but not limited to):

- Employer covenant risk;
- Liability risks: Interest rate risk, Inflation risk, Longevity risk;
- Asset risks: Equity risk, Property risk, Currency risk, Credit risk, Interest rate risk, Inflation risk;
- Strategy risks: Asset allocation risk, Liquidity risk (including collateral risk), Growth asset risk (including currency risk);
- Implementation risks: Investment manager risk, Counterparty risk, Operational risk, risks associated with the use of derivatives.

The trustee and their advisors assess investment manager risk. This is measured by the expected deviation of the expected return, as set out in the investment managers' objectives, relative to the investment policy. The risk is mitigated through the diversification of the Scheme's assets between investment managers and the ongoing monitoring of the investment managers' performance relative to the objective and factors supporting the managers' investment process.

Liquidity risk is measured by the level of cashflow required by the Scheme over a specified period. This is managed by the Scheme's administrator, who monitor the level of liquidity in order to limit the impact of the cash flow requirements on the investment policy.

Risks associated with derivatives, Basis risk – the returns from the backing assets used to meet the payable leg of the derivatives may not exactly match. This risk is addressed through the investment policy adopted for the backing assets and the investment managers' asset management capabilities;

Liability risk – pension scheme liabilities can only be estimated and there is a risk of unanticipated changes in the assumptions used to project the Scheme's liabilities, hence there may be a divergence between the performance of the derivatives and the amount expected to be required to meet the liabilities;

Legal and operational risk – the successful implementation of derivative strategies is dependent on various legal documents governing the derivative contracts and the accuracy and appropriateness of operational tasks. The Trustee has taken and will continue to take advice in putting in place legal documents and appointing providers capable of carrying out the required operational tasks.

Counterparty risk – in the use of derivatives this risk is mitigated through the exchange of collateral and diversifying exposure among a number of counterparties.

These risks are measured and managed by the Trustee as follows:

- The Trustee has set an investment strategy that adheres to the contents of this SIP.
- The Trustee receives strategic investment advice from the Investment Consultant that may include risk modelling and quantification (e.g. Value at Risk) whenever strategic changes are considered.
- The Trustee undertakes regular monitoring of the Plan's investments supplemented by information provided by both the Investment Managers and Investment Consultant, as well as advice from the latter.
- The Trustee periodically assesses the strength of the Employer covenant and uses external expertise where appropriate.
- The Trustee delegates the day-to-day management of some of these risks to the appointed Investment Managers.
- The Trustee considers the Investment Managers' role and approach to managing risk is considered when selecting appropriate Investment Managers.
- The Trustee utilises custodian relationships to ensure Plan assets are held securely.
- The Trustee assesses whether appropriate controls are put in place by themselves, the Investment Consultant, Investment Managers and Custodians (where there is a direct relationship).

The trustee assesses solvency risk and mismatching risk are measured through triennial actuarial valuations of both assets and liabilities, as well as more frequent interim estimates.

Realising Investments

The Trustee recognises that assets may need to be realised to meet Plan obligations at any time.

The Trustee will ensure that an appropriate amount of readily realisable assets are held at all times, and this will be part of the assessment for including new investments within the strategy.

The Trustee will from time to time agree a policy for sourcing cash from the investments as required.

Responsible Investment

The Trustee has considered its approach to ESG factors and does believe there can be financially material risks relating to ESG. Reflecting this, the Trustee has delegated the ongoing monitoring and management of ESG risks to the Plan's investment managers. The Trustee requires the Plan's investment managers to take into consideration ESG factors within their decision-making recognising that how they do this will be dependent on the asset class characteristics.

The Trustee will take their views on the potential for ESG factors to lead to financially material risks into account in any future investment manager selection exercises for the underlying investments that the Plan makes. Further to this, the Trustee will monitor the ESG integration practices of the managers they are invested in to ensure they remain appropriate and in line with the Trustee's requirements as set out in this Statement.

The Trustee has delegated responsibility for the exercise of rights (including voting rights) attached to the Plan's investments to the investment managers and encourages them to vote whenever it is practical to do so.

> Signed on behalf of the Trustee:
> Signature: ....
> Printed Name: ....
> Date: ....

Overall strategy

In addition to the above assets, the Trustee secured the benefits for the then, uninsured current pensioners through the purchase of an insurance policy. This was achieved through a buy-in arrangement whereby the insurer reimburses the Plan for payments made to the insured pensioners in return for a premium paid by the Plan.

The investment strategy is expected to provide returns of 1.25% pa above gilt yields over the long term.

Liability hedging and Rebalancing investments

The investment strategy has been designed to mitigate 100% of the interest rate and inflation risk inherent in the Plan's liabilities. However, the trustee recognises that re-balancing the portfolio may become appropriate. Currently the Plan does not have any formal rebalancing arrangements in place. However, the Trustee will review the allocation from time to time and as often as necessary. If required the trustee will instruct the Investment Managers to rebalance towards the strategic allocation.

Realising investments

Where assets need to be realised, the Trustee will consult with the Investment Consultant regarding the source and timing of disinvestments. It is envisaged that where assets need to be realised, the primary source of disinvestments will be from liquid short-term assets.

Additional Voluntary Contributions (AVCs)

The Trustee has made several AVC investment options available to members of the Plan.

The Trustee will review the AVC providers, as well as the funds available, in the light of their performance on a periodic basis. Performance of these funds will be measured relative to the individual benchmarks and objectives for the funds offered and/or to other providers offering similar fund options.

The Trustee is aware that members' AVC funds are subject to the same risks faced by the Plan's investments, such as inflation risk eroding real returns. In addition,

AVC members face the risk that their investments will not meet their future expectations (for example, if they are planning to purchase an annuity at retirement), lack of transparency on how their fund is managed and also that their AVC fund may fall in value.

The Trustee considers that, in making a number of funds available, they provide these members with sufficient options to meet their reasonable expectations and to mitigate the risks faced.

Liability-Driven RoboAdvice and the Development and Digitisation of the Industry

In the following section; we look at the future of investment services, in particular at the growth of Robo Advice. We explore how greater uptake of technology driven solutions is changing the way we interact with the financial services industry. Financial Advice is moving from the relationship driven analogue processes of the last century to more modern digital and automated processes capable of reaching larger markets than ever before. We explore how the use of this technology is already changing Risk and Wealth Management and will continue to do so in the future. Introducing the concept of Wealth Technology or WealthTech. Robo-Advice is still in its infancy but is likely to radically alter the financial landscape over the next ten years. Although the current crop of robo-advisors mainly rely on algorithms generated by Modern Portfolio Theory, the next batch of digital solutions are likely to rely on more holistic solutions. This is likely due to the continuing rise of Goal Driven Investing and LDI and likely regulatory pressure that will require increasingly complex solutions that more closely match consumer needs.

WEALTHTECH: HOW WEALTH MANAGERS AND THEIR CLIENTS ARE EMBRACING NEW TECHNOLOGIES

With many forms of consumption becoming 'Digital' financial services are no exception. Technology is rapidly changing the nature of our commercial relationships, and these changes are happening more rapidly than ever before. The way we shop, socialise and communicate have all changed radically over our lifetimes and will continue to do so.

The financial services industry is in many ways behind the curve, with many product lines unchanged in decades. We are about to enter an increasingly online and digital-only age, and it is unfortunate that insurers and the asset managers of large banks have been so slow to adapt to the new era. Innovations from outside traditional finance will change the sector in the near future with relationships between institutions and consumers likely to be disrupted as new products in banking, financial management and investment are unveiled, creating more options and convenience for the end-user.

With regulators anxious for technological take-up to facilitate lower cost financial services and to stimulate competition, we look at the concept of 'WealthTech,' and see how the application of digital wealth management will change the user experience (UX), and look at how WealthTech may force financial services to evolve.

The age of data and information transparency has already impacted our financial lives. Historic commercial connections are breaking down (or being disrupted in Tech speak) and it looks likely that traditional relationships in the finance ecosystem will be changed by the powerful twin forces of technology and regulation. Revenue streams and business models of legacy institutions such as asset managers, life insurers and banks are in danger of being replaced by newer more innovative market entrants such as the digital asset managers (also known as robo advisors), peer-to-peer lenders, and disruptive new financial products. These new entrants or startups to the investment space have become categorised as WealthTech or InvestTech firms and are part of the 'FinTech (financial technology) revolution'.

With its traditional strength in Financial Services, the United Kingdom has become home to many of these startups, with incubators such as Level 39 – based in Canary Wharf, and owned by Canary Wharf group – creating an ecosystem in London that acts as a catalyst for technological growth. London alongside New York is currently considered the global home of FinTech.

The UK regulator, the Financial Conduct Authority (FCA), has done much to support innovation generally, and WealthTech specifically. As a result, it has found itself emulated worldwide for its entrepreneurial approach, particularly the regulatory Sandbox and Project Innovate. These projects allow WealthTech firms to experiment with new financial products which don't obviously fit into a narrow regulatory category. The FS firms then can receive regulatory support before achieving full and direct authorisation. The sandbox has been a way for companies to test propositions in the real world. This makes it easier for younger companies to go to market with more clarity on their product suite will work in the regulated marketplace. The Sandbox has had firms as small as Bud (UK Startup) to HSBC (Global Megalith) receive advice and support and for new firms offering digital advice Project Innovate can be a first step to market.

Perhaps the best-known player in the UK WealthTech space is Nutmeg, a digital asset manager which now manages approximately $1 billion for UK investors despite no branch network or physical presence. Newer entrants to the market for Digital Wealth Products include RiskSave, which I founded and is part of the Level 39 ecosystem, and the peer-to-peer lending platform Zopa.

WealthTech has become defined as the FinTech sector that focuses on enhancing wealth management and the retail investment process. The most visible players are applications called robo advisors, but other concepts are deserving of attention. Technology derived from wealth management firms, research tools that generate investment solutions, and platforms to support financial advisors – all fall under WealthTech.

Whilst the term robo advisor has gained traction, few of the current crop of digital asset management firms appreciate the label. This is as few players match the regulatory definition of 'advice' and not all parts of the process are automated. The term 'semi-automated digital guiders,' whilst more accurate, isn't quite as snappy and newer players to the robo-advice space have been using the term Digital Asset Managers to describe their proposition.

An offering of automated financial advice from the retail banks will see Wealth-Tech go mainstream. Indeed, this is happening in the UK and new entrants emerge monthly. Santander and HSBC have already launched product offerings in this space, with HSBC trialling its service using the regulators Project Innovate. In addition, RBS, after trialling a service through its Coutts' sub-brand, launched a mass-market Wealth-Tech proposition through its NatWest subsidiary. Eventually Lloyds (with a quarter of the UK market), which has been embracing Digital Transformation (at least in its investor strategy presentations), will enter the market. Mass market low cost financial advice could soon be on our doorstep.

But with the distribution potentially available it's likely wealth management is about to enter a period of change. The smaller wealth managers and banks are looking at the space. Investec, which traditionally serve the more affluent end of the market, has launched a robo-advice offering 'Investec Click and Invest', aimed at millennials and those who can't afford full financial advice. Similarly, UBS has launches its SmartWealth digital platform in the UK.

The technology originated in the US with Wealthfront. The company was founded in 2008 and is considered to have been the first to develop the robo-advice concept. Wealthfront has since been followed by a number of entrepreneurial start-ups and replicators around the world. Hundreds of thousands of investors worldwide have embraced these platforms, and the enthusiasm of users contrasts markedly with that of legacy wealth management providers. Nutmeg has a score of 9/10, according to the TrustPilot customer review platform. More traditional wealth managers consistently score lower, many much lower.

Consultants and investors estimate that within the next five years those who have been 'robo-advised' will climb from an estimated 50,000 now into the millions. It is likely that existing financial service firms will pick up the bulk of custom. This is important as it means that those involved in retail bank technology or operations will have to consider the impact of this on their processes.

Integrating a WealthTech solution will depend on the provider and other factors, but most solutions will offer modular processes and financial services firms will develop many of the features in-house. Indeed, established players like the aforementioned Investec, Charles Schwab and Vanguard all developed platforms internally.

Many firms are embracing the FinTech mantra and claiming to be part of the 'FinTech revolution' and whilst receiving an email from a financial advisor might be defined as 'WealthTech' for us simply having an online presence in an asset management or advisory firm doesn't reach true 'WealthTech'. We believe that, not only must the technology work and meet the needs of the business, but it should also be novel, surprising and transformative. In our view the risk to the FinTech sector is that this innovative disruption comes from outside the industry – firms that place technology at the forefront, with almost unlimited R&D resources and without one eye on the clock for the next funding round. Indeed, many non-financial firms are entering the space with ideas and concepts for both user experience (UX) and customer onboarding, or acquisition. With FinTech's relentless focus on innovation we see it likely that artificial intelligence (AI) interfaces and seamless onboarding experiences are likely within the next five years. But because of this they are likely to be: a) commoditised, and b) supplied by a non-financial player, IBM being the go-to choice at the moment for legacy players for their AI needs, rather than a FinTech startup.

Traditional financial firms have put developers as a back-office function separate from the front-office business line. This was fine when technology was considered a support role. However, for a WealthTech (or any FinTech), we question whether this back-office approach is likely to yield the desired result. WealthTech seeks to replicate or enhance processes currently performed by a finance professional. This requires developers to understand intricately how the front-line/customer needs work. This knowledge would ensure that the developers have a better grasp of customers wants. Developers will struggle to replicate a process, let alone innovate without this commercial knowledge. Some of the larger players are seeking to integrate the technology team with distinct revenue lines. Indeed, Goldman Sachs is seeking – perhaps unconvincingly – to position itself as a technology player.

This, of course, brings new responsibilities to both technology teams and the multiple revenue producers, who have to commit time and effort to communicate and understand new concepts in different areas to their own expertise. This presents both a challenge and an opportunity.

The challenge will be in establishing this more integrated way of working. The opportunity, however, is access to the vast and varied knowledge base that exists in any professional organisation. If the two can be successfully combined then some real WealthTech may actually emerge.

For us the most exciting changes will be the use of AI as part of the customer experience (although more limited in the investment process) and the relentless rise of passive. Passive investments are approximately ten per cent of retail distribution currently – we could see this become a majority in the next decade. The main benefit of the changes in the investment ecosystem will be the continued slashing of fund management charges, but it is a struggle to give WealthTech the credit for this, with Vanguard being the ultimate driving force and a child of the 70s.

Interestingly wealth management technology will benefit not just the traditional clients of financial advisors and Private Banks, i.e. the ultra-rich and mass affluent, but will hopefully reach more members of society. The lower costs of leveraging technology enable a mass-market solution creating a larger market place. Financial advice has typically cost £100 per hour or more and, unless you are dealing with large sums, tailored financial advice is likely to be unaffordable, with negative outcomes from both a social and governmental perspective. This issue has become known as the 'financial advice gap'. Throughout Europe, it has typically been uneconomic to receive advice on sums less than €100,000 or £100,000 even if financial education or guidance is sorely needed. These new technologies and digital platforms are vital in ending the financial advice gap. In its Financial Advice Market Review (FAMR), published in June 2016, the FCA stated that up to 16 million people in the UK could be trapped in this financial advice gap – they need or would benefit from advice but were unable to afford it.

Due to this trickle-down effect regulators and governments globally are encouraging the growth of digital asset managers and the uptake of WealthTech as a way of increasing financial inclusion and eliminating the financial advice gap. As such these new technologies have a social as well as commercial purpose, in fact within the next decade (some say sooner) it is likely that the majority of your colleagues, friends and family will utilise some form of WealthTech product.

FROM WEALTHTECH TO ROBO-ADVICE

As discussed previously, the FinTech revolution and the development of WealthTech has left the asset management industry in a state of flux, and the manner in which individuals and institutions interact with their wealth managers is on the cusp of dramatic change. Digitisation and increased use of technology should mean that we are at the point of a low-cost revolution for financial advice. This is likely to impact job security in financial services and will radically re-shape the industry with dramatically lower employment likely across all major centres. Automation is likely to lead to less financial service professionals covering a larger number of clients.

The level and impact of automation will impact all sections of the financial community. From guidance/advice through to investment and distribution and at both firms large and small. However, on a social level the importance of robo-advice is how these changes will alter how society consumes, saves and invests in the future, and how much we pay for this (much less, hopefully!).

Many wealth managers are currently buoyed up by record profits generated through five years of ever-increasing asset prices caused by loose monetary policy and ultra-low interest rates. Asset managers still have share prices and enterprise values implying further good times ahead and no exit from the land of plenty. But these numbers hide the upcoming storm. A different story of new market entrants using automation to slash costs while at the same time leveraging technology to improve risk management and compliance has been emerging for some time. The new digital era will make the future more of a challenge for older financial institutions.

Currently the asset management process is unwieldy, with multiple steps between end-users and financial professionals. An investor will typically deal with several separate firms paying fees at every step of the investment process. This convoluted and complicated approach is time-consuming as well as costly. There is hope that a growing number of FinTechs can change this.

This evolution has been supported by regulators worldwide, but particularly by the FCA in London. It is hopeful that increased use of technology could finally enable the provision of advice to mass-market segments, including segments that have previously been unreached by financial advice. They estimate this could be as many as 16 million people in the UK alone, and have set up a dedicated Robo-Advice Unit to support digital or tech-led asset managers bring products to market. Here we outline the key points of Robo-Advice, which is being hailed as the 'future of asset management'.

Robo-Advice in Ten Points

Robo-advice is online: Rather than an expensive to maintain branch network, robo-advisors save money and can increase customer convenience by allowing a digital first experience.

The key is probably cost: Although robo-advice has significant regulatory support, and a smoother customer journey and ease of use will create momentum and growth.

The cumulative effect of compounded cost savings is likely to be the main driver of consumer uptake. Robo-advisors can be 60–70 per cent cheaper than traditional solutions and can provide savings of one percentage point per year of assets under management. Over a lifetime of investing, this would make £100,000s of difference to millions of investors in the UK alone.

Growth is strong: Whilst still only a fraction of the market, the assets under management of major players are growing between 50 and 100 per cent per year, and new entrants and concepts are developing all the time. There are currently over 100 robo-advisors in Europe with most based in either Germany or the UK. Commoditisation of the underlying technology is likely to create more digital first advice concepts and allow even more brands to market, maintaining growth in the medium term.

There is a long way to go: Nutmeg, the UK's largest robo, has $1bn in assets, but Legal and General, the UK's largest traditional asset manager, has over $1 trillion – a thousand times larger. Data in the US is similar, with BlackRock having $6 trillion under management and Betterment, the largest US robo, having a fraction of this. Even conservative estimates of future Robo-Advice market share would indicate incredible growth ahead for the sector.

On-boarding is a noted differentiator, but also a concern: On-boarding, the process of bringing new customers to the platform, is conveniently and efficiently done online, but there are regulatory worries concerning know-your-client rules and suitability. The faster process and fact-finding may not always be up to date with regulations or as rigorous as it should be. Indeed, the commercial teams at robo-advisors often sacrifice regulatory rigour to decrease drop off rates in the on-boarding process.

Millennials are less important than predicted: Most of the original players in this nascent market targeted millennials. But older, wealthier and still tech-savvy baby boomers have become core clients.

Robo-advisors mainly use ETFs: To create diversified and low-cost investment pools, robos have mainly been using exchange traded funds (ETFs) which are generally passive, low-cost, liquid investments.

Future robo-advisors will be more sophisticated: A portfolio solely consisting of ETFs can be generated quickly and easily but doesn't allow more tailored risk matching or factor exposure. Comparing the recommended portfolio of a robo-advisor to the recommended allocation of an investment consultant to a large institution would demonstrate the lack of sophistication of much of the current offering. A narrow portfolio of listed funds (for the robo-advisor) contrasts poorly to the much broader selection of assets available to institutions. For example, by staying in listed assets the digital asset managers restrict access of their users to the illiquidity risk premium – indicating that an improvement in portfolio risk return characteristics would be possible with the simple addition of more asset classes.

Robo-advice aids financial inclusion: Large sections of society, typically the financially less literate, have been excluded from the best investment solutions by the high initial costs of financial advice. Both the regulator and the industry are hoping that robo-advice will improve participation and access to the investment process. With the marginal cost of providing advice approaching zero as technology brings the benefits of scale to a currently fragmented industry, previously uneconomic clients can benefit from financial services.

Robo-advisors typically use Modern Portfolio Theory: Robo-advisors typically use mean-variance optimisation for asset selection, but future solutions are likely to use Liability Driven Investment (LDI) frameworks for portfolio construction.

With strong growth and regulatory support, robo-advisors are here to stay. The cost-advantage of these financial technology firms is likely to create a great deal of social utility over the next few decades. By stimulating interest in saving for the future and widening access to investment with an easier customer journey, their products can increase financial security, stability and knowledge across multiple stakeholders. But despite all the attention from press, venture capitalists, banks and regulators globally, digital wealth managers currently represent less than one per cent of the savings market so the journey is only at the beginning.

A BRIEF INTRODUCTION TO ROBO-ADVICE

Robo-advice is a hotly debated topic, both with regard to the term itself and the future it represents. The term has been broadly used to describe any digital asset management firm whose main presence is on-line, but can include offshoots and subsidiaries of established institutions. In practice most robo-advisors or robos are semi-automated services with some human interaction in both the on-boarding and investment process. Confusingly, given the popularity of the term many robo-advisors do not meet the regulatory definition of advice. Most in fact fall under the regulatory term of 'investment guidance'. Understandably, however, the more accurate descriptor 'Semi-Automated Digital Guiders' has not been taken up by the industry or trade press. The somewhat unwieldy but slightly snappier portmanteau 'Robo-Advisor' has gained favour instead.

The term was first used to describe the on-line, self-led investment propositions developed by several start-ups in the US, with the most notable being Wealthfront and Betterment. These early pioneers have since been followed by a numerous entrepreneurial start-ups and replicators around the world. Although it is interesting to note that now nearly a decade after the first robo-advisors had emerged nearly 100% of assets under management by robo-advisors consist solely of narrow portfolios of exchange-traded-funds (ETFs). It seems likely if not inevitable that, in the near future, Robos or 'semi-automated digital guiders' capable of investing in a wide array of funds, ETFs and individual securities will emerge. RiskSave with a B2B offering using individual securities and UBS SmartWealth which invests in actively managed funds are both UK examples of these. Moving beyond ETFs would have numerous advantages. Investment portfolios generated from a wider array of assets would be considered an improvement on the current model. As in accordance with Markowitz and Modern Portfolio Theory they will be more efficient with superior risk–return characteristics. The addition of a wider ranger range of investment instruments would also be able to incorporate LDI pooled funds and similar strategies that would enable more precise risk hedging and liability matching. A robo-advisor with the ability to select individual securities would be able to create a bespoke LDI (or similar) solution to individual investors with liability matching to an almost granular level.

However, the emergence of robo-advice has been met with some concern from financial advisors around the world. In their opinion, an automated solution cannot be a personal solution and is likely to lower the quality of advice available. Many IFAs view digital solutions as removing the core value of personal advice which is individualised recommendations based on personal knowledge often formed over decades of personal relationships. The robo-advice community argues that traditional financial advisors' arguments are, however, tainted as they fear disruption and the impact of digital disruption on their livelihoods. It is likely that for all but the wealthiest clients there will be a disintermediation of the traditional face-to-face business models. But in the eyes of some IFAs, the new technology could also be an opportunity for improving traditional methods. New systems allowing advisers to better engage with clients with more detailed, frequent and accurate reporting. There is also huge potential for stream-lining processes, enabling more time for marketing, content creation and client engagement and creating a superior customer experience.

There has also been the real hope that robo-advice or digital asset management could finally enable the provision of advice to mass-market segments, in particular those on low incomes who have some ability to save but lack the knowledge to begin their savings journey. The broader reach of technology could open up new markets, including segments of the population that have previously been unreached by financial advice. The FCA estimated in 2016 that this could be as many as 16 million people in the UK alone. We believe that advanced digital advice models are likely to have wide market appeal and certainly has regulatory support.

Many savers or potential investors will be attracted by the educational aspects and simplicity of these new financial services enabling them to move at their own pace and at a price they can afford. Similarly, for highly experienced investors or the cash-rich but time-poor could be attracted by the lower costs, automated rebalancing and higher levels of data that robo-advice services typically offer. Over time technology-led digital distribution will be used to deliver an expanding range of financial services to an increasing variety of consumer segments and, as such we expect that digital advice is will come to dominate financial services at some stage in the future.

There is currently no regulatory subset of permissions labelled 'robo-advice'. Although this may change and the UK regulator in its Guidance discusses 'Streamlined Advice' and 'Simplified Advice'.

Within the robo-advice industry different providers often differ regarding which regulatory definition they apply to themselves:

- Some provide advice, taking investors through an on-line process which leads to specific recommendations.
- Some provide simplified advice. Simplified advice models are typically automated, process-driven advice services, typically delivered over the internet. They are not designed to provide advice on a consumer's existing financial products.
- Some provide 'guidance' which is intended to leave the ultimate responsibility for choice with the customer.

As well as appealing to fintech entrepreneurs and financial advisors – financial institutions are also engaging with the concept. There a multitude of attractions to existing players in financial services entering the space:

- Generation of AUM (assets under-management);
- Increased 'stickiness' and client retention;
- An enlarged client universe;

- Improved client engagement;
- Lowering of operational risk with standardised processes;
- Lowering of regulatory risk with standardised processes;
- Low marginal cost of client service.

After a decade on the sidelines many large institutions are now seeking to enter the market, disrupting the disruptors. The legacy institutions are unburdened by high customer acquisition and marketing costs and have pre-existing distribution pipelines. It will be likely be the incumbents that become the future of the digital advice market and with regulatory support help close the 'financial advice gap'.

Whilst there had been hope, particularly from venture capital investors, for the arrival of an 'Uber-style' disrupter that will change personal finance forever, our belief is that collaboration between those with investment expertise and those with a distribution platform is the way forward.

The start-ups have created a buzz around the space and creating a new market and developing customer awareness. But the (presumed) low barriers to entry which led to their creation, have led to a situation where there are over a hundred robo-advisors in Europe, with more unveiling every day, and with none yet to turn a profit despite various iterations and evolution of business models. However, it still seems reasonable that a digital approach is the future of financial advice and that the financial services industry will soon experience dramatic change. The bulk of robo-advisor AUM will likely be a value add for larger institutions in response to a combination of increased competition and regulatory pressure creating downward pressure on fees. Financial advice may become a means of increasing client retention and, for the better offerings, lower the cost of client acquisition. This would have significant social benefits with consumers enjoying the benefits of improved risk management near (or even possibly below) the cost of provision.

The largest financial institutions already have millions of customer relationships, including customers that have been identified by the regulator as being excluded from the world of Financial Advice. Market conditions and demographics mean that low interest rates and an aging population create an increased desire for saving and investment products. it is likely that financial advice will soon be readily available through these channels. To the millions previously unaware of, or excluded from, the most appropriate financial products.

Pricing Structures for Digital Advice

One of the more obvious benefits of the digital advice revolution is the ability of these new digital asset managers to offer investment and advisory services at a significantly lower cost than traditional analogue distribution channels. The new technology driven advisors have always put fair pricing and simplicity at the front of their marketing and product message. The robos pride themselves on simple pricing and tend to be less opaque in both product offering and fees than high street IFAs, they are notably more transparent about the total fees that are ultimately paid by users. Although, as ever with Financial Services, some portions of fees are still unclear: for example, slippage and other implicit costs may not be obvious.

For a typical digital advisor, the platform will levy a simple management charge as a percentage of assets under management. The level of this charge can differ from one platform to another, and from jurisdiction to jurisdiction. The fee may also depend on the type of service offered: i.e., where the service sits on the spectrum between 'guidance' and 'full advice'. Currently the range of pricing in the UK is typically between 0.5% and 1.0% annually, and this is charged on an accruals basis monthly. Charges are notably higher in the UK than in the US due to the US having a more developed ecosystem for Financial Technology and larger, more liquid financial markets encouraging more competitive pricing.

Conversely charges in Asia are higher across the board. As here there are more fragmented markets and less regulatory requirement for clarity of pricing, alongside weaker suitability requirements.

The numerous charges and fees whilst seemingly negligible will still have a negative effect on user outcome. Due to the long holding periods and investment horizon, even low charges will become significant cumulatively. With the effects of compounding exacerbating the negative effect. Nevertheless, the new models represent a significant improvement on the status quo.

Even for mass-affluent clients the charges within traditional analogue distribution channels can be staggering. In the United Kingdom charges for independent financial advice are estimated to be between three and five per cent of assets. Although it is difficult to get a precise number, both due to the opacity of charging and the difficulty of collating many different providers and charges, some of which are implicit, not explicit. These charges are split between fixed and variable costs and typically include; a platform charge (to hold assets, similar to custody in institutional markets). A running percentage fee for managing assets, and an hourly rate for ad-hoc advice (typically £150 per hour but sometimes notably higher).

There are also cases of charges significantly higher than the 1 per cent within robo-advice. The annual charge can also be quoted in terms of a flat fee, although this structure is currently less common, but may more accurately reflect the cost of providing the service. Examples include Moneybox in the UK, Stash in the US and Acorns in Australia. These propositions, which describe themselves as Savings Apps or savings applications, charge approximately $1 or £1 per month for access to their service, in addition to the other typical charges users face.

On top of the numerous platform charges are the expense fees of the underlying funds which the robo-advisors purchase on the investor's behalf. For robo-advisors minimising the cost of external fund providers is a strength and a core part of their marketing message. The majority of providers concentrate on offering exchange traded funds (ETFs), whose fees are significantly lower than the active managed funds typically selected by human advisors. Fees for ETFs typically come in at 0.1–0.3 per cent on average, but are sometimes even lower. An example being the Vanguard S&P 500 tracker, which currently charges just four basis points, or 0.04 per cent.

ADVICE OR GUIDANCE: ROBO-ADVICE OR PARTIALLY AUTOMATED DIGITAL GUIDANCE

As discussed previously in this book, and debated at more than a few FinTech conferences, many of the new breed of robo-advisors and digital advice platforms do not actually provide financial advice. In the eyes of the financial regulator the digital asset managers will often provide a much simpler service which the FCA describes as guidance. Robo Guidance whilst a more accurate descriptive term for these platforms is not yet in common parlance. For comparison the term 'Robo-Advice' is now widely seen in the national press and has even been included in the OED (Oxford English Dictionary), robo-guidance is so far only discussed by investment compliance consultants and regulators and has yet to trend on Google.

Both the regulator and provider hope that a consumer attracted to a fintech asset manager with their simpler customer journey and simpler message should be able to understand the products available. However confusingly the service received when using a digital advice platform may not be clear, even to a regulatory expert. The terms 'advice' and 'guidance' are explained in different ways by different providers, and even a compliance specialist can find this confusing.

The term 'guidance' is considered less encompassing than 'advice' and is often seen to be explained in negative language. Descriptions of guidance in standard Terms and Conditions frequently listing items that the service did not offer rather than outlining the benefits.

Examples below are the standard disclaimers seen on providers anxious not to be seen advising:

> We do not provide advice
> We do not provide recommendations on investments
> We will not advise you about the merits of a particular investment
> This is not advice
> We do not give you a personal recommendation

The FCA's take on what constitutes guidance is included below:

- Guidance is an impartial service which will help you to identify your options and narrow down your choices but will not tell you what to do or which product to buy; the decision is yours.
- Providers of guidance are responsible for the accuracy and quality of the information they provide but not for any decision you make based on it.
- Guidance is free unless your provider clearly tells you otherwise.
- It will suggest what you *could* do.

For comparison the regulators take on the broader advice product:

- Advice will recommend a specific product or course of action for you to take given your circumstances and financial goals. This will be personal to you, based on information you provide.
- Advice will be provided by a qualified and regulated individual or online by a regulated organisation.
- Providers of advice are responsible and liable for the accuracy, quality and suitability of the recommendation that they make and you are protected by law.
- You will usually pay a fee for advice. Fees will be disclosed before you are asked to commit yourself.
- It will recommend what you *should* do.

Interestingly, the FOS (Financial Ombudsman Service) has stated that if a consumer feels that they have received advice the service would be minded to agree with them. And that the blurred lines between inconsistent disclaimers ('This is not advice', etc) may not be enough to ensure full compliance or that advice has not been given.

The inconsistency between these two product types is creating a situation where both the consumer and the platform provider could easily be confused as to which product or service they are transacting. Clearly this is not ideal, and the regulator and the industry need to work together on creating commonly accepted standards. A clear explanation of the differences would encourage competition in addition to promoting a better understanding of the services available. By making services more directly comparable the consumer can better find value for money or find the service most appropriate for their needs.

From the FCA

What is Guidance?

- Information and options, often tailored to your personal circumstances. It does not include a recommendation as to the course of action you should take – this will be for you to decide.
- It is what you could do.

What is Advice?

- A recommendation which is personal to you, based on your personal situation, needs and objectives.
- A recommendation of what you should do.

The Financial Advice Working Group has performed market research to understand consumer opinions on the matter, their findings supported the need for more communication on the matter:

- *Participants had conflicting views on what constitutes 'advice' and 'guidance', with many transposing the meaning.*
- *Participants lacked understanding of what services to associate with 'advice' and 'guidance'.*
- *Participants were unfamiliar with the concept of 'guidance' in a financial context.*

It seems that 'financial guidance' is not yet a familiar term, despite the simpler process being a valuable addition to the financial product range available to the consumer. The industry will need to work harder to communicate its benefits to the small saver.

If the asset manager recommends a specific product or course of action for to take to take given individual circumstances and financial goals – then it is likely that the provider has crossed a line and is providing 'Financial Advice'. This requires more detailed reporting, a greater regulatory cost and the need to create a 'Suitability Report'.

Under the now ubiquitous MiFID II, a suitability report will have to be issued 'before the conclusion of any contract' recommended in it. There has been some debate in compliance circles around when a contract is concluded. But best practice should be providing the report to clients before they make a decision on how to proceed and also provides relevant information to the client allowing them to make a more informed decision. (Hopefully) leading to a better customer experience.

The need for a Suitability Report is one of the more obvious differences between advice and guidance. If you have received a suitability report it is likely that you have received some form of advice and a recommendation that is personal to you. Although, naming no names, we have opened trial accounts at some of the entrepreneurial robos that offer financial advice and not received a report!

FURTHER DEVELOPMENTS IN LDI

The Evolution of LDI and the Creation of Cash Flow-Driven Investment

In the past few years LDI has taken hold of the long-dated investment market, with a near 100 per cent hold on the institutional pensions market (for Defined Benefit at least). In this environment Investment consultants have sought to differentiate themselves in what looks to become a more commoditised market. The fees for monitoring a portfolio or strategy whilst valuable are a fraction of the value of the fees for implementing a strategy, as such we have seen the development of overlay strategies to support LDI frameworks. One such strategy is Cash Flow Driven Investment, aka CDI. CDI has also arisen organically to meet the needs of many pension funds who are declining in membership and resultantly paying out more than they are receiving from active members; ie, they are cashflow negative. Currently in Europe approximately half of Defined Benefit schemes are cashflow negative, but this proportion can only increase, and indeed could reach 90 per cent within the next 15 years. This is because nearly all Defined Benefit schemes are closed to new members, and current members will continue to retire and leave the workforce. This dynamic has added an extra layer of complication to trustees' already complex goals. The investment team at a pension fund in this situation must worry, not only about long term investment performance, but in addition short term cash flow needs; hence, we are seeing more focus on managing cash flows.

WHAT IS CASH FLOW-DRIVEN INVESTMENT?

A CDI framework aims to complement LDI and achieve stable funding positions whilst also concentrating on short term cash flow needs. Similarly to LDI, some may view Cash Flow Driven Investment as a luxury only available to schemes that a strong funding position. This is as frameworks utilising CDI rely on Fixed Income, rather than the traditional equity holders common in long term portfolios. Savers in these schemes are expected to sacrifice investment returns for more certain cash flows. One can see differences and similarities between the two frameworks in terms of focus and need.

The Liability Driven Framework will:

i. be long term – 20 years or more typically;
ii. rely on AAA-rated Government Debt to hedge the liabilities or Cash flows;
iii. possibly use Cash and Synthetic Derivatives;
iv. rely on the expertise of Interest Rate Specialists for execution;
v. need less frequent monitoring due to the longer time horizons;
vi. be relatively commoditised with the availability of pooled funds.

The Cash Flow Driven Framework will:

i. complement long dated strategies with a focus on short term needs – typically ten years or less;
ii. rely on a broad range of credit instruments with a broad range of credit ratings;
iii. possibly use Cash and Synthetic Derivatives;
iv. rely on the expertise of Credit Specialists for execution;
v. need more frequent monitoring as cash flow needs can and will change – typically annually or semi-annually;
vi. likely need to be bespoke, with the expertise currently needed for implementation only available to the largest schemes.

With a constant need for short- and medium-dated assets to match cash flows, execution can be tricky and clearly CDI frameworks create a layer of re-investment risk. But this risk is compensated for by the extra yield obtained from the credit instruments utilised.

Many actuaries consider CDI to be a development of LDI rather than a field in its own right. With more and more large funds becoming cash flow negative we can expect to hear more about CDI in the next few years.

THE EVOLUTION OF LDI

Over the next few years, we expect LDI to be an increasingly important part of the investment landscape. As followers of, and investors in the FinTech revolution, we also expect technology to help democratise many of the processes currently only available to institutions. We see a lot of 'mores'. LDI will become more digital, with more asset classes, and become more relevant to an aging population, with Liability Driven Investment's dominance of the Defined Benefit market now assured, we can expect increasing market share for LDI mandates or lifestyling strategies in the market for Defined Contribution schemes and hopefully a gradual uptake in the retail sector. As discussed in the previous section, better funded pension schemes (both DB and DC) will continue to mature and hedging needs of LDI portfolios will naturally look towards cash flow matching as many schemes become cash flow negative (and as schemes currently in this predicament better understand their cash matching needs). Cash flow-driven strategies are likely to become increasingly important. We can expect to see pooled funds launched from the major asset managers with CDI components to match the already existing ranges of LDI pooled funds.

We expect to see further reductions in cost, which will be a boon to end users punished by high asset prices and low interest rates. When choosing service providers or investment teams, Manager Selection will likely be increasingly driven by cost for all but the most complicated use case. This will be augmented by the increasing rise of passive strategies; we expect passive techniques to dominate the LDI landscape in the near future.

The rise of Digital Solutions will complement the rise of superior risk management, product aggregators and digital dashboards will make the markets more transparent and consumers better educated and more alert to their own needs. As advice becomes more and more digital, bespoke goals-based investment with some degree of personalisation should become available to the retail market in the next few years.

Currently, if we look at digital solutions for the retail market, risk is a one-variable factor. So, for example, Nutmeg (the UK's leading 'robo-advisor' at the time of writing) shows risk as a number between one and ten. Future providers or evolutions of current solutions will likely see risk in more dimensions, with the timing of cash flows and the maturity of investment goals of a (fairly) real impact on portfolio construction.

The past decade has seen tremendous growth in both take-up and awareness of LDI frameworks; the last step is the final mile of distribution, with pooled schemes and the like feeding down to individual investors. It is likely that technology will enable this within the next few years.

Index

60/40 split 33
70/30 portfolio 30

acid test 43–4
Acorns 148
active managers, reason for using
   51–6
   alignment of values or values based
      investment 54–6
   bespoke risk management 54
   customer experience 52–3
   downside protection 53–4
   excess returns or alpha 52
active vs passive 23, 48–56, 56–7
Additional Voluntary Contributions
   (AVCs) 136–7
advanced risk management 3
advice, definition 150
Age in Bonds rule 36
Alpha 27, 60–1, 111
alternative funds 61–2
Alternative Investment Market
   (AIM) 30, 31
Aon Hewitt 60
artificial intelligence (AI) interfaces 141
asset allocation 71
   decision making 30–1
   fund selection 27
   individual security analysis 27
   portfolio construction 27
   risk 134
asset backed securities 30
asset classes, range of 115
asset efficiency 43
asset gatherers 68, 69

asset-liability management
   (ALM) 5, 27, 32
asset managers 68, 69
asset risks 134
assets under management
   (AUM) 57, 147
asset valuation 63

Barclay's Global Aggregate for
   Fixed Income 31
basis point 81
basis risk 134
Behavioural Finance 47
Berkshire Hathaway 42
Beta 27, 29, 35
Betterment 3, 144, 145
BlackRock 5, 106, 107, 144
Bogle, Jack 36
bonds 20, 30, 78–81
   key features 79
   maturity 79
   coupon 79
   coupon type 79
   credit rating 79
   pricing 80
Boots Pension Scheme 2, 94, 95–6
Bud (UK Startup) 140
Buffett, Warren 41, 42, 60
Business Angels 66
business continuity 64

Cambridge Associates 61
capital risk 16
cash 30
cash equivalents 30

Cash Flow Driven Investment (CDI) 79,
123–5, 128–9, 133
  ABC plan 128–9
  creation of151
  definition of 151–2
  vs LDI 125–6
cash ratio 44
cash--risk profiles 20
Chartered Financial Analyst (CFA) 42
Charting 45–7
Chartists 45
Chief Risk Officer (CRO) 18
collateral risk 134
collectables 30–1
commercial real estate 31
commodities 31
Commodity Trading Advisors
  (CTAs) 46
compliance with current guidelines 64
conflicts of interest policies 64
convertible bonds 79
corporate and social
  responsibility (CSR) 118
costs 76
counterparty risk 129, 34, 135
coupon rate 78
Coutts 141
Cowan vs *Scargill* 119–20
credit 126–8
credit risk 134
Crowd 66
cryptocurrencies 25
cult of equity 6–7
currency risk 134
current assets 43
current liabilities 43
current ratio 43
customer onboarding 141
cybersecurity 65

data 64
data mining 45
Data Protection Act (DPA) (1998) 64
data validity 63
Debt Management Office
  (DMO) (UK) 87
debt ratios 44

debt-to-assets ratio 44
debt-to-capital ratio 44
debt-to-EBITDA ratio 44
debt-to-equity ratio 44
defined benefit (DB) pension schemes
  5, 6, 12, 25, 101, 151
  Boots Pension Scheme 2, 94, 95–6
  checklist for Trustees 97–8
  definition 25–6
  example 93–100
  liabilities 98–100
  stakeholders 97–8
defined contribution (DC) pension
  schemes 5, 6, 12, 25, 26, 101
digital advice, pricing
  structures for 147–8
digital advice platforms *see*
  Robo-Advisors
digital asset management *see*
  robo-advice
digital asset managers *see* robo-advisors
Digital Solutions 152
Digital Transformation 141
Digital Wealth Products 140
disaster recovery 64
diversity 64
Dow Jones Sustainability Indices 112
duration 81

Efficient Market Hypothesis
  (EMH) 1, 48–51
  behavioural 47
efficient market argument 55
efficient market theory (EMH) 45
emerging markets 31
employer covenant risk 134
environmental, social and governance
  (ESG) 101–3, 123
  funds 54
  history of 119–20
  incorporating into SIP 121–2
  increasing importance of 105–7
  integration-based approach
    111–14
  investing, impact-based 114–17
  representation by 106–7
  revised statement 122

screening approach 108–11
  best in class positive
   screening 112–13
  implementing 110–11
equities 30
equity convertibles 79
equity investment 21
equity risk 134
  profiles 20
equity securities 20
ethical investing 54, 103, 107–8
  see also environmental, social
   and governance (ESG); socially
   responsible investing (SRI)
excess return 18
Exchange Traded Funds (ETFs) 23, 51
  rise of low-cost 2

factor analysis 111
fair return on investment 18
Fama, Eugene 49–50
fat tails 19
fees charged for investing 42
final salary pension scheme 7
financial 'risk', definition 15
financial advice gap 12, 142, 147
Financial Advice Market Review
  (FAMR) 142
Financial Conduct Authority (FCA) 12,
  68, 140, 142, 150
financial leverage 43, 44
financial ratios 42–3
Financial Services Authority (FSA) 12
Financial Technology *see* FinTech
  (financial technology) revolution
Fink, Larry 106
FINRA (US) 15
FinTech (financial technology)
  revolution 24, 140
Fischer Equation 86
fixed income 5, 20, 25, 30–1
  immunization 82
  securities 20, 78
floating rate bonds (floaters) 79
Foreign Exchange 31
Forward Rate Agreements (FRAs) 84, 85
FRCPI index (INSEE) 90

Freshfields Bruckhaus Deringer 120
Friedman, Milton 86
Fright, Tim 116
FTSE 100 31
fund domicile 64
fund selection 52, 57, 59–71
fund structure 64
Fund Twenty 8 66
fundamental analysis of
  securities 40, 41–4
fundamental analysts 57

General Data Protection
  Regulation (GDPR) 64
GigaInsurer 68
gilt edged securities see gilts
gilts 34, 79
gilts minus model 76
Global Financial Crisis (GFC) 1, 47, 66,
  95, 105, 127
global market 90–1
Gold, Ben 128
Goldman Sachs 142
Goobey, George Ross 6
Graham, Benjamin 41
groupthink 64
growth asset risk 134
growth capital 115
guidance, definition 150

hedge funds 31
herding 64
HICPxT index (Eurostat) 90
high grade bonds 78
high investment risk 21
high yield credit 30
holding period 70
home country bias 31, 32–3
  costs 33
  currency 33
  exposure to multi-nationals
   32–3
  familiarity 32
  governance 32
homo economicus 21, 102
HSBC (Global Megalith) 140, 141
human resources procedures 64

IBM 83, 142
ICI pension scheme 94
idiosyncratic risk 34–5
illiquid credit 126–8
immunisation theory 81–2
impact investing 115
impact measurement 115
impact reporting 116, 117
intentionality 115
Impact Reporting and Investment
  Standards (IRIS) (Global Impact
  Investment Network) 116
Imperial Tobacco Pension Fund 6
implementation risks 134
Independent Financial Advisor
  (IFA) 3, 60
index linked defined benefit
  pension plan 85
index-linked gilts 79, 89
index ratio 88–9
indexation lag 89
inflation 85
inflation and credit linked
  fixed income 30
inflation-linked bonds, reason for
  issuing 87–8
  demonstration of commitment to
    stable monetary policy 88
  diversification of funding sources 87
  removal of a risk premium 88
  UK Debt Management
    Office (DMO) 87
  widening investor universe 87
inflation linked fixed income 30
inflation-linked government securities 85
inflation linked liabilities 85
inflation-linked securities 85–91
inflation-linked swaps 89–90
inflation risk 134
inflation swap
  market 90
  mechanics of 88–9, 90
Insight Investment (BNY Mellon) 5
institutional pension market (UK
  DB market) 2
interest coverage ratio 44
interest rate risk 134

interest rates 82
interest rate swaps 82–5
  definition 83
  mechanics 83
internal rate of return (IRR) 62
Invesco 109
Investec Click and Invest 141
investing, engagement-based 117–18
investment due diligence 60
Investment Grade Credit 30
investment guidance 145
Investment Management
  Agreement (IMA) 118
investment manager risk 134
investment risk 15–21

Legal & General Investment
  Management (LGIM) 5, 103, 144
legal and operational risk 135
Lehman Brothers 18
leptokurtosis 19
liability-driven investment (LDI)
  rise of 1–2
  retail market and 12
  vs CDI 125–6
  evolution of 151, 152–3
liability hedging 136
liability risk 134
LIBOR (London Interbank
  Offered Rate) 84
linear algebra 69
linear optimisation problem 71
Linkers 85
liquidity 29
liquidity and solvency ratios 43
liquidity risk 134
Lloyds 141
long dated fixed credit 30
long position 83
longevity risk 134
longs 79
long-term investment, risk and 21

Macaulay duration 81
manager selection 52, 61–2
market efficiency, forms of 50
market portfolio 28, 31

market risk 16, 19–20, 34
market value ratios 43
Markowitz, Dr. Harry 2, 5, 12, 27, 28, 36, 41, 48, 145
Markowitz Efficient investments 5
Markowitz Theory of Portfolio Management *see* Modern Portfolio Theory
matrix algebra 71
mean-variance optimisation 29
mediums 79
MegaBank 68
Markets in Financial Instruments Directive (MiFiD II) 25, 29, 64, 150
Millennials 141, 144
Modern Portfolio Theory (MPT) 2, 12, 24, 25, 27–9, 102, 145
  definition of efficient portfolio 4–5
  limitations of 3–4
modified duration 81
Moneybox 148
Moneyfarm 3
Moody's 127
Multi-Asset Class investing (MACI) 12, 24, 48, 96
multi-asset strategy 33–5
Munger, Charlie 42
Myners (2001) Report on Institutional Investment 93

National Coal Board 119
National Union of Mineworkers (NUM) 119
nominal interest rate 77
nominal value 20
non-'suitable' portfolios 25
non-systematic risk 19–20
normal distribution 19
notional 84
Nutmeg 3, 103, 140, 141, 144, 153

Occupational Pension Scheme (Investment) Regulations 2005, 132
Office of National Statistics (ONS) 4
onboarding 141, 144

operational checks 63–9
  asset valuation 63
  business continuity/disaster recovery 64
  compliance with current guidelines 64
  conflicts of interest policies 64
  cybersecurity 65
  data 64
  data validity 63
  diversity 64
  fund structure and domicile 64
  IT and physical security 64
  outsourcing 63
  regulatory change 64
  remuneration policies and HR procedures 64
  research process 63
  trading compliance 63
  trading process 63
operational due diligence 63
operational risk 134
outsourcing 63
Oxford English Dictionary 16

par 20
partially automated digital guidance 148–51
passive investing 27, 29, 42, 48
passive investors 48
passive vs active 23, 48–56, 56–7
payers vs receivers 91
Peak LDI 2
peer-to-peer lenders 140
pension deficits 12
Pension Protection Fund (UK) 7–13
Pensions Act (1995) (UK) 93, 132
Pensions Act (2004) (UK) 7
physical security 64
Plenitude.io 116
portfolio construction 57
portfolio managers 47
portfolio selection 69–71
Portfolio Theory *see* Modern Portfolio Theory
precious metals 31
Preqin 61
present value (PV) 73

PRIIPs regulations 33
principal 78
private equity 31, 61, 62, 65–9, 115
profitability 43
Project Innovate 140, 141
property risk 134
Purple Book 125

quantitative analysis 3, 47–8
quantitative analysts 47, 57
quantitative practitioners 47
quantitative strategies 57
quants 47
quick ratio 43–4

Ralfe, John 94
ratings momentum 113
ratio analysis 42–3
RBS 141
real estate 25, 31
real interest rate 77
real versus nominal discounting 77–8
realising investments 136
rebalancing investments 136
receivers vs payers 91
regulatory change, systems and
    procedures 64
remuneration policies 64
research process 63
Redington, Frank 60, 81–2
regulatory burden 66
Responsible Investing 103, 119
Retail Distribution Review (RDR) 12
return, definition 29
return of capital 23
return on capital 23
return on equity (ROE) 44
return vs risk 18–19
risk
    capacity 18
    definition 29
    management 18, 29
    profile, creating 20–1
    quantifying 19
    tolerance 17–18
    vs return 18–19
    see also under types

riskless asset 34, 35
RiskSave 140, 145
robo-advice 12–13, 143–5, 145–51
robo-advisors 3, 140, 141
Robo Guidance 149
Rolls Royce Pension Scheme 94
RPI index from the ONS 90
Rule of 100 36
running yield 80

S & P 127
S & P 500 31
S & P GSCI (Goldman Sachs
    Commodity Index) index for
    Commodities 31
Sandbox 140
Santander 141
Scalable Capital 3
Scargill, Arthur 119–20
Schwab, Charles 141
sector classification 110–11
sector exposure 110, 111
secured fixed income 115
security selection 57
seed capital 114–15
Semi-Automated Digital Guiders
    see Robo-Advisor
semi-automated digital guiders 141
semi-strong form market efficiency 50
senior debt 79
Sharpe Ratio 56, 61, 67
Sharpe, William 56
short dated fixed credit 30
short position 84
shorts 79
short-term investment 21
sin stocks 109, 110
single stock selection 40
Smart Beta 111
Smith, Terry 42
Socially Responsible Investing (SRI) 105
Socially Responsible
    Investment funds 54
SONIA (Sterling Overnight Interbank
    Average Rate) 85
Soros, George 60
Sortino Ratio 61

Sovereign Wealth Funds of Commodity producing nations 54
standard deviation of asset prices 19
standard deviation of returns 19, 29
Stash 148
Statement of Investment Principles 16, 118, 131–7
  ABC plan 132–7
    Additional Voluntary Contributions (AVCs) 136–7
    investment objective and strategy 133
    investment restrictions 134
    investment risk 134
    investment strategy 133–4
    realising investments 135
    responsible investment 135–6
  drawing up 131–2
  essential elements 131
  incorporating ESG into 121–2
  preparation 132
  sample 132
statistical analysis 46
stock-picking 39
stocks 30
strategy risks 134
strong form market efficiency 50
strong governance 55
structured notes 25, 31
subordinated bonds 79
suitability 26
swap spread 84
swaps 84–5
Syndicate Room 66
Systematic ESG Integration 112
systematic risk *see* market risk
Taskforce on Climate-Related Financial Disclosures (TCFD) 121
technical analysis of securities 40, 45–7
technical analysts (think traders) 57
technical factors 45
technicians 45
think economists 57
time value of money 73–7
Total Expense Ratio (TERs), high 33
tracking error 29
trading compliance 63

trading process 63
traditional long only managers 61
Treasury Inflation Protected Security (TIPs) 89
Trend is your friend school of investing 46
trend-following 46
trustees 97–8
  communications strategy 98
  compliance 98
  investment objectives 97
  operational effectiveness 98
  risk management 98
  trustee appropriateness 97

UBS 141
UBS SmartWealth 145
UKSIF 122
uncertainties within liabilities 76
undated gilts 79
United Nations Environment Programme Finance Initiative 120
United Nations Principles for Responsible Investment (UN PRI) 103–5, 122
US Securities and Exchange Commission (SEC) 15
user experience (UX) 141
value add 60
value proposition 60

Vanguard 36, 42, 67–8, 105, 141, 142
  Life Strategy and Target Retirement product suite 3
  S & P 500 ETF 51
variance 29
venture capital 31, 61, 62, 65–9, 114–15
venture capitalists 66
volatility 25, 27, 29
Volcker, Paul 83

Wall Street Crash (1929) 41
weak form market efficiency 50
Wealthfront 141, 145
Wealthify 103
WealthTech 139–43
Williams, John Burr 41

Willis Towers Watson 60
Woodford Equity Income 67
Woodford, Neil 109
Working capital loans 115
World Bank 83

XPS 60, 128

yield 80
yield to maturity (YTM)
  80–1

zero-coupon securities 78
zero-coupon swap 91
Zopa 140